Women in
the Politics of
Postcommunist
Eastern Europe

Also available from M.E. Sharpe, Inc.

Women in
the Politics of
Postcommunist
Eastern Europe

Revised and Expanded Edition

Edited by
Marilyn Rueschemeyer

M. E. Sharpe, Inc.

Armonk, New York
London, England

Library of Congress Cataloging-in-Publication Data

Women in the politics of postcommunist Eastern Europe / edited by
Marilyn Rueschemeyer.—Rev. and expanded ed.
p. cm.
Includes bibliographical references and index.
ISBN 0-7656-0295-4 (alk. paper).—ISBN 0-7656-0296-2 (pbk.:alk. paper)
1. Women in politics—Europe, Eastern. 2. Europe, Eastern—Politics and government—
1989–
HQ1236.5E852W66 1998
320′.082   dc21
98-15195
CIP

Printed in the United States of America

The paper used in this publication meets the minimum requirements of
American National Standard for Information Sciences—
Permanence of Paper for Printed Library Materials,
ANSI Z 39.48-1984.

BM (c) 10   9   8   7   6   5   4   3   2   1
BM (p) 10   9   8   7   6   5   4   3   2   1

Contents

About the Editor and Contributors

Marilyn Schattner Rueschemeyer is Professor of Sociology at the Rhode Island School of Design and Adjunct Professor of Sociology at Brown University. She is a Fellow at Harvard University's Russian Research Center. Her publications include *Professional Work and Marriage: An East-West Comparison* (1981); *Soviet Emigré Artists: Life and Work in the USSR and the United States* (with Igor Golomshtok and Janet Kennedy, 1985); *The Quality of Life in the German Democratic Republic: Changes and Developments in a State Socialist Society* (edited with Christiane Lemke, 1989); and *East Germany in Comparative Perspective* (edited with David Childs and Thomas Baylis, 1989). Rueschemeyer has been a Senior Associate Member of St. Antony's College, Oxford University, a Visiting Fellow at the Hebrew University in Jerusalem, and a Fellow at the Stockholm Institute of Soviet and East European Economics.

Branka Andjelkovic did graduate work at St. Antony's College, Oxford. She received an M.A. in European Studies and International Relations at the Central European University, Budapest, where she wrote a thesis on civil society. She is currently a news analyst for the Belgrade newsweekly *NIN*.

Mary Ellen Fischer is Professor of Government at Skidmore College. She is the author of *Nicolae Ceauşescu: A Study in Political Leadership* (1989) and of many articles on political developments in Romania, on national inequality, and on women.

Eva Fodor is Assistant Professor in the Department of Sociology at Dartmouth College. She studied at ELTE University in Budapest and the University of California, Los Angeles, where she received her doctorate.

Jill Irvine received her Ph.D. from Harvard University and is assistant professor of political science at the University of Oklahoma. Her publications include *The Croat Question: Partisan Politics in the Formation of the Yugoslav Socialist State* (1994), and *State-Society Relations in Yugoslavia, 1945–1992,* coedited with Melissa Bokovoy and Carol Lilly (1997).

Eva Kolinsky is Professor of Modern German Studies and director of the Centre for the Study of German Society and Culture at Keele University, England. Professor Kolinsky is co-editor of *German Politics.* Her books include *Companion to German Culture* (edited with W. van der Will, 1998) and *Jewish Culture in German Society Today* (edited with D. Horrocks, 1998).

Dobrinka Kostova is a Fellow at the Institute of Sociology of the Bulgarian Academy of Sciences, Sofia. She has published articles on the challenges and risks for women in the transition to democracy.

Silva Mežnarić is Senior Researcher in the Institute for Migration and Ethnicity Research at the University of Zagreb. She has written extensively on migration and ethnic problems in Yugoslavia.

Carol Nechemias is Associate Professor of Public Policy in the Division of Public Affairs at the Pennsylvania State University, Harrisburg. She has written extensively on the women's movement and women's political participation in Russia.

Joanna Regulska is Associate Professor of Geography at Rutgers University and director of the project Local Democracy in Poland. She has edited *Warsaw: Space, People, and Politics* (with A. Kowalewski, 1990) and *Socialist Cities* (with G. Demko, forthcoming).

Fatos Tarifa is Dean of the Faculty of Philosophy and Sociology at the University of Tirana. He has written several books and articles on family issues in Albania and Europe, and on the impact of economic and political reform on the status of women in Eastern Europe and the former USSR.

Anna Titkow is a sociologist in the Institute of Philosophy and Sociology at the Polish Academy of Sciences, Warsaw. She has written extensively on the family and women in Poland.

Mirjana Ule is Professor of Social Psychology at the University of Ljubljana. She has published books and articles on the psychology of youth, on the self and personality formation, on the private sphere of women in communist societies, and on abortion.

Sharon L. Wolchik is director of the Russian and East European Studies Program, Elliot School of International Affairs, George Washington University. She is the author of *Czechoslovakia: Politics, Economics, and Society* (1991) and editor of *Women, State, and Party in Eastern Europe* (with Alfred G. Meyer, 1985) and *Domestic and Foreign Policy in Eastern Europe in the 1980s* (with Michael Sodaro, 1983).

Acknowledgments

This volume has greatly benefited from the support and encouragement of the International Research and Exchanges Board (IREX). Through the years Vivian Abbott of IREX provided help for scholars working on the problems of women in Eastern Europe. It was her office that arranged the original contributors' first meeting in Prague in the summer of 1992. Beate Dafeldecker, the Senior Program Officer for East European Programs at IREX, gave us extensive help with the organization of our meeting, for which we are most grateful. We also thank several East European women prominent in political life who joined us in Prague: Dorottya Buky, Dagmar Burešova, Smaranda Enache, Virginia Gheorghiu, Andrea Ivan, Elka Konstantinova, Eda Kriseová, Ewa Letowská, Iveta Radičová, Eva Sahligerová, and Jiřina Šiklová. This book is dedicated to them and to all women in Eastern Europe now engaged in political life.

Other scholars who took part in our discussions were Gail Kligman, Janet Reineck, Hanna Beate Schöpp-Schilling, Brigitte Schulz, Luann Troxel, Jason Parker of the American Council of Learned Societies, and Vladimir Hancil of the Czechoslovak Academy of Sciences.

The first edition of this book was completed when I was a guest at the Stockholm Institute of Soviet and East European Economics. I am most grateful to Anders Åslund, then director of the Institute, for his invitation to work there and to my other colleagues for their welcome and support. Michael Wyzan of the Institute provided interesting comments on the Bulgarian chapter. During the same semester, Dietrich Rueschemeyer was at the Swedish Collegium for Advanced Study in the Social Sciences in Uppsala (SCASSS). I thank the directors and fellows of SCASSS for their kindness to both of us and for their interest in and support of this project. Dietrich Rueschemeyer made good observations on this manuscript, and I thank him—once more—for his help.

This new, expanded edition was completed in 1997. At that time, I was at St. Antony's College, Oxford, and the Academy of Sciences in the Czech Republic. I thank Archie Brown and Michal Illner, respectively, for their welcome and support.

Finally, at M.E. Sharpe I am grateful to Elizabeth Granda and Ana Erlić for their help in preparing this volume for publication and to executive editor Patricia Kolb for the intelligence and commitment she brought to the project.

Women in the Politics of Postcommunist Eastern Europe

1

Introduction

Marilyn Rueschemeyer

This volume focuses on the political scene, on what has happened to women during the various stages of transition from communism to a market economy and a multiparty political system, to societies in which nationalism has increasing appeal and legitimacy or where the church has gained in power. We seek to understand the relations of political institutions to these developments and the emerging conceptions of women's place in the new social and political orders.

The contributors to this book are social scientists who either live and work in Eastern Europe or have spent long periods doing research there, both before and after the fall of communism. Our past experiences and our present work in that part of the world lead us to see the new policies that are emerging in the postcommunist societies of Eastern Europe as neither simply reprises of precommunist procedures nor new imitations of the West. They also reflect the changes that have taken place in these societies since World War II. Therefore, an assessment of the position of women in communist societies is crucial for our understanding of what is happening now.

The writings of early socialist theorists advocated that women be brought into the labor force and into the public sphere so that they could contribute their energies and intelligence to the creation of a more egalitarian society. Private household responsibilities were eventually to become public responsibilities. And women would no longer be forced into marriage and dependence on men with whom they would rather not live. This broad framework of ideas for the participation of women in work outside the household strongly influenced the policies of communist societies. These policies have been criticized by feminists from a wide variety of perspectives: the primary goal of communist societies was to gain the labor of women, rather than to achieve gender equality; support for the participation of men and women in the labor force were inadequate; the policies were generally geared to women, rather than to men and women, parents, and families; the obligations of men in the household were seldom discussed; and the very process took place in an authoritarian state where women had little influence on the policies that affected their lives. These criticisms contain much more than a grain of truth, but they are not sufficient for our understanding of a variety of important changes that took place in the lives of many women in Eastern Europe.

It is probably safe to say that very few people, men or women, would choose to return to life in the authoritarian systems of Eastern Europe. But important expectations associated with the role of the state are now threatened, and women especially feel that threat. Here it is important to note that the situation of women in communist Eastern Europe varied considerably, and women's assessments of this period also vary within each country.

Among the factors to which we pay particular attention are differences among the various countries in the composition of sectors of the labor force and in education level, in the status of women, and in the tensions and conflicts—latent or open—surrounding former policies on women. Even the public discussion of these issues varied from place to place. Thus we try to guard against the tendency to see the later years of communist rule and "the transition" as a single process with a few minor variations.

Within any society the positions and the experiences women have had influence their current concerns and hopes for the future. And these positions and experiences are not all the same. We must take into account, for instance, the fact that women in the former German Democratic Republic and at least the Czech part of what was Czechoslovakia grew up and worked in societies that had been industrialized before World War II. It is also true, though, that even in a country such as Albania, with its religious traditions and a population that was two-thirds rural, and Romania, with its pervasive rural past and small educated urban elite, large numbers of women moved into the public sphere during the forty-five years of communist rule and became skilled workers and professionals. We are not suggesting that it was always better to be an urban worker than a peasant, but many women found new opportunities to change and develop when they left the traditional setting.

The reaction to the communist policy of educating women and bringing them into the work force also varied over time. In some countries both men and women were horrified by a policy that forced women to join the labor force and devote their time and attention to their jobs rather than to their families. Other women embraced work outside the home with intensity and enthusiasm but later became bitterly disappointed by the continuing inadequacy of the state's services and supports.

Since nearly all women worked outside the home and since nearly all women had families, several of us refer to their "double burden" or "double duties." What these added responsibilities entailed, however, also varied from country to country. Some countries have experienced slow but definite changes in the relations between men and women; young and educated couples especially have increasingly tended to share child care and some household tasks. In other countries the women have been responsible for everything that goes on in the household. We deal with this issue in considerable detail.

During the early years of communist formation, official organizations encouraged the education of women, their political training, and their participation in the work force. It was several years before nearly all state-socialist societies could establish the structure of economic and social supports that citizens of these societies now take for granted. While the details and the overall level of these supports varied enormously from country to country, these policies were part of the overall economic and social agenda of East European communism, which also included supports for socially weaker strata and classes. They were also in line with socialist ideas on gender relations from Engels on, even if this transformation was not complete and was not programmed and processed according to criteria many of us might use now. But the quality of the services—nurseries, kindergartens, medical care, and so on—was directly related to the burdens shouldered by families, and particularly by women. Here, too, we find variations in access among and within countries.

One question that has captured the attention of scholars and others interested in Eastern Europe is whether women will "choose" to stay at home, rather than participate in the labor force. The choice that women really have now is limited for a variety of reasons, as we shall see. But it is clear to all of us that something important did happen during those forty-five years that changed the lives of large numbers of women. We observed, as scholars who studied workers in the West did, that during the communist period the more skilled the woman was or the more involved she became in her profession, the more she identified with the place where she worked, the more interested she was in keeping her job, and the more reluctant she was to become a full-time homemaker. The percentage of women involved in the labor force was much greater in communist societies than in most Western countries, includ- ing—until recently—the United States. Indeed, many women in Eastern Europe developed a changed sense of self, a more independent voice, and expectations of partaking in public life. As several of the contributors suggest, these past experiences strongly shape their reac- tions to current developments.

In most East European countries, men and women participated in the labor market in almost equal numbers during the communist pe- riod. Work in some occupations, however, was of a gender-specific character, with more women than men doing less prestigious and poorly paid work. In some countries—in Hungary and Poland, for example—women's education was more general than men's. Men were trained for vocations and given greater access to jobs after their schooling. Few women held managerial and leadership positions in industry and in the professions. We have observed that, as in the West, professions that are considered female or that become largely female are usually characterized by lower prestige and earnings. Here, too, however, the issue is more complicated than it may seem. In Poland, for example, though medicine became a feminized profession and was not very well paid, it retained its high social prestige. More than half of all Polish doctors were women, as were more than three-fourths of all dentists and pharmacists. Evidence suggests that despite the low mone- tary compensation, such women felt confident and independent, and that many retained certain expectations with respect to social policy and the responsibility of the state. Silva Mežnarić and Mirjana Ule note that the very understanding of the term "modern" among women in Croatia and Slovenia incorporates a view of the state as the provider of services for the community, for society.

The increasing equality of women and men in education and labor force participation was not matched in political life. In nearly all the countries of Eastern Europe, few women advanced beyond mid-level positions. They accounted for from a quarter to a third of the members of their parliaments, but very few women were to be found in the Central Committees and Politburos, though more in some countries than in others. At both the local and national levels women were seen as representatives of official organizations, present because of quotas. In some countries they were considered tokens and looked down upon because they differed from their male colleagues in their educational or occupational backgrounds. But even their comparatively small role in political life during the communist period is more complex than it appears at first glance. We will have to return to the way the authority and legitimacy of women politicians during that period was evaluated later, how that evaluation was used in the formation of a new political milieu, and what has changed since the early years of the transformation.

The conditions under which the transition from communism to a multiparty system and market economy took place varied significantly from country to country, and these variations influenced the formation of parties, social policies, and modes of economic development. In Hungary the communist party itself introduced a variety of reforms, and by the time the communist system had essentially ended in Eastern Europe, Hungary had the strongest links to the outside, with a larger number of investors than the rest of Eastern Europe. In Poland the church played a powerful role in the transition, along with repeated and persistent union action, while the financial and other supports that West Germany provided East Germany and the complex relation between the two states strongly affected the unification process. These differences in the ways communism came to an end and new political and economic orders were approached had direct and indirect consequences on the position of women.

Although we all deal with similar themes, an issue that is salient in one country is not necessarily so in another. All societies in Eastern Europe strive for economic development, but whether abortion or the role of the church or of ethnicity is of major concern varies from country to country. Mežnarić and Ule's contributions illuminate the importance of a modernized, democratic state with a strong civic culture for the position of women.

In view of the chaotic developments in this part of the world, especially the states of the shattered Yugoslavia, we are grateful to have so many Eastern European countries represented in our analysis. With the inclusion of chapters on women in Russia and Germany we gain perspective on the full sweep of the region, from north to south and west to east. We only regret that we were unable to include chapters on more of the former Soviet states.

2

Women and Politics in Post-Soviet Russia

Carol Nechemias

Years of far-reaching political reform and socioeconomic upheaval, beginning with Gorbachev's perestroika and continuing through the breakup of the USSR and the establishment of a newly independent Russian state, did not draw women into the halls of power. Indeed, women's low level of representation in newly reformed legislatures quickly led women activists to charge that "democratization without women is not democracy."[1] Commentators regarded the plummeting numbers of women in the postcommunist parliaments of Eastern and Central Europe as evidence of women's declining political status. But a closer examination reveals an ostensible, rather than a real, decline in political influence. Comparing communist legislatures with their postcommunist counterparts masks the persistent marginalization of women from political decision making.

It is the position of the legislature in the overall political system that has changed, while women's place in politics has remained stable. Women played a marginal role in the political life of the Soviet Union, and their exclusion from high-level decision making in the Russian Federation constitutes an element of continuity, not a break with the past. Discontinuity has occurred, however, with respect to the establishment and growth of independent women's organizations, some of which seek to enhance women's role in decision making. This chapter explores these aspects of continuity and change by reviewing the legacy of communism and of perestroika before focusing on women's political participation in the Russian Federation.

The Legacy of Communism

An examination of high-level party and state institutions under communism demonstrates women's lack of access to key decision-making bodies. Within the Communist Party, the Central Committee, and above all the Politburo, were the key centers of policymaking, while upward mobility within the party apparatus provided the surest path to political power. The Central Committee, generally regarded by scholars as the best measure of the party elite, had a female membership that hovered at the 3 percent mark for decades, finally inching above 4 percent in 1986. Moreover, the women's contingent on the Central Committee disproportionately contained individuals selected to lend a rank-and-file flavor to that institution: honored textile workers and collective farmers, rather than high-ranking party or state officials.[2]

The record of female membership on the Politburo, the pinnacle of the party apparatus, shows a similar dearth of women: between the passing of the old generation of Bolsheviks to the eve of perestroika, only one woman—Ekaterina Furtseva, from 1957 to 1960—served on the Politburo.

Few women reached the top because few women traveled the path of upward mobility within the party apparatus. As is the case with many pyramid structures, women congregated at the bottom. At the lowest level of the party—primary party organizations or party cells—women frequently held the position of first party secretary. As early as 1966 women held one-third of these positions, which generally did not involve full-time party work. But women typically did not ascend the party ladder: they constituted only 7 percent of all regional and county level party secretaries in 1988.

Women likewise failed to secure more than token representation within influential state institutions. At the all-union or national level it was rare to have more than one woman minister on the Council of Ministers; overall, women ministers generally held positions associated with women's roles, such as health, social security, and culture.

Women did achieve a substantial presence in the soviets, holding 33 percent of the seats in the USSR Supreme Soviet in 1984 and even higher proportions in soviets at lower federal levels. Unfortunately, however, the Supreme Soviet functioned more as a facade of democracy than as a center of lawmaking. The high proportions of women deputies reflected a quota system, rather than public opinion. Roughly

40 percent of the Supreme Soviet's members were persons who held significant party and/or state positions; but women generally were found among the other 60 percent, chosen according to quotas that kept the sexual, professional, and party composition of the legislature within proportions set by the party leadership. Soviet propaganda proudly pointed to the "democratic" character of the Supreme Soviet by noting its high proportion of women, workers, and collective farmers.

While some groups may have had access to high-level decision making through bureaucratic politics, like the military and industrial managers, organizational structures formally charged with "speaking" on behalf of women carried little weight in the Soviet system. In the post-Stalinist era one all-union structure representing women existed—the Soviet Women's Committee (SWC). But the SWC functioned as a mouthpiece for Soviet propaganda, representing the USSR at international conferences and hosting foreign delegations of women. Its functions were oriented toward foreign affairs and echoing Soviet policy positions.

At the local level, women's councils (*zhensovety*) were active at some work sites and engaged in such activities as organizing the purchase of food at work, exchanges of children's clothes, social gatherings for young people, and help for pensioners. Like the SWC, the women's councils were state created, part of the "old" system of state-sponsored activism.

Within society women's absence from politics evoked little concern. The Communist Party had proclaimed women's struggle for equality won as early as 1929. The communist conception of women's emancipation highlighted the central role of work in securing women's independence and social status. And it is in the spheres of work-force participation and educational opportunities that sweeping change did take place, though after 1928 the Soviet state's mobilization of women into the labor force occurred more for demographic and economic reasons than ideological considerations. By the close of the Soviet era, women had more formal education than men and represented 51 percent of the work force. Despite women's impressive achievements in the professions and their entry into many sectors of industry, women tended to fade out in the upper reaches of managerial hierarchies.

Women took on new roles without abandoning old ones, as suggested by official images of women, which often portrayed them as mother-workers. Traditional familial roles were bolstered by a "biology is destiny" approach to gender differences, and the everyday lives of women trying to combine work and family duties were marked by crushing burdens and difficulties. Indeed, the impact of marriage and childrearing on women's political activism is revealed in the startling statistic that, as students, young women were more likely than young men to take leadership in Komsomol (the Communist Youth League).

Insofar as women's issues did figure in the popular press and in specialized academic literature, debate in the decades preceding perestroika centered on women's reproductive and productive roles. Key issues involved demography: unacceptably low birthrates among European nationalities and looming labor shortages in the developed, European part of the Soviet Union. Some scholars did draw attention to women's exhaustion and lack of leisure time, but this generally was treated, especially by politicians, as a problem that would go away as economic development produced modern appliances and improved consumer services. Moreover, rarely did commentators point a critical finger at the household division of labor and call on men to share more of the burden. The view of women as a productive and reproductive resource easily meshed with the state's paternalistic approach to women: through protectionist legislation the state sought to ensure the reproductive health of working women; and through social policies such as preschools and maternity leaves the state sought to ensure women's work-force participation.

The Era of Perestroika

With the advent of perestroika new opportunities and challenges faced women. Political reform brought the first competitive elections since 1917, freedom to establish organizations operating independently from government control, and open debate over "women's place" in society. At the same time, Gorbachev's pursuit of partial economic reform generated yet more severe shortages, the rationing of such goods as sugar, and still longer lines, conditions that kept the day-to-day lives of women entangled with enervating, time-consuming domestic tasks.

Competing in the Electoral Arena

The wave of political reform carried out in 1988–90 emphasized a flow of political power from high-level party institutions to revitalized state institutions. A centerpiece of this effort involved transforming the USSR Supreme Soviet, a pseudo legislature, into a genuine, working parliament. Constitutional changes replaced the USSR Supreme Soviet with the Congress of People's Deputies (CPD), which, in turn, elected from among its members a smaller, standing Supreme Soviet. The CPD included 2,250 deputies, two-thirds of whom were elected via two traditional routes: one-third from districts based on population; one-third from districts based on the federal structure. A novel procedure involved allotting 750 seats to all-union public organizations, which would fill their mandates through internal procedures such as conferences or plenums.

The elections held for the CPD in the spring of 1989 captured public attention as the contests conducted in electoral districts generally were multicandidate, the first since 1917. For women political activists, however, the results were disappointing.[3] In contrast to the last USSR Supreme Soviet chosen in 1984, in which women held 33 percent of the seats, women's proportion fell to 15.7 percent. And even this figure overstates women's representation. Of the three routes to the CPD, women depended heavily on public organizations for access to the newly reformed legislature. Fifty-six percent of women deputies secured their status through public organizations; within the CPD as a whole, 21 percent of the women deputies came from the Soviet Women's Committee, an organization associated with the "old politics" of a mass organization created by the Communist Party leadership.

Public dissatisfaction with built-in representation for public organizations resulted in the abandonment of reserving seats in thirteen of the fifteen union republics that held elections in 1990. The absence of seats allocated to women in the 1990 Russian republic election meant electoral disaster for women, as their level of representation fell from 35.3 percent in the prereform era to 5.4 percent. Of the fifty women serving in the Russian republic Supreme Soviet, only three were chosen to serve on committees. For women activists this election was a wake-up call, a blunt reminder of where women stood in the absence of quotas.

New legislative committees were formed to address women's issues. These included committees on Women's Affairs, the Defense of the Family, Motherhood and Childhood in the Supreme Soviets of the USSR and the Russian republic. Discussions of women's issues flowed from the perspective that women are mothers and wives, rather than individuals. As the chair of the USSR committee, Valentina Matvienko, noted, "it is very difficult to separate out the problems of children, the problems of women and maternity."[4] The chair of the Russian republic committee, Ekaterina Lakhova, stated that women's prime mission is propagation of the human species and called for greater protection for families, children, and women. She expressed disgruntlement with Soviet-style equality between men and women, contending that "we have already experienced equal right to swing the hammer. Nothing good came of it."[5]

The dominant theme raised by women deputies involved women's poor working conditions and how those conditions impinge on women's health, particularly their ability to give birth to healthy children.

Competing in the Party and State Machinery

The severe underrepresentation of women in high party and state office continued under Gorbachev, though it would appear that tokenism, the presence of a lone female, occurred more often. Two women served, though not simultaneously, on the Politburo. Alexandra Biriukova held candidate or nonvoting status on the Politburo from 1988 until her retirement in mid-1990. During her stint in the top domain of Soviet officials, she had served as a party secretary from 1986 to 1988, when she gave up her work in the Secretariat to become a deputy chairman of the USSR Council of Ministers and chairman of the Bureau for Social Development. She was the sole female member of the Council of Ministers.

After Biriukova's retirement two women reached high political posts in the waning days of the USSR. The overhaul of high party institutions in July 1990 led to the establishment of a new position within the Party's Secretariat: that of secretary for women's affairs, a slot filled by an editor of a popular women's magazine, Galina Semenova, who also gained Politburo membership. On the state side, Bikhodzhal Rakhimova, a former secretary of the Tajik Party Central Committee, was brought in as the lone female cabinet member, serving as the deputy chairman in charge of social affairs. It should be noted that in the Russian republic the position of women in high government office was similarly bleak: under President Yeltsin in 1991 no women served among the twenty-six members of the Council of Ministers.

Women's Organizations and Public Debate

As part of the reform process, Gorbachev transformed the roles of the SWC and women's soviets and allowed new women's organizations to emerge. He called for the revitalization of the women's soviets and their subordination under the SWC, which was granted the power of legislative initiative and later was slotted for 75 seats in the CPD. The numbers of women's soviets grew dramatically, from only 15 in the Moscow region before 1986, for example, to 600 by 1987. A reorientation in the SWC's responsibilities took place: formerly isolated, the organization found itself coordinating the activities of an extensive grassroots network of women's councils. Moreover, domestic policy issues replaced foreign policy as a primary concern at a time when far-reaching criticism of Soviet society had become fashionable. And most important of all, the SWC found itself thrust into "high" politics, charged with representing women within the newly created CPD.

The SWC did not earn high marks in the legislative arena. With the country glued to their television sets in the spring of 1989, the SWC's caution and its status as one of the public organizations slated for reserved seats garnered public scorn and ridicule. Zoia Pukhova, who took over as leader of the SWC in 1987, did deliver hard-hitting speeches stressing women's need for state protection, especially the goals of moving women out of arduous and heavy physical labor, improving maternal and infant health, ending night shifts for women, and creating better working conditions for pregnant women.[6] But it is striking that none of the women who gained public recognition, women like Galina Starovoitova, Evdokia Gaer, and Kazimiera Prunskiene, were from the SWC or identified themselves with women's issues. Starovoitova spoke of the SWC women deputies as the weaker part of the women's corp in the CPD,[7] while the journalist Evgeniia Albats expressed her outrage in the popular magazine *Ogonek* at the SWC's claim it represented her and, by implication, other women.[8]

If the SWC smacked of the "old politics" of mass organizations associated with the Communist Party, the reform process saw the founding of new, independent women's organizations. These organizations were nongovernmental; foreign sponsors, foundations, and governments have provided crucial financial support to many of them. With the burgeoning growth of women's groups, a particularly noteworthy development took place in the spring of 1991: the holding of the first Independent Women's Forum in Dubna, which brought together about 200 participants from forty-eight women's organizations. The Forum added a new and distinctly feminist flavor to the debate over women's place, with its motto of "Democracy without women is not democracy" and its firm stance against social, economic, political, and cultural discrimination against women.

Gorbachev's policy of *glasnost* opened up a wider range of debate over women's issues. The flavor of this public discussion to a large extent reflected a backlash against the emancipation of women, a policy closely associated with the Communist Party. "Sending the women back home"—reducing women's participation in the work force and enhancing their roles as wives and mothers—emerged as a popular theme. Yet a variety of other views also were beginning to find expression, including an emphasis on women deciding for themselves what they wish to do, on a vision of women as individuals and citizens, rather than as "mother-workers."

Post-Soviet Russia and Women's Political Participation

In the aftermath of the breakup of the USSR, severe economic and political crises continued to plague the newly independent Russian Federation. Runaway inflation, though largely established by the mid-1990s, and the erosion of such safety nets as free health care and day care, threatened women and their families with impoverishment. The era of perpetual shortages of basic goods and services gave way to a flood of available products but also to a shortage of money in the pockets of most citizens. On the political front a strong sense of political instability punctuated by extraordinary crises, like President Yeltsin's use of military force to disband parliament in the fall of 1993, gradually has given way to a more relaxed atmosphere, though one still full of uncertainty regarding the economic and political future of the country.

Within this context women's groups have sought to carve out a niche for themselves in Russia's developing political system. We next examine women's successes and failures in the electoral arena, within the Yeltsin administration, and among the burgeoning numbers of nongovernmental organizations seeking to achieve particular goals, often including the influencing of public policy.

The 1993 and 1995 Elections: The Women of Russia Electoral Bloc

The 1993 parliamentary elections, held in the aftermath of a bloody showdown between President Yeltsin and parliament, contained surprising results. The biggest surprise involved the success enjoyed by Vladimir Zhirinovsky's Liberal Democratic Party. But there was another unexpected outcome that did not draw as much media attention: the fourth-place finish in the party-list balloting of Women of Russia (*Zhenshchiny Rossii,* or ZhR). The proportion of women in Russia's parliament soared from 5.4 percent in the 1990 Congress of People's Deputies to 13 percent in the State Duma elected in 1993. Of the sixty women elected to the Duma, twenty-three were from ZhR. Women of Russia secured just over 8 percent of the vote, finishing ahead of many of the stalwarts of perestroika and the post-perestroika period, like Mikhail Lapshin's Agrarian Union, the Yavlinsky-Bodyrev-Lukin (Yabloko) bloc, Sergei Shakrai's Russian Party of Unity and Accord, and Nikolai Travkin's Democratic Party of Russia.

A women-only electoral bloc—above all, a successful one—is virtually unprecedented in the worldwide history of women's movements. In reality, ZhR had deep roots within the Soviet system, and in the eyes of many represented the "old" politics of communist public organizations, rather than the "new" politics of an independent women's movement. ZhR's "pedigree" traces directly back to the SWC, which, in the wake of the August 1991 coup, moved quickly to register as a nongovernmental union of women's public organizations with a new name, the Union of Women of Russia (UWR). Aside from the women's councils, some newly formed women's groups—artists, mothers-of-many-children, entrepreneurs, and so on—affiliated themselves with the UWR. It should be pointed out that the UWR's leader, Alevtina Fedulova, who had succeeded Pukhova, had tremendous organizational experience but a tainted reputation due to her extensive links with Komsomol, the Pioneers (a children's organization), and the Soviet Peace Committee.

The UWR continued its political work, lobbying the constitutional conference and the Russian Supreme Soviet on behalf of women's issues. In the fall of 1993 the UWR reviewed the programs of thirty parties planning to participate in the December parliamentary elections and concluded that none addressed women's issues. As a result the

UWR sent letters to these parties, inquiring about their positions on women's issues and informing them that their responses would shape the organization's stance toward them during the campaign. Only three parties responded, all with superficial statements. Moreover, an examination of party lists revealed few women; it appeared that women's representation in the Duma would be paltry.

In interviews Fedulova stated that the disinterest of the "establishment" in women's affairs, the "send-the-women-home" sentiments expressed in society, and the belief that women must decide their own fate and have an equal voice in politics generated the decision to create a women's electoral bloc, Women of Russia.[9] Sheer political ambition may also, of course, have played a role. The UWR invited two other all-union organizations—the Union of Women Entrepreneurs and the Union of Women of the Navy—to join together to form ZhR and enter the electoral fray, a decision made less than three months before the election. Of the three constituent groups, the UWR was the dominant element.

The woman who held the second position on ZhR's party list did not come from any organizations that formed the women's bloc. This was Ekaterina Lakhova, formerly chair of the Russian republic Supreme Soviet Committee on Women's Affairs and the Defense of the Family, Motherhood, Childhood, and by 1993 President Yeltsin's adviser on family and women's issues as well as head of a presidential commission on women, family, and demography. By background a pediatrician from Sverdlosk, Lakhova's political career has been closely tied to that of Boris Yeltsin.

ZhR did not spring from a wave of grassroots activism but from a combination of organizations whose origins lie in the top-down politics of the communist past as well as in the Kremlin, given Lakhova's key role. At ZhR's first press conference the slogan "Democracy Without Women is not Democracy" was put forward, only to be swiftly dropped in favor of the less contentious "Women of Russia—for Russia." The bloc stressed populist appeals stressing social policy and the restoration of social benefits, as well as the contention that women could raise the moral standards in political life and bring peace and consensus to society. Lakhova, who over the years became increasingly open to feminist ideas and to a wider vision of women's issues, embraced a pragmatism that ruled out any open references to feminism. She noted in a National Public Radio interview that Russian society is not prepared to discuss the feminist movement and women's issues, and that it was therefore better to approach the problems of women through family and children.[10] In many ways ZhR proved to be the follower, rather than the leader, on women's issues: it generally adopted mottoes and issues that had already been pioneered by more feminist groups associated with the Independent Women's Forum.

Analysts have identified several factors as crucial to ZhR's electoral success. A key factor involves the times—with men apparently all too willing to settle their differences on the barricade, women's image of seeking peace and consensus rather than power may have stood them in good stead. As one man who voted for ZhR said, "Better the rolling pin than the automatic."[11] Extreme anger at and distrust of political parties also favored rank outsiders like ZhR (as well as Zhirinovsky). Thus, voting for ZhR represented a protest vote, and a rather exotic one at that. Moreover, the change in the political rules of the game aided ZhR, with half of the members of the Duma being elected from a party list and half from single-member districts. Twenty-one of the initial twenty-three members of ZhR gained their status as deputies through the party-list ballot. Finally, ZhR had inherited from the communist past a fairly extensive network of grassroots organizations—the women's councils—that gave the electoral bloc a presence that few other political groups, with the major exception of the Communist Party of the Russian Federation, could muster.

ZhR had two short years to establish a legislative record before the 1995 elections. With the election of Fedulova as deputy chair of the Duma, the leadership of the faction fell to Lakhova. ZhR emphasized its moderate and centrist nature, fiercely maintaining its independence by refusing to enter alliances with other parliamentary parties or blocs. A faction member chaired the Duma Committee on Women, Family, and Youth, and the centerpieces of the faction's accomplishments flowed from the work of that committee. These legislative achievements included Children of Russia, a multifaceted program that focused primarily on children but also included family planning. A new Family Code was adopted, which drew little public attention. Interestingly, ZhR members cited a new attitude toward women politicians—men taking them seriously—as a key result of their electoral success.

In contrast to the 1993 elections, ZhR entered the 1995 electoral fray as one of the electoral blocs favored to clear the 5 percent barrier in the party-list ballot. But ZhR finished just below the 5 percent mark, in fifth place among forty-three electoral blocs. The number of ZhR deputies fell from twenty-one to three, all of whom secured election in single-member districts. The reasons behind ZhR's electoral eclipse include the failure to take a clear and principled stance against the war in Chechnya; the failure to deliver on promises that, in reality, could not be kept with respect to social benefits; the failure to work effectively with the growing numbers of nongovernmental women's organizations; and the failure to refute attacks by other electoral groups effectively. Finally, the passage of time had brought greater civic calm and undercut ZhR's appeal as an outlet for a protest vote.

Overall, the proportion of women in the Duma fell from 13.5 to 10.2 percent. It might have fallen further had it not been for the impact of ZhR's earlier success. In 1993 ZhR had drawn 14 to 15 percent of the women's vote and 3 percent of the male vote.[12] As a result, other political blocs in 1995 sought women politicians to include on their party list to counter the pull of ZhR. Excluding ZhR, 7 percent of candidates running on party lists were female in 1993, compared with 14 percent in 1995.[13] The names of the top three candidates on the party list appear on the ballot, and it is striking that two major contenders, Yabloko and the Communist Party, included women within this top grouping. Although electoral blocs may have wished to show their sympathy toward women politicians, only ZhR included in its platform a commitment to equal opportunity for women. Other party programs, if they addressed women's issues at all, spoke in traditional terms about defending motherhood and childhood. Moreover, some of the flurry to find a woman candidate focused on famous actresses, an approach actually pioneered by ZhR in 1993.

It is unclear whether the 1995 election returns represent more than a temporary setback for women. The proportion of women deputies within the Duma did fall, and women parliamentarians continue to work largely within the confines of the traditional female sphere of social policy. Lakhova has withdrawn from her alliance with Fedulova and the UWR, choosing to register a new organization, one more clearly committed to the democratic camp, and with a slightly different name—the All-Russian Social-Political Movement of Women of Russia—as opposed to the Political Movement "Women of Russia." It is too early to tell whether a future women's party will emerge from this organization. Other women's groups are pursuing alternative approaches to enhancing the numbers of women officeholders by lobby-

ing, so far without success, the Central Electoral Commission to introduce new rules that would require parties and electoral blocs to adopt
quotas for women candidates.

Women in the Yeltsin Administration

Women have had little opportunity to influence policymaking by holding high-level positions within the Yeltsin government. In one analysis
of Russia's political elite in 1995, Olga Kryshtanovskaia found that
while 44 percent of the employees of the government apparatus were
female, only 3.9 percent of those in responsible government posts were
women.[14] Curiously, the one ministry that exhibited an interest in
women's affairs, the Ministry of Social Protection, has been abolished
and its programs transferred to the Ministry of Labor. After the 1996
presidential election, one woman served at the ministerial level, Minister of Health Tatiana Dimitrieva, and of 152 deputy ministers, only 2
were female.

   In judicial organs the picture has been similarly bleak. In 1996 only
two women served among the nineteen judges on the Russian
Federation's Constitutional Court, and only four women among the
eighty-six judges on the Supreme Court and the territorial and regional
courts.[15]

   Although Russia has a long history of words but not action when it
comes to women's rights, there are recent signs of a greater openness
to appointing women to high office. In June 1996 President Yeltsin
issued a decree "On Increasing the Rule of Women in the System of
Federal Bodies of State Powers . . ." and invited representatives of
women's organizations, with whom he met on July 21, 1996, to submit
names of women candidates for him to review as possible administrative candidates.[16]

   The year 1997 witnessed some favorable signs. Yeltsin nominated
Liudmila Zharkova to the Constitutional Court, appointed Natalia
Dementeva as minister of culture, Natalia Fonareva as head of the State
Monopoly Committee, and Viktoriia Mitina as the Kremlin's deputy
chief of administration. Dementeva informed the Russian press that she
sees an increased willingness to appoint women to governmental posts
and vigorously defended women as worthy of public trust.[17] In early
1998 yet another appointment, that of Duma deputy Tatyana
Nesterenko as head of the Federal Treasury, suggested that women's

access to high-level appointive positions might be on the upswing. Women's underrepresentation in the corridors of power remains severe, but these recent appointments do suggest an improvement in women's access to high-level positions within the Yeltsin administration.

The Political Influence of Women's Organizations

There has been a tremendous growth of women's organizations and the gradual emergence of a women's movement. While some women's groups chose to participate directly in the electoral campaigns of various parties in 1995, the best-known independent women's groups committed to women's rights have refrained from supporting any particular political bloc. In 1993, for example, the Independent Women's Forum expressed its support for all women candidates and nominated its own members to run as candidates in different blocs, thus maintaining the political pluralism within the organization.

Women's organizations exhibit a growing institutionalization oriented toward public advocacy. The Committees on Soldiers' Mothers and the Russian Association of Crisis Centers for Women represent single-issue groups whose goals include, respectively, the passing of laws relating to military service and to violence against women. Women connected with the Moscow Center for Gender Studies, in particular its Gender Expertise Project, as well as the Information Center of the Independent Women's Forum, and the Consortium of Women's Non-Governmental Organizations, have lobbied through Duma hearings, the provision of reports and commentaries to government officials, and at times direct membership on working groups charged with developing legislation. The growing use of the Internet to spread information to women's organizations about government programs and pending legislation represents a major breakthrough in a society where basic knowledge about government laws and activities has been a scarce commodity.

Another effort at coalition building occurred in March 1997, when, at the behest of Lakhova's Women of Russia, a variety of women's organizations signed a Charter of Solidarity. The goal involves coordinating and consolidating the strength of women's organizations in order to influence public policy. The outcome of this effort remains unclear as actual mechanisms for achieving joint action have yet to be determined. Moreover, many young women activists view the entire scheme with skepticism, as part and parcel of Lakhova's own political ambitions.

Conclusion

Women's political participation in post-Soviet Russia shares much in common with the communist past—especially marginalization. Despite far-reaching political and economic change, women's exclusion from key political institutions remains a constant. Indeed, in October 1996, the only woman appearing on the list of 100 top political figures published periodically by the newspaper *Nezavisimaia gazeta* was Tatiana Dyachenko, Boris Yeltsin's daughter.[18] Politics remains a male domain, but a lively and growing women's movement, increasingly institutionalized and sophisticated, seeks to inject women's voices into the Russian political arena.

Notes

I would like to thank several organizations for supporting my research on women's participation in Russia in recent years. These include an IREX Short-Term Travel Grant in 1994, an American Political Science Association research grant in 1995, and a Short-Term Grant for research at the Kennan Institute for Advanced Russian Studies of the Woodrow Wilson Center in 1995. The University of Illinois Summer Slavic Workshops also have proved enormously helpful.

1. The slogan "Democracy Without Women is not Democracy" was used by the Independent Women's Forum, meeting at Dubna in 1991.

2. See my article "Women's Participation: From Lenin to Gorbachev," in *Russian Women in Politics and Society,* ed. Wilma Rule and Norma C. Noonan (Westport, CT: Greenwood Press, 1996), pp. 15–30.

3. See my article "Democratization and Women's Access to Legislative Seats: The Soviet Case, 1989–1991," *Women and Politics* 14, no. 3, 1–18, for a review of women and the 1989 election.

4. As cited in Rolf H.W. Theen, ed., *The U.S.S.R. First Congress of People's Deputies,* vol. 3 (New York, NY: Paragon Press, 1991), p. 699.

5. "Out Interview with Lakhova. . . ," Women's Discussion Club newsletter, Interlegal Research Center, January–March 1991, p. 6.

6. "Vystuplenie tovarishcha Pukhovoi Z.P.," *Pravda,* July 2, 1998, p. 11.

7. Galina Starovoitova, "A Woman in Politics," *Moscow News* 10 (1990): 3.

8. Evgeniia Albats, "Po polovomu priznaku," *Ogonek* 10 (1990): 9.

9. For an explanation of the origins of ZhR, see Tatiana Khudiakova, "Alevtina Fedulova: "Nashe dvizhenie sledovalo by nazvat' 'Zhenshchiny dlia Rossii'," *Izvestia,* December 2, 1993, p. 4.

10. See transcript of "All Things Considered," National Public Radio, December 10, 1993, p. 19.

11. As cited in El'vira Novikova, "Zhenshchiny v politicheskoi zhizni Rossii," *Preobrazhenie,* no. 2 (1994): 18.

12. The figures were given by Professor Jerry Hough at a roundtable panel on the 1993 Russian parliamentary elections at the American Political Science Association Meeting on September 2, 1994.

13. Elena Kochkina, "Nastupaet pora sufrazhizma," *Nezavisimaia gazeta,* December 28, 1995, p. 6.

14. Olga Kryshtanovskaia, "Zhdem svoiu Margaraet Tetcher," *Argumenty i fakty* 39 (September): 10.

15. For data on women's representation in government, see Nadezhda Kuznetsova, "Women's Rights: Realities and Prospects," *You and We,* no. 1 (1997): 8–10.

16. Mariia Krobka and Natalia Buniakina, " 'Zhenshchiny Rossii' vedut aktivnyi obraz zhizni," *Uchitel'skaia gazeta,* July 30, 1996, p. 5.

17. "Culture Minister on Women in Government," RFE/RL Newsline 1 (106), part 1 (August 21, 1997).

18. "100 vedushchikh politikov Rossii v Sentiabre," *Nezavisimaia gazeta,* October 2, 1996, p. 1.

Poland

3

Polish Women in Politics

An Introduction to the Status of Women in Poland

Anna Titkow

When the results of Poland's historic parliamentary elections of June 1989 were tabulated, discussions with an American colleague from Rutgers University focused on the influence that the upcoming political changes would have on the status of Polish women. While I felt great concern, an American colleague expressed optimism. Unfortunately, the events of the next three years supported my view. The changes in the political system that Poles so eagerly awaited were not positive for women. Developments since then have not dissipated concern, but they do provide some cause for optimism about the future for Polish women.

Women as Resources: Employment

Polish women are now in a paradoxical position. Women's equality with men has been legally guaranteed since 1918. The post–World War II political system encouraged increased levels of education for women and ensured their massive participation in the labor market. The educational level of women is the same as that of men—11.1 years (Domański 1992)—and women's participation in the labor market is stable. Women accounted for 43.4 percent of the work force in 1979, 45 percent in 1988 (*Demographic Yearbook of Poland* 1988), 46 percent in 1996 (Kowalska 1996).

The 120 years since independence have been a difficult period for women and have created a social genotype in attitudes and behavior.

Women were perceived as persons capable of meeting the most difficult requirements of social reality in the name of sacrifice to the Motherland and to the family. They expected no gratification beyond acknowledgment of their importance to the family and to society.

Polish women adopted another characteristic of self-effacement. They were "like the sediment of a good wine, they have sunk to the bottom" (Fuchs-Epstein 1970). Girls chose, and they continue to choose, specializations that prepare them for traditionally female occupations. It is as if they knew that some professions were not proper for them.

Stabilized, educational preferences of Polish women are among the factors that contribute to meaningful and lasting inequalities between men's and women's wages. Women work principally in the worst-paid "unproductive" sector of the Polish economy, where 70 percent of them are employed (Domański 1992). Even in the better-paid sectors women are primarily lower-status administrative employees or semiskilled workers.

The occupations of women and men follow the stereotypical division of labor, and their average monthly earnings reflect these divisions. During the years between 1982 and 1993 women earned on average between 66 and 67 percent of the wages earned by men (Domański 1996).

Nevertheless, because wages in Poland were generally low, Polish women's participation in the work force contributed substantially to the well-being of the family and the increased life span of its members. After 1945 the occupational activities of women were accepted as part of the pattern of everyday life. These changes, however, were regarded not as an expansion of the social roles of women but merely as an extension of their established duties.

The relative stability of women's participation in the labor market under communism has disappeared. Unemployment of women and of men emerged in Poland after 1989. The longer duration of unemployment and the longer time of looking for work—especially for less educated women—are specific characteristics of that phenomenon. In December 1991, for every 100 women who held jobs, 13 were unemployed and the number of job openings was seven times smaller for women than for men (Olczyk 1991). Women now account for 55 percent of the unemployed population. Most of the unemployed women—63.3 percent—are between 18 and 34 years old. Many women in this age cohort are heads of households. Every tenth unemployed woman is between the ages of 45 and 54. The 18–24 age group represented 34.4 percent of all unemployed women in 1995. The largest group of unemployed women has a basic vocational education (33.4 percent); the next largest group has only a grade school education (28.6 percent) (*National Work Office* 1995).

Women as Resources: Common Survival and Invisibility in Public Life

Women's responsibilities did enhance their self-esteem. Their ability to cope with difficult living conditions, both under the communist regime and later, enhanced their sense of competence. As they carried heavy net bags of food and suffered from lack of sleep, they were compensated by their knowledge that they were the indispensable managers of family life who performed, alone, duties and tasks that would be burdensome for several persons. Success in managing daily survival was won through both personal sacrifice and indomitable perseverance. "Without us" they rightly said "everything would collapse." This perception afforded Polish women tremendous psychological gratification. For the majority of them, this gratification is more important than the satisfaction that comes from occupational and social status.

Unfortunately, this gratification now prevents women from perceiving the symptoms of discrimination in social and occupational life. It may also be part of the reason why women have remained, with few exceptions, outside the decision-making processes of public and political life.

In 1986, 11 percent of the members of the Central Committee of the Polish United Workers' Party were women, yet women accounted for only 5 percent of the members of President Wojciech Jaruzelski's Consultative Board. The sixty participants in the 1989 round-table discussions included only one woman. Few women in the Solidarity movement became nationally known. The low representation of women in Solidarity (28 percent of members) corresponds roughly with female membership in the political parties and the pre-1980 trade unions (Sokołowska 1987). Women expressed their overwhelming support for Solidarity outside of organizational structures. Innumerable invisible female supporters at various levels of the movement were responsible for its basic needs and efficient operation. They were instrumental in the printing and distribution of underground publications. They provided essential liaison with the sympathetic Catholic church.

In the winter of 1981–82 it was primarily women who, with the assistance of the church, aided detained and imprisoned persons, many of them women.

Looking at women's status after 1989 we continue to see symptoms of *unfinished democracy*. In 1990 only four women were selected to sit on the ninety-six-member National Solidarity Committee (Kuratowska 1991). A 1990 government report revealed that women in public service are promoted to executive posts less often than men, although women form the majority of the government's clerical staff.[1] After 1993, women represented 13 percent of the members of the Sejm (the lower house of parliament) and 13 percent of the senators. In 1995, the proportion of women who were presidents of the board of joint Stock/Exchange was 4.4 percent and the proportion of women presidents of the board of directors of joint Stock/Exchange was 8 percent (Dukaczewska-Nałęcz 1997).

These observations suggest that the great part of society and women themselves have not recognized, have not expected, and have not been interested in the political, economic, and social contributions of women.

The Present Situation: Paradoxes of Transition

The June 1989 parliamentary elections signaled the beginning of a series of threats to women's health and their personal, public, and political autonomy.

The ideological context of the transformations emphasizes a drastic, complete break from postwar history. There is, first and foremost, a situation favorable to the filling of the vacuum that has arisen by a new ideology that constitutes the only right ideology and that would be obligatory for the entire society: the ideology of the Catholic church. The danger for the status of Polish women resulting from this situation is obvious, particularly since the leaders of national Christian organizations (who played a considerable role prior to the 1993 parliamentary elections) give the impression that locking Polish women in the worlds of the "Church, the Kitchen and Children" is for them the most important political, strategic, and personal problem. The Catholic church has historically bred an unfavorable climate for the establishment of equal rights for women. The church's influence on the definition of women's role in a society in which 85 percent of the population are practicing

Catholics has always been strong, but since 1989 it has taken the offensive against the social and political advancement of women. It constantly proclaims that a woman's domain is the home and family, whereas the world of a man revolves around his job, politics, and activities outside the family circle.

The 1991 Senate draft of the act to abolish access to abortion expresses the essence of the church-supported effort to reduce women to stereotypical sex roles, treats women as incubators and incapacitated persons, and contests their right to make responsible decisions for themselves. It contradicts international conventions ratified by Poland and offends the historically and culturally determined position of women in Polish society. The abortion debate is politically involved, long, and continuing. No recent debate in Poland has been comparable in emotional intensity, pervasiveness of discussion, or depth of division provoked (Fuszara 1993).

On July 1992 the Sejm decided to send to a specially established ad hoc working commission a document sponsored by the National Christian Club titled "On the Legal Protection of the Conceived Child." According to this bill, each person involved in the death of an embryo or fetus (with the exception of the doctor who saves the life of the mother) commits a crime that carries a prison term of up to two years. The bill, "On Family Planning, the Defense of the Human Fetus and Conditions of Abortion Permissibility," which was voted through on January 5, 1993 (213 persons for, 179 against, 29 abstaining) and introduced on March 16, 1993, was a less radical version of earlier propositions. It permits abortion only when the mother's life or health is seriously threatened, when prenatal diagnosis will show severe and irreversible defect of the fetus, or when a pregnancy is the result of rape or incest. It requires the administration and local authorities to assure access to all contraceptives. The "mildness" of the bill is equivocal, however, because in all other cases every person (except the pregnant mother) responsible for abortion will be sentenced to two years in prison. Physicians are authorized to perform abortions in public clinics only.

On August 30, 1996, the lower house of parliament, over strong Catholic church opposition, voted to amend the restrictive 1993 abortion law. It would allow women to end unwanted pregnancies for social reasons in the first trimester provided they undergo counseling and a three-day period of reflection. Pregnancies caused by rape or incest could be terminated beyond the twelfth week. The procedure would be free of charge for women meeting specified conditions. Abortions could again be performed in private clinics. The bill also instructed the Ministry of Education to enforce sexuality education programs in the schools beginning in September 1997. The liberalization of the abortion law was rejected by the Senate in October 1996. After coming back (as required) to the lower house of parliament, it was again accepted on October 24, 1996 (with 228 voting for and 195 against) and signed officially by President Kwasniewski on November 20, 1996.

The realities of political life in Poland after 1989 and the "bargain" role of women's reproductive rights do not allow us to treat the actual liberalization of the antiabortion law as a stable solution of long-lasting controversies. Tensions continued after the 1997 parliamentary elections.

The attacks on the social position taken by Polish women concentrate primarily on two areas: participation of women in the labor market and their reproduction rights.[2] I dare to say that in both areas, the effects of antiwomen activities stay unproportionally small in comparison to the intensity and range of the attacks.

The latter statement may seem false or at least improbable at first. We do have chronic unemployment of women, and the restrictive antiabortion law has been enforced.

At the same time, however, we are witnessing phenomena and facts showing that the main goal of "transitional backlash"—which is to subordinate women and return them to the traditional model of society and family—cannot be reached.

One of the questions in the Polish General Public Opinion Poll in 1992, 1993, 1994, and 1995 (Cichomski and Sawiński 1995) was this: "If you were to get enough money to live as comfortably as you would like for the rest of your life, would you continue to work or would you rather stop working?" In 1995, 76.2 percent of women answered, "Yes, I would continue to work" (figures in 1992, 1993, and 1994 were 70.1 percent, 72 percent, and 72.2 percent). For men, the 1995 rate was 83.7 percent, as compared to 80.9 percent in 1994.

In recent years (1991–94) we have noticed a remarkable decrease (from 20 percent to 13.5 percent) in the number of women who think that a woman should, first of all, take care of the family and not go out to work (CBOS 1993a, GUS 1994a).[3]

For decades, Polish society has been realizing its procreative plans with a minimum consideration for modern contraceptive techniques. Neglecting sexual education and a limited availability of contraceptives—the heritage of real socialism, which forced the society to use abortion as the only way of birth control—gave a really wide range of arguments to the followers of life-protection ideology.

Neither the antiabortion law itself nor the accompanying procedures or explanations could trigger any particularly "pro-family" or "pronatalistic" behaviors. The number of births in Poland has been decreasing since the mid-1980s. The year 1995 was the sixth consecutive one in which human reproduction level was below that which guarantees simple generation reproduction (Population Commission of the Government 1995). After 1990, the number of marriages decreased, too. Procreation plans of young married couples are much smaller than those declared in the 1980s. Families with one child are dominant in urban areas (GUS 1994b).

After several decades of a nonsubjective citizenship, Polish people are learning to treat themselves as subjects and not as objects of the state. Both men and women are now learning to articulate their interests by taking part in political parties, associations, local government, and so on. But only 5 percent of Poles are engaged in any form of such activities and only 0.5 percent of Polish men and women belong to political parties (CBOS 1993b, Domański and Rychard 1997).

The year 1989 was a turning point in this area. The change in the political system was enough of a reason to instigate fast and rapid creation of what we would call the new women's movement. This new movement is not of a massive character. It does not mark its presence in statistics or in sociological research conducted on representative samples. And this is really not what we would expect. The movement is of a diversified character, however, and the dynamics of its initiative and growth are extensive. It is enough to compare the contents of two consecutive directories of women organizations and initiatives in Poland published by the Center for the Advancement of Women (1993, 1995). In 1993 the directory listed approximately 100 such organizations; in 1995 there were 170 of them.

The diversity of initiatives seems promising. Probably it means that women who are united by certain ideas, assisting other women, addressing a common problem, or trying to reach any common goal can get organized and cooperate with each other.

Also, a coalition is being formed. An impressive spectacular example is the Federation for Women and Family Planning, which unites organizations as different ideologically as the Polish Feminist Association and the Association of Christian Women and Girls. Joint actions are being taken, such as the Report on the Situation of Women in Poland prepared by the Committee of Non-Government Organizations—Beijing 1995. It was a spectacular event and a very important one in that it publicly proved that women want to and are able to speak of their problems in a way that is different from what was previously done "on their behalf."

Notes

1. Figures from the Report of the Government of Poland on the progress made in implementation of the Convention of 1979 on the elimination of all forms of discrimination against women, in the period from June 1, 1988, to May 31, 1990.

2. The following part is based on my research supported in 1994–96 by an Open Society Institute grant coordinated by Gail Kligman and Susan Gal from University of California Center for the Study of Women, Los Angeles.

3. According to information published by GUS (Main Statistical Office) at the end of September 1997, women accounted for 63.2 of the unemployed by the end of August 1997 (*Rzeczpospolita* 28 September 1997).

References

CBOS [Public Research Center]. 1993a. "Postawy wobec pracy i aspiracje zawodowe kobiet" [Attitudes toward work and women's professional aspiration]. Research report, Warsaw.

———. 1993b. "Reprezentacja interesów kobiet" [Representation of the women interest]. Research report, Warsaw.

Centrum Promocji Kobiet [Center for the Advancement of Women]. 1993, 1995. "Informator o organizacjach i inicjatywach kobiecych w Polsce" [Directory of Women's organizations and initiatives in Poland]. Warsaw.

Cichomski, Bogdan and Zbigniew Sawiński. 1992, 1993, 1994, 1995. "Polski Generalny Sondaż Społeczny" [Polish General Social Survey]. Warsaw: Warsaw University.

Demographic Yearbook of Poland. 1988. Warsaw: Main Statistical Office.

Domański, Henryk. 1992. "Zadowolony niewolnik? Studium o nierównościach między kobietami i mężczyznami w Polsce" [The grateful slave? Inequality between men and women in Poland]. Warsaw: Institute of Philosophy and Sociology, Polish Academy of Sciences.

———. 1996. "Na progu konwergencji. Stratyfikacja społeczna w krajach Europy środkowej" [On the verge of convergence. Social Stratification in Eastern Europe]. Warsaw: Institute of Philosophy and Sociology Polish Academy of Sciences.

Domański, Henryk and Andrzej Rychard. 1997. "Elementy nowego ładu" [Elements of a new deal]. Warszawa: IFiS Publishers.

Dukaczewska-Nałęcz, Aleksandra. 1997. "Aktywność kobiet w sferze prywatnej jako substytut dominacji mężczyzn w sferze publicznej" [Private and public. Female activity as a substitute for male dominance]. Unpublished Ph.D. thesis, Warsaw.

Fuchs-Epstein, Cynthia. 1970. *Women's Place: Options and Limits in Professional Careers.* Berkley: University of California Press.

Fuszara, Małgorzata. 1993. "Abortion and formation of the Public Sphere in Poland." In: *Gender Politics and Post-Communism,* eds. N. Funk, M. Muller. New York, London: Routledge.

————. 1994/95. "Równe prawa, równie szanse?" [Equal rights, equal chances?]. *Roczniki Nauk Społecznych,* 22–23, no 1.

GUS [Main Statistical Office]. 1994a. "Sytuacja społeczno-zawodowa kobiet w 1994 r." [Social status of women in 1994]. Warsaw.

————. 1994b. "Kobieta w statystyce" [Women from a statistical perspective]. Warsaw.

Kowalska, Anna. 1996. "Aktywność ekonomiczna kobiet i ich pozycja na rynku pracy" [Women's productive activity and labor market]. Warsaw: Main Statistical Office.

Kuratowska, Zofia. 1991. "Present Situation of Women in Poland." Paper presented at Regional Seminar on the Impact of Economic and Political Reform on the Status of Women in Eastern Europe and the USSR, Vienna, April 12.

National Work Office. 1995. "Bezrobocie Kobiet" [Women's unemployment]. Warsaw.

Olczyk, E. 1991. "Wyjść z Kuchni" [To leave the kitchen]. *Życie Warszawy,* April 4.

Sokołowska, Magdalena. 1987. "Women and the Social Crises." Paper presented at the International Conference on Inequity and Development, Salt Lake City, August 11.

4

Transition to Local Democracy
Do Polish Women Have a Chance?

Joanna Regulska

On January 23, 1991, after a two-day meeting, the National Women's Section of Solidarity released a statement addressed to President Lech Wałesa:

> The principle that guides Poland's social and economic policy, which gives priority to material goods over human needs, carries serious dangers for the entire society, but in particular for women. Concerned about our country and about the future of independent Poland, and in order to counter these negative processes, the National Women's Section (NWS) sees the need for women to be included in the decision-making process in regard to social and economic policy.
>
> Because men are overrepresented among union officers at all levels, the NWS requests the establishment of a quota system, its implementation to be guaranteed by the Union Charter.
>
> Because men are overrepresented among the highest public office-holders in the country, the NWS demands the creation of a new office at the ministerial level to represent women. The NWS demands establishment of a Ministry of Women's Affairs, headed by a minister who will be a member of the Council of Ministers. The activities of such a person would concentrate on matters related to the status of women in society, in the family, and in the workplace. The participants in this meeting do not approve the proposed creation of a Bureau for Family Matters, Women, and Youth.
>
> We request a meeting with the President of Poland and with the members of the government to discuss the above matters.

Although they are only one of many groups caught in the middle, women in post-1989 Poland are faced both with unprecedented opportunities and with challenges. On the one hand, the collapse of communism made room for free expression of dissatisfaction and for requests for dialogue such as the one issued by the NWS; on the other, it permitted the recognition that the so-called equality of the sexes in politics, economy, and the family is far from real.

Under communism, women were present in formal politics, and although fewer of them sat in the parliaments, the proportion of regional and local offices held by women was among the largest in the world (Shaul 1982). Yet a women's agenda was absent from political deliberations; women's organizations, except for a few that were ideologically controlled, were nonexistent; and a woman political leader seemed an impossibility (Bystydzienski 1989; Siemieńska 1990).

The revolution of 1989 created new political and economic circumstances for Polish women (Bellows 1996; Fuszara 1993; Gontarczyk-Wesoła 1997; Nowakowska 1997; Regulska, 1998a; Kuratowska 1991). Women lost heavily in elections held without controls (and without quotas): parliamentary and local elections increased women's unemployment rapidly; the state withdrew its support and delivery of child care, medical services, and educational opportunities, all within a few years—and all in the name of the transition to democracy and a market economy.

Not surprisingly, increasing, albeit still limited, attention has been paid to the impact of the current political and economic changes on women in Central and Eastern Europe. While empirical studies are still rare, scholars, activists, and a few women parliamentary leaders are voicing their concern that women are the primary victims of the progress that has attended the fall of communism (Einhorn 1995; Fuszara 1991; Weschler and Thomas 1992; Tarasiewicz 1991; Bishop 1990). But existing studies focus largely on the national context of the transition and the future prospects for women's employment, the political dimensions and implications of women's rights and status, and the relationship between democratization and the transition to a market economy (Moghadam 1992; Funk and Mueller 1993; Kolaczek 1992; Leven 1991; Janowska et al. 1992; Wolchik 1992; Einhorn 1992; Renne 1997). What is absent from these analyses is a close look at the transition process from the perspective of women involved in local politics.

I have argued extensively elsewhere about the importance of the emergence of local self-government and the formation of a local political arena in the transition period (Regulska 1993); here I shall point only to the most important of my conclusions. First, fundamental political and economic restructuring cannot take place and ultimately claim success unless a local government is recognized as a legitimate partner in this process. And second, any attempt to design the new Polish state from the top, without participation and dialogue with local society, will not succeed. Neither of these principles has been initially recognized in Poland, and the consequences were clearly indicated in the alienation of the society from its leadership (Mason, Nelson, and Szklarski 1991; *Nowy Dziennik* 1992a, 1992b, 1992c). Although over the last few years local government has gained endorsement by citizens, it still remains unacknowledged as an equal partner by the national institutions and politicians (Grzelak 1995; Kulesza 1995; Rabska 1995). This failure to attend to the local level is especially important to women. Research on the determinants of women's participation in politics points to the local level as an indispensable step for women entering politics. By entering local politics women gain experience and skill and build their own networks; in short, they develop a base that facilitates their political participation. Such resources help their candidacies for higher posts, where they can serve as role models for other women who contemplate entering politics (Carroll, Dodson, and Mandel 1991; Clarke, Staeheli, and Brunell 1995).

These issues spurred my research on Polish women leaders at the local level. While I was interested in finding out who these leaders were, I wanted above all to learn their views on the problems that Polish women have faced during the initial stage of the transition and on the barriers they have had to overcome in order to hold leadership positions in local government. Finally, I wanted to explore those women's political agendas. These were the questions I hoped they would answer when I conducted a survey among women local leaders in the summer of 1991.

Polish Women in Local Politics Under Communism

In the era of communism there was a particular notion of equality. As Barbara Jancar (1985) has pointed out, the political posts offered to women in communist government administration frequently appeared comparable to the places women occupied in the economy. Thus, women were systematically more evident on government committees dealing with light industry, education, health, arts, and culture. In general, women were more visible at the local level than in higher posts in the government (Reszke 1991). When Daniel Nelson (1985) studied women active in Polish local politics in the 1970s, he concluded that women had proportionally fewer opportunities to rise in the local political hierarchy; even if they did rise, they were concentrated in a narrow spectrum of duties. This finding reinforces Jancar's argument that the more powerful a political body, the lower the representation of women in it.

The issue, however, is not only placement within the governmental hierarchy; it is also about the existence of opportunities to this career path. Several observers have pointed out that such opportunities were almost nonexistent for women (e.g., Jancar 1985; Nelson 1985; Siemieńska 1990). The absence of women in high-level managerial and professional jobs drastically restricted women's access to power positions and presented fewer career options with opportunities for advancement. Given the view in Poland, as well as in other Central and East European cultures, that politics is "not for women," is "dirty" and unfeminine, women were less likely than men to invest in acquiring the kinds of skills and knowledge that would enable them to become political actors (Jaluśić 1994; Regulska, 1998a). As a result, women were not generally enthusiastic about entering political life, although Nelson has pointed out (1985, 163) that for some women politics was an ultimate calling and career path.

Thus, under the communist rhetoric of "sameness," women not only had unequal access to positions within political structures, they also lacked the resources associated with the pursuit of political activism (Graham and Regulska 1997). Networking, volunteer work, opportunities to build support groups around issues of concern to local societies—all are considered to be of great value to people entering political life in Western societies (Center for the American Woman and Politics 1978; Kelly 1988). The absence of these opportunities and the restrictions imposed by the communist regime with respect to freedom to organize prevented Polish women from coming together; without question, this situation has hampered their participation in politics (Graham and Regulska 1997; Regulska, 1998a). Without their own supportive network, women have relied for promotion and support on political parties or, more often, on mass organizations such as the League of Polish Women. In direct competition with men, however, women were bound to lose.

If women did exert political pressure in communist societies, the pressure was indirect and localized, in part because of the double burden of work and family responsibilities. To sustain active party membership women had to make a large commitment of time, and this requirement kept many of them out of the party. As a result, they were automatically precluded from advancement and the possibility of holding public office. Without public office, they could not sustain political activism. Over the years this pattern was translated into a lack of a tradition among women of public officeholding and involvement in politics. The lack of women's political identity translated into a lack of agency. In the end, it precluded development of a women's agenda that would be separate from the state-enforced ideology of false equality.

A final factor that should be considered as an impediment to women's participation in local politics is the role of the Catholic church and its authoritarian rule. The focus on family values and on the role of women as mothers reinforced women's position in the private sphere and weakened their role outside the home. This was especially true in rural areas, where adherence to "family values" has been a tradition for centuries. Here we see why more women participate in politics in the cities than in rural areas. The economic situation in the countryside may also have played a significant role; the private ownership of agricultural property may simply have made women's role at home seem more important.

This is not to say that women played no role in Polish politics under communism. They were definitely present, and not by accident; communist regimes needed them to support the claim of gender equality in representation. Under the quota system, women's presence in local authorities grew from 7.6 percent in 1958 to its peak of 25.6 percent in 1978 and was maintained at over 20 percent during the 1980s (Regulska 1992). A similar pattern of participation is visible at the regional level. But women were not perceived as powerful leaders at the national level. In general, the party was likely to support a few women for mid-level political positions during periods of internal stability but to overlook them for such positions during periods of domestic crisis (Jancar 1985). Women's actual lack of skills, the invisibility of women in the higher ranks, and the perception of women as unreliable because of their family obligations have combined to limit women's political careers to the middle rank of the political hierarchy.

The conservative outlook on marriage and the family alongside imposed communist "equality" constructed a lifestyle for Polish women that did not permit them to discover that their problems were not theirs alone. Here economics, ideology, and societal values intertwined. The answer to this problem has to come through political mobilization and increased activism by women. In theory, the events of 1989 presented an opportunity to women. In practice, however, from the beginning difficulties begun to unfold.

Post-1989 Transition: Are Women Still There?

The collapse of communism moved Poland as well as other Central and East European countries on the path of transition. Poland was among the countries that entered this road by negotiation, rather than by confrontation (as in Romania) or containment (as in East Germany) (Osiatyński 1990; Sajo 1990). The 1989 round-table negotiations brought not only the collapse of the communist regime but also, at least initially, a new common political agenda for the entire polity. A process by which a new political culture could be created and a new attitude formed was initiated.

These events were of extraordinary importance for the establishment of a democratic Polish state. They brought to an end the period of hidden political mobilization, which developed elaborate underground channels of communication and resistance. Women had been very active in the opposition, in part because of the informal structure of those organizations, though in only a few cases can we point to leadership positions that were held by women (Regulska 1992; Penn 1994). In fact, women's limited visibility in Communist Party structures was to a large extent mirrored in the underground. Women were motivated to act, to engage, but their activism, throughout the entire Solidarity period, remained invisible. In the end, according to Penn, "their invisibility ultimately limited their political effectiveness" (Penn 1994, 67). As a result, women's involvement during the opposition years did not translate into an invitation to the negotiating table; none of the groups that negotiated with the regime was chaired by a woman.

Although the first round of elections in June 1989 was widely viewed as an overwhelming victory, they could not be regarded as such from the perspective of women. The few women elected to parliament (13 percent in the Sejm and 7 percent in the Senate) were neither strong enough nor prepared to formulate a women's agenda; nor were they eager to do so. Thus, while the process of shaping a political and economic agenda for the nation was extremely intensive at that time, women's interests were not adequately protected. The first fully democratic parliamentary elections in 1991 resulted in no improvement; only forty-five women were elected to the Sejm (9.5 percent) and eight to the Senate (8 percent) (Regulska 1992). The Democratic Union sent twelve delegates to parliament, the Christian National Union and the Confederation for an Independent Poland each sent seven women, and the Alliance of the Democratic Left elected ten women. The remaining women delegates were distributed among the other parties. Hence the process of political marginalization of women became a fact. It was not until almost three years later, in January 1992, that Barbara Labuda, a leader among women deputies, achieved a major success by establishing a Parliamentary Women's Group that brought together women deputies from five parties. The group immediately became a watchdog to protect women's interests in the legislative process and a supporter of gender-related legislation (*Kronika Sejmowa* 1992). By 1993 women's representation in both Sejm and Senate had increased to 13 percent. Similar slow improvements in the representation of women have been experienced at the local level. The first round of local elections in 1990 brought 10.4 percent women to local government offices; after the second, in 1994, 13 percent of local officials were women.

The euphoria produced by the downfall of the communist regime did not last long. Spirits sank as the society began to respond to the difficulties produced by the transition to democracy and the market economy (*Nowy Dziennik* 1992a, 1992b; Engelberg 1992; Przeworski 1991; Elster 1992). The increasingly high costs of the transition began to show in rapidly growing unemployment (Fuszara 1991; Kolaczek 1992; Semprich 1992). Women unfortunately became "leaders" in this respect. Often the fact that a woman's husband still had a job was counted against her, since the family did have some income. A lack of adequate statistics at the national level prevents our determining how many of those unemployed women are actually single mothers and their families' only breadwinners. What statistics do reveal is that, contrary to widespread belief, younger women, aged 18–24, are becoming the largest pool of the female unemployed (BSE 1997). For them, the transition has been an especially difficult period of adjustment, and their difficulties may be an important indicator of a grim future and the end of a never-existing "communist equality." In fact, the continued rejection of everything that was created under communism has permitted the reimposition of restrictions on women's reproductive rights and a revival of the traditional view that women should remain in the home. In this case it would seem that the replacement of an old ideology by a "new" and "free" one would give men the "freedom" to discriminate against women (Graham and Regulska 1997).

Women's Emerging Local Leadership: Survey Results

Who are the women leaders? Where do they live? How do they assess the needs of Polish women in general and the women of their communities in particular? Do they perceive any special barriers that Polish women need to overcome in order to become involved in local politics? These are a few of the twenty-four questions in the first post-1989 exploratory survey I administered to women who held public offices as a result of the local elections of May 1990.

The survey focused on three areas: the respondent; the municipality in which she resides; and her perception of the problems and barriers that women face. Each respondent was asked to answer several sets of questions related to (1) her characteristics (age, education, occupation, number of children); (2) the municipality she serves (size and type of economic base); (3) problems that the municipality faces and kinds of skills or knowledge that the respondent might need in order to address them; (4) problems that face Polish women in general and specifically in the area under the respondent's jurisdiction, and barriers that Polish women will need to overcome if they wish to enter local politics; and, finally, (5) existing women's organizations and the respondent's participation in their activities.

I originally intended to send the questionnaire to a sample of women elected, directly and indirectly, to offices within the local government structure. The holders of such positions were defined as mayors of urban and rural municipalities and, in the case of large urban municipalities, presidents of a city (total of 2,500 mayors in Poland); chairs or vice-chairs of the National Voivodship Assembly (total of 5); representatives of individual voivodship assemblies (2 representatives from each of 50 voivodships, for a total of 100); and chairs of municipal councils, both rural and urban (total of 2,500). Although this definition may not appear rigorous, my goal in conducting this survey was simply to gain some insight into the emergence of women's local leadership during the transition period. These positions required a woman to be elected as a council member in direct local elections and then to be elected by her peers or appointed by the municipal council to the post she now occupies. The process required the candidate to be known in the local community and to possess certain skills and knowledge that people consider to be of leadership quality. The Office of the Ministry for Local Government, the Council of Ministers, and the Office of the General Commissioner for Local Government Elections were asked to assist in the preparation of such a list.

I knew that the proportion of women elected to local offices was smaller in 1990 than in the past, when a quota system was enforced (10.4 percent vs. 22.0 percent achieved in the last local elections held under communism, in 1988), although it would be misleading to interpret these numerical results as a major failure for women. Clearly women officeholders under communism, even twice as many women, could not exercise greater power in a parliament that had no power. What I did not anticipate was that the past pattern of women's political marginalization was reinforced so strongly during the 1990 local elections. First, women continued to be a minority among local leaders. Only 320 of 5,105 local leadership posts (6.2 percent) were held by women. Second, a woman was three times more likely to be elected mayor of a small rural community than of an urban community. Third, most of the women in the group held the lowest leadership position in the local government structure, that of chair of the municipal council. A total of 177 women, or 55 percent of the women in local leadership posts, were chairs of municipal councils. Thus the past pattern—the higher the position and more prestigious the place, the fewer women present—remained constant.

These findings had major implications for the design of this study. Small overall numbers of women local leaders and even smaller numbers in particular categories (mayors of urban municipalities) led me to decide to send the questionnaire to *all* women who fitted the category of "local leader" as I defined it for the purpose of this study. The questionnaire was mailed at the end of May 1991, a year after the local elections took place. I received 238 responses, a response rate of 74.4 percent, and used 220 of the responses in my analysis.

Who Are Women Local Leaders?

My respondents are middle-aged women, very highly educated, and two-thirds of them have at least one child. Only 3 percent have more than three children. A majority of women local leaders (94 percent) are between the ages of 30 and 59; almost half of them in their forties (Figure 4.1). My findings confirmed the well-established fact that Pol-

Figure 4.1 **Age brackets of respondents**

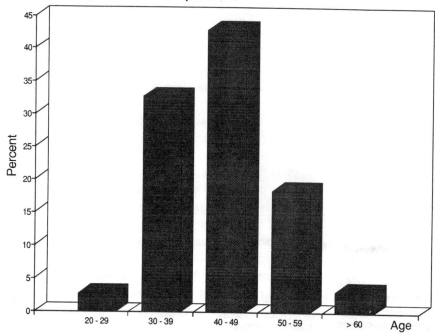

Figure 4.2 **Respondents' educational attainment**

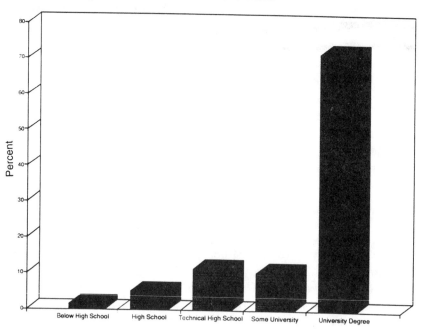

Figure 4.3 **Occupational status of respondents**

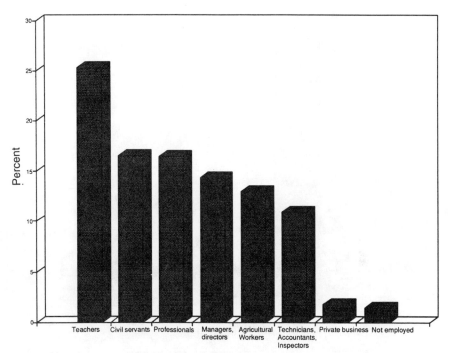

ish women are very highly educated. Only 1.5 percent of respondents did not have a high school diploma; over 71 percent had university degrees. An additional 22 percent had professional or vocational education beyond high school or had completed two to three years of university study (Figure 4.2).

The largest occupational categories of women in the survey consisted of teachers (25.3 percent) and civil servants employed in local public administration (16.5 percent). Women holding professional degrees and employed as lawyers, doctors, academics, and engineers were almost equally represented (4 percent in each occupation, for a total of 16.5 percent). Only slightly higher was the proportion of managers and directors (6.9 percent and 7.4 percent), occupations in which women were not very likely to be found under communism. Women employed as agricultural workers accounted for over 13 percent and those working as accountants, technicians, and inspectors constituted fewer than 12 percent of respondents. Equally few women had their own businesses (1.8 percent) and did not work in paid jobs (1.4 percent) (Figure 4.3).

Figure 4.4 **Economic base of respondents' municipalities**

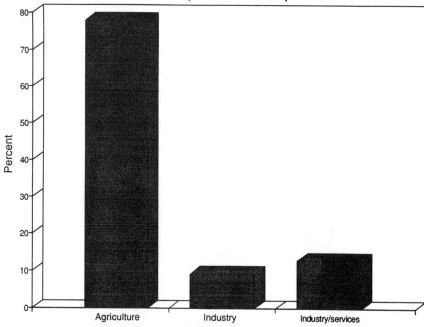

Figure 4.5 **Size of respondents' municipalities**

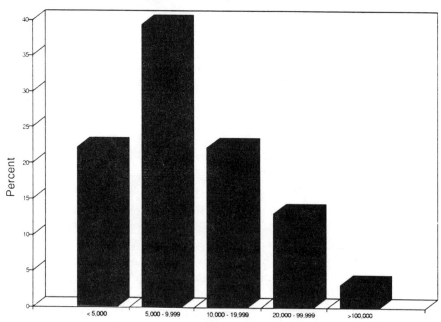

The municipalities where my respondents lived are predominantly rural and small. Agriculture is the primary economic base of almost 78 percent of their communities. The remaining 22 percent have a mixed industrial and service-oriented base (Figure 4.4). Sixty-two percent of respondents are leaders of municipalities with populations between 5,000 and 20,000 inhabitants, and an additional 22 percent reside in communities with fewer than 5,000 people (Figure 4.5).

Current Concerns of Polish Women

Polish women have little money, their economic situation is unstable, and their living standard has declined. They feel overburdened and overworked. These were the issues my respondents mentioned most frequently when I asked them to identify "the problems that in your opinion are most prevalent among Polish women." Sixty-nine percent mentioned financial and economic concerns and over 57 percent spoke of being overburdened and of having too many conflicting demands. More than 42 percent of respondents mentioned lack of adequate services, poor infrastructure, and a lack of housing. The women expressed great concern about the lack of adequate gas and telephone services, water, and roads in rural areas, and about the increasingly frequent closings of day-care centers. Unemployment was singled out by more than one-third of the respondents (38.7 percent). Some of these pressures, such as unemployment, are new for Polish women, but others are all too familiar and now are intensified.

Two forces appear to be responsible for poor infrastructure in rural areas. First is uneven development. The wide gap between the living conditions of urban and rural areas is an outgrowth of forty-five years of intensive and rapid industrialization and of a general lack of political interest in rural development. These policies continue today; austerity programs do not favor rural areas. Second, under the new law on local self-government, the responsibility for most local services falls on local governments. Though many municipalities are in much sounder financial condition than the central government, it is extremely difficult for municipalities with small budgets even to maintain the level of services to which people became accustomed under communism. Moreover, the priorities established by local councils, while initially focusing on infrastructure development, increasingly emphasize economic development and business growth and shy away from

investing in services that would "only" meet the needs of the population, but would not bring direct economic returns (Regulska, 1998b;
Grobelna and Łyszkowska-Cieślik 1995). The increasing activism of
local groups results in small improvements, however, and this force
should be seen as an alternative to state-supported intervention (Foundation in Support of Local Democracy 1992; *Biuletyn Informacyjny*
1992; Graham and Regulska 1997).

Much lower in the hierarchy of problems cited were equality between men and women (20.5 percent), family problems (18.2 percent),
and the attitudes of society toward women (11.4 percent). It is not clear
whether these issues are indeed of lesser importance in general to
Polish women or whether the sense of instability and lack of security
for themselves and their families leads women to focus on problem
areas more readily amenable to practical action. Whatever the explanation, women are fully aware that they are discriminated against, and
they point to two factors.

First is the fact that women have become symbols and are subjected
to careful scrutiny; second is the legacy of communism and the negative side of the perceived benefits of "communist equality." One
woman responded, "In my opinion, if a Polish woman is to get ahead,
she needs to be much better educated and more effective in her work
than a man." Others echo this perception. "A woman who talks loudly
should know twice as much if she wants to be respected among men."
"The greatest barrier is gender. From the moment they [women] are
given leadership positions, their expertise and decisions are under
more rigorous evaluation." Women thus feel that they need to prove to
everybody that they have knowledge, skills, and abilities, that they are
not merely "housekeepers." They recognize that they have become
symbols—that what one woman does or fails to do reflects on all
women—and that as a consequence their actions are frequently interpreted in terms of the larger question of who Polish women are. This
sense of collective responsibility seems, unfortunately, to have an in-
hibiting effect on women's leadership potential. Women recognize the
legacy of the communist era as adding to their discrimination: "After
the period of 'security,' both economic and social, 'Polish Woman'
feels threatened and powerless in the face of economic difficulties";
"Women are penalized for the so-called equality of women." Yet, the
previously mentioned sense of collective responsibility does not seem
to be translated into the women's collective development of women's

agenda, the prerequisite for women's collective action (Eduards 1994). One possible explanation is that women, along with the rest of Polish society, are attempting to construct the opposite, the individual, the autonomous identity, which they see as not shaped by ideological constraints. The experiences of the communist past forced all to be alike; now, with the new freedoms, people seek the opposite (Regulska, 1998a).

Because respondents see themselves as symbols, I was interested in determining the extent to which newly elected women officeholders do represent women. Studies completed in the United States suggest that women, both those involved in the legislative process and officeholders at the local level, tend more than men to express an interest in such issues as child care, education, family policy, employment discrimination, and what Susan Carroll and her colleagues (1991) have called "women's rights bills"—pay equity, domestic violence, and maternity leave, among other issues (Antolini 1984).

The survey responses suggest that Polish women local leaders are concerned with issues that directly affect their families, their homes, and their living conditions. At the same time, the responses yield very little evidence that the presence of women in local government is being translated directly into a specific women's agenda. The most interesting of my findings is the interrelation between the issues of traditional concern to women and the issue of equality with men.

The initial analysis of responses argued for a purely economic interpretation of what women meant when they wrote about equality and discrimination. Both rural and urban women were concerned with equality, but to different degrees. When they discussed their economic difficulties, over one-third (36 percent) of urban local leaders expressed concern about equality, while only 18 percent of rural woman officeholders cited this issue. A partial explanation may lie in the differences between rural and urban women's occupations; the evidence suggests that many women in rural areas hold jobs in which the difference between men's and women's pay is small—teaching, clerical work, technical support. Very few hold the high managerial and professional jobs in which differentials in pay are blatant. Finally, while few women anywhere owned and operated small businesses (where the income gap can be enormous), the number who did so in rural areas was negligible.

Discrimination and lack of equality, especially in respect to promotion and pay, were mentioned more frequently by younger women (under age 40) with children. Their frustration may be explained by the fact that women often do need to interrupt their career paths to take care of small children. In theory, laws guarantee women up to three years of leave when their children are small, with the right to return to their jobs, but in practice the story is different, and the transition period has pointed out the negative effects of these laws (Fuszara 1997a, 1997b).

The Polish parental law permits both women and men to take time off, for example, but social norms do not. This is even more evident when these results are compared with the findings of a more recent survey on "Career Aspirations of Women and Family Life," conducted by CBOS in 1997. The survey's major findings pointed out that women's professional engagement is treated to a large extent by women themselves as an addition to their primary responsibilities in the home. This was indicated despite the respondents' preference for the partnership model of marriage (CBOS 1997b). In real life they continue to practice the traditional division of gender roles. Thus, in my survey in 1991, as well as in the 1997 CBOS results, in the vast majority of cases it is the woman who is the full-time caregiver. When she returns to her job after three years, her skills and experience, as well as her pay, are no longer comparable to those of the co-worker who has been on the job throughout her absence. What is even more discouraging is that employers are increasingly firing women who return to work after a long leave of absence or who become pregnant. Lack of appropriate legislation to prohibit such practices represents, de facto, their reinforcement. My respondents are aware that these disruptions do have negative consequences on women's careers, and that often it is only when the children are grown that a woman can begin a more stable professional engagement. One respondent directly addressed these issues when she charged that "men . . . have more time, because they don't take parental leave and medical leave for sick children, and as a result they are seen as better employees." Another claimed, "In my case I could begin my activism only when the last of my four children left home."

I also asked my respondents to look at their own communities and to determine "which of these problems should be dealt with as a first priority." The answers revealed a very practical and focused approach to the problems. Unemployment (30 percent), improvement of living standards (22 percent), and improvement of the quality of services (19 percent) and of infrastructure (12 percent) were considered to be the most pressing needs. Equality and discrimination ranked lower on the list of things to be changed (5.5 percent and 13 percent). Surprisingly, many other issues discussed frequently by the Polish media, such as public safety, were not raised by the respondents. In fact, street crime, youth violence, robberies, and other social pathologies were not mentioned at all. Similarly, alcoholism among Polish men is a much-discussed problem, but only 5 percent of respondents acknowledged its existence. Moreover, alcoholism among rural women, although acknowledged by some public institutions (e.g., Union of Rural Gminas), was not mentioned at all by respondents.

A comparison of responses regarding problems confronting Polish women in general with comments on the problems that women in the respondents' communities are facing revealed in more detail how women local leaders perceive the status of women in Polish society. It is not true that women are concerned only with material improvements. On the contrary, it appears that women directly link their economic well-being with their positions in the society: to them the way they live and the way they are treated are not mutually exclusive matters.

As I mentioned earlier, at first glance it appears that my respondents measured equality and discrimination primarily along the economic dimension. Among the women who saw inequality as a major problem for Polish women, for example, 53 percent claimed that economic considerations should be given priority at the local level. Issues such as unemployment, household poverty and financial instability, pay, and deteriorating living conditions were mentioned. When I looked at the responses of women who indicated equality as an issue to be handled at the local level, I found that more than 51 percent pointed to the economic situation as a problem that faces Polish women in general. These findings suggest that there is more than a 50 percent probability that equality is indeed perceived as an issue of economic justice.

Further analysis, however, introduced new dimensions and indicated some negative correlations between the groups. Only 15 percent of the respondents who mentioned economic issues, both those important to Polish women in general and those important at the local level, claimed equality to be an issue at the national or local level. This finding suggests that in the consciousness of Polish women, equality and discrimination are not reducible only to economic terms. While a majority of respondents indicated that the position and status of women will not change unless economic conditions improve significantly, their expectations go beyond the immediate sphere of living and working conditions: "The parliamentary elections are coming up, and I must say right now that there are no women in political life and in civic organizations; no political party or women's organization has been created during this period of building democracy. Very often women are the primary caregivers in their family; they have no time to be active. This is very sad. We will not have our representation in parliament."

These issues are of crucial importance and should be heard by the policymakers at the national level. Women clearly need to have access to the decision-making process, to formulate policy agendas that will result in direct improvement in their lives. But do women themselves recognize this need? My survey seems to indicate that this is not the case. Despite the fact that there are no women's organizations at the local level, except for the still-existing mass women's organizations instituted by the Communist Party (for instance, the League of Polish Women [LPW] and the Circle of Rural Women [CRW]), very few women pointed to the lack or weakness of women's organizations. Only 6.5 percent mentioned the issue at all, and an even smaller group (3 percent) pointed to this factor as something that should be addressed at the local level. This lack of awareness that civic organizations are essential for the functioning of a democratic country is not new. The fact that 62 percent of my respondents claimed that women are organized at the local level demonstrates further that the purpose and role of civic organizations are not yet understood. One may argue that, despite the lack of women's organizations, such a high positive response does reflect to a large extent the perception that urban women have a greater number of women's groups and organizations at their disposal than rural women do. Yet, the fact that more than 84 percent of respondents come from rural communities disputes this assumption. Women's interests are occasionally addressed through labor unions, but over the last few years more failures than successes can be listed (Tarasiewicz 1991). The old communist organizations offer very little in the way of political activism, and only recently has the LPW joined an organization that promotes planned parenthood (Federation for Women and Planned Parenthood in Poland 1992). What is needed, then, as one of the respondents wrote, is "greater representation of women when decisions that directly affect them are made."

Obstacles to Women's Political Involvement

Women who hold local offices were united in identifying five main barriers that they need to overcome in order to perform their leadership function. The single most clearly identified theme, mentioned by 47 percent of respondents, was lack of time and the feeling of being overwhelmed by the responsibilities of paid employment and work at home. The second barrier was lack of trust in women holders of public office, and the assumption that men can do those jobs better (46 percent). The third obstacle, less strongly identified than the first two, is a belief that women are not assertive enough, that they lack trust in themselves and, in general, lack self-esteem (14 percent). The two other barriers mentioned were lack of a tradition of active participation in public life among Polish women (9.5 percent) and women's lack of interest in participating (7 percent).

There is no question that the majority of respondents are very much aware of the traditional attitudes toward women's participation in local politics. Only nine women claimed that they recognized no barriers and an additional twelve respondents believed that although barriers exist, they are not based on gender.

In regard to the first theme, women respondents were pointing to the traditional values of a society that sees women primarily as mothers and wives and thus expects women first of all to fill the homemaker role. At the same time, the "equality of women and men" proclaimed by communism added to these constraints the responsibilities of paid employment. Thus many women wrote about the pressure of raising children, of feeling trapped and forced to make choices. They pointed to the very limited availability of household equipment that would shorten the time needed to prepare food and take care of the home: "It's a matter of time availability; that is, it's a choice of home and children or paid job." "The challenge lies in balancing family, professional work, and volunteer work responsibilities." "Women in our society spend too much time on household activities." "Only women without family responsibilities can allow themselves to work in local government."

Obviously several of these respondents are nonetheless combining professional responsibilities, political activism, and work at home, even when they feel that the task is impossible: "It is impossible to combine my job [in a factory] ... with my duties as chair of the municipal council and my role as a mother and wife. You can't do everything adequately—if I do one of those things right, the others are sacrificed. My employer sees no difference in the fact that I'm chair of the city council, but the performance of this function takes a lot of time, especially during a period when such important changes are taking place in this country."

Very few women argued, however, about specific things that might help them in their efforts to combine their multiple roles. Things such as child-care facilities that stay open in the evenings were mentioned rarely, as was the need for more household appliances. Moreover, what remained as a silent and not addressed obstacle was the traditional gender roles. In this respect none of the respondents indicated a need for change. Still, although I did not ask the question specifically, women gave no indication that they would like to return home and be released from the responsibilities of work and political activism.

The fact that a lack of time and overwork were cited as the main difficulties faced by women in public office did not come as a surprise. The traditional gender division of labor in the household has already been well documented under communism. Women spend three times more hours than men performing household tasks (Siemieńska 1992). A lack of time has not been widely cited by researchers in Western Europe or the United States, but it's an old story in developing countries, and the similarity between East European countries and the Third World in this respect is increasingly being pointed out. Only a small group of predominantly urban women have dishwashers or washing machines, and very few can afford household help. In many respects the situation has been getting worse during the transition period. At first the problem was shortages and the need to spend hours standing in queues. Now the goods and services are available, but the problem is to find ones that people can afford. In effect, access remains restricted.

The withdrawal of the state from its protectionist role and the persistent cutbacks in the number and extent of public services have gone on for many years, but they intensified during the transition years (Lake and Regulska 1990; Regulska 1997b). Medical services are provided at fewer and fewer workplaces; the responsibility for maintaining child-care facilities has been shifted to the municipalities, with the result that their funding is often the first to be cut; school budgets are so severely curtailed that many schools now operate on two shifts, morning and afternoon. The social programs established under communism no longer exist. As a result, women are faced with increasing and conflicting demands on their time, are subjected to more stress, and must overcome new obstacles in their efforts to meet the needs of family and work. When political activism is added, the pressures can be overwhelming.

Clearly women's political participation and activism are new experiences both for Polish women and for the society at large. On the one hand, the ideological and political barriers have been removed so that men and women can openly participate in political and social institutions; on the other, the removal of the "enemy" brought to the surface traditional perceptions of the place that women should occupy within the social structure. In regard to this barrier my respondents can be divided into two groups: those who feel that women are perceived to be unable to do the work required of a holder of public office and those who point to the perception that the ideal public officeholder is a man. The first group argues that there is "a lack of trust in women who hold leadership positions"; that "everybody believes that women do not know how to make concrete decisions." As one woman respondent put it, "The greatest barrier is the fact that one is a woman, a person who can't be trusted, and whether she has the right characteristics, such as being systematic, loyal, and having professional expertise." The second group sees men's characteristics as contributing to the creation of barriers that prevent women's political participation and reinforce the preference for men as holders of public office. The responses range from clear statements that the major barrier for women is "male prejudice" to those declaring that "men see themselves as the only ones qualified to govern effectively." "In most cases men are the decision makers. They believe that women are less appropriate for those positions." "The absolute majority of men believe that it is not appropriate for women to hold leadership positions." As I did not specifically ask men what they think about women in leadership positions, I can only speculate as to the accuracy of those perceptions. The evidence in the form of election results and emerging trends in governmental appointments established by all postcommunist governments is sufficient, though, to suggest that, as Jiřina Šiklová has expressed it, a transition to male democracy is taking place. At the same time, however, an important shift seems to be taking place in Poland in regard to public attitudes toward women's representation and women politicians. Respondents to the 1997 CBOS survey indicated that women are underrepresented in public and political life and that specific actions should be undertaken to increase their presence (CBOS 1997b; Fuszara 1997b; Kuratowska 1996). One may then speculate what factors foster the invisibility of women as political actors: is it the way we understand the nature of politics (or have patriarchal values been combined with new liberal philosophy?), or could it be possible that women themselves contribute to their invisibility (Regulska, forthcoming a)?

Female personality traits are seen by women respondents as a barrier. Women are passive and quiet, they are weak and fold under stress, and in general they are not assertive enough to make decisions. Our respondents wrote: "Women are difficult to communicate with." "The inability to overcome [heavy psychological burdens] forces women to resign from leadership positions." Women are too "scared to take risks and are too sensitive to criticism." "They are not brave enough." The main barriers are "psychological, fear of responsibility, fear of decision making, and fear of discrimination by men."

The systematic exclusion of women from high positions in politics has made women less visible and has limited their opportunities as well as their ability to claim a place in public office. Over time, the lack of role models has reinforced the feeling that there is no "tradition of women holding positions in local government," in "public offices," or in "any type of leadership position." Respondents pointed to a general "lack of tradition of appointing women to public office."

But not everyone blames the system alone. The respondents believed that Polish women themselves are contributing to the current situation by their reluctance to participate in public life. Some see justification for this reluctance in the fact that "women have too many responsibilities" or that "the job is stressful and requires a certain psychological predisposition" or simply that "women are not interested in public life and do not want to get involved in public service activities." Although these arguments may have lost some of their power, in 1997 they persisted among women from small towns and rural areas (for a detailed discussion, see recent survey results in Graham 1997 and CRCEES 1997).

Many respondents stressed that the traditional attitudes toward women should be changed, especially in rural areas, which they saw as especially conservative with regard to women's participation in public office. There are two problems with this observation. First, because so few of the respondents were from urban areas, it is impossible to

determine statistically whether rural areas are indeed more conservative in respect to women's participation in public office. Second, the
belief in rural conservatism flies in the face of the fact that 84 percent
of the respondents lived in rural and small communities. My data
suggest that women can actually enter leadership positions more easily
in small towns than in cities.

This proposition does not contradict the observation that traditionally rural areas have lagged behind in accepting new ideas. My data
may suggest additional explanations, however, that reinforce that notion. Societal values are not the only determinants of women's political
participation; such factors as access to networks, information, previous
experience, and skills play important roles in one's ability to gain a
position in local government. As Polish women, both under communism and during the period of active opposition, have been
marginalized politically and professionally, they do lack some of those
resources. Cities are the places where "inner circles" are formed, and
these are the all-important circles to which men have had access and
women have not. In rural areas, skills and access to information and
networks are more uniformly inaccessible to everyone, so the gap between men and women, if indeed it does exist, is not necessarily significant. It is quite possible that in view of the high level of education
among women, this gap actually favors women. Yet there is another
dimension that should be considered: who is more likely to recom-
mend women candidates? Obviously, as women are reluctant to belong
to parties, and parties are equally uninterested in involving women in
their activities and listing them as candidates, areas where parties serve
as the predominant source of candidates will have fewer women on
their lists. (The left-oriented parties are more likely to include women
on their lists. For the discussion of the survey results regarding women
candidates of particular parties, see Kuratowska 1996.) Indeed, in the
1990 elections, over 81 percent of women candidates came from the
lists presented by nongovernmental organizations, civic committees,
citizens' groups, and various local organizations. In urban areas, where
the political scene is dominated by parties, few women end up on party
lists. In rural areas, however, where the party control over the electoral
processes was much weaker in 1990, NGOs and citizens' groups have
a greater impact on selecting candidates. This fact may further explain
why women were more likely to be elected to leadership positions in
rural areas than in urban.

Finally, it should be noted that the type of function a woman performed influenced her view of the obstacles to political life. Lack of time, the need to combine the responsibilities of home and job—in short, the double burden—were more frequently cited by women who were chairs of municipal councils and thus had been elected as council members. Women who were mayors (regardless of the size and type of the municipality) underlined the preference for men as officeholders, and they cited the lack of trust in women as a barrier to their political advancement. These findings seem to indicate, then, that the lack of a political culture supportive of women's political activism is more visible when women need to make executive decisions in daily affairs and use their negotiating and bargaining skills.

The Future for Polish Women Local Leaders

The responses of these local leaders suggest both the continued impact of the communist legacy and the emergence of new conditions during the transition period. First, women continue to be politically marginalized, but their marginalization is being redefined. Under communism, women were present in formal politics but had no real power; under the free electoral system, even fewer women are visible, and those few are still relegated to the lower positions. Thus the old pattern prevails: the higher the position, the less likely it is to be filled by a woman.

Yet the perception that nothing is changing may be false. The results of this survey and other scattered evidence suggest to me that something new is indeed emerging: a struggle for the redefinition of women's position in Polish society. This effort, unorganized though it is, can be seen in various forms throughout the society. At the local level, and in contrast to the situation in the past, women hold more leadership positions in rural areas than in cities, and these women are well aware that they are being discriminated against and marginalized. At the national level, parliamentary women have become more vocal, and the threat to the right to abortion has galvanized a significant majority of women throughout the nation to join in the struggle to retain it.

The second conclusion that we may draw is that the problems Polish women have to deal with are symptomatic of the tensions created in the attempt to build a democratic state and establish a new economic order. Women are questioning the current allocation mechanisms, which assign the costs of the transition disproportionately to women.

They are the ones who are increasingly unemployed; they are the first to feel the lack of needed services and infrastructure; and they are the ones expected to carry the emotional burden of the effort to preserve patriarchal family values. The economic strategy advanced by Polish politicians ignores the social costs of the reforms under the assumption that women will manage somehow, as they always do.

Third, women in Poland do not face any special barriers that might prevent them from holding public office, but the context is marked by Polish culture, the legacy of the past, and the new circumstances created by the transition period. Extensive studies on the subject carried out mainly in Western Europe and the United States (only to a limited extent in other regions of the world) point to the same obstacles facing women who want to became politically involved: the need for electoral systems that advance women's chances for election; gender consciousness of political parties; the existence of role models; and especially, women's willingness to run for public office (Outshoorn 1996; Wadstein 1996). What is different in the Polish situation is the context within which the electoral process is taking place. With respect to women's identity, the role of the Catholic church, the traditional role of Polish women in maintaining national values in times of crisis, and the image of the heroic Polish Mother are only a few of the social forces that erect these obstacles. Yet, at the same time Polish identity, too, is being redefined. How are these two processes interrelated? How is the process of constructing national identity affecting gender relations in Poland? Who are Polish women, and what is their place? Feeling almost apologetic for impinging on the public domain, women respondents often attempted to relegate themselves to the private sphere of home. Though the public/private dichotomy has been called into question by feminist theory and shown to lack validity as an analytical tool in practice, Polish women nonetheless seem to perceive this dichotomy as one of their constraints when they consider political activity. This focus on public and private spheres is among the new forces that shape the new identity of Polish women within the transitional period. Paradoxically, for women, rejection of the past regime also meant rejection of the forced, socialist public life and an almost automatic yearning for the establishment of a new private/public divide. As a result, many women are faced with conflicting forces, ideologies, and agendas. Only when they themselves acknowledge their political activity, however, will women be in a position to begin to redefine this divide.

Fourth, the study indicated that the process of redefining the political sphere is already taking place among Polish women local leaders. Surprisingly, one of the sites where the process of testing women's new political space is taking place is in the rural areas, as indicated by the much higher level of women occupying leadership positions. While these numbers are small, and various studies have indicated that the small number of women officeholders is a problem because it reinforces the perception of women's absence from the political arena (and thus possibly inhibits the power of women already in positions of leadership), my respondents indicated that they are very conscious of their role and that they have a new sense of responsibility. These responses suggest that a renegotiation of gender relations is already taking place in the household, in the workplace, and in the community. Questions remain, however: How, and by whom, should these new processes be translated into the empowerment of Polish women? What are women themselves doing to change the current political structures and practices?

Finally, one the most important implications of this study focuses on the process of policy transformation during the transition period. How can Polish women achieve policy transformations, and how can we ensure women's participation in this process? In short, what place, if any, do gender relations play in the democratization process, and how can we secure their lasting effect on this process? The experiences of other countries during transition periods, especially in Latin America, suggest a certain evolutionary process during which the increasing participation of women in civic associations and numerous other nongovernmental organizations begins to be translated into increasing numbers of women in local office. The crucial question is how to achieve recognition of the importance of women's contributions at the local level and how to translate this local activism and representation into visible participation in the political decision-making process at the national level. This is not merely a matter of political participation. It is a question of the creation of new democratic institutions that will recognize and legitimize women's efforts and will foster the formation of policies that address a women's agenda. Under the communist regime, policy was determined by the state's needs and not by political, economic, and social rights that are equally accessible to all citizens. If a redefinition of those rights is what we are seeking, then the emphasis should be on the development of new strategies and on a discussion of their implications for the policy-formation process. My respondents emphasized the connection between economic and social well-being and the issues of equity and discrimination. Indirectly they thereby argued that, while it is important to address the issues of immediate economic concern, the road to success lies in going beyond daily crises. They clearly claimed that women's experiences in Polish society have been different from men's. Despite this, the majority of respondents overlooked another crucial connection: a simple legal guarantee of social and economic rights is insufficient. The execution of these rights depends on one's ability to claim them. This, however, cannot take place without guaranteed *de jure* and *de facto* political rights to participation and representation. It is this latter dimension that requires greater women's attention.

These findings suggest two important areas for future research on women's leadership in Poland. First, research needs to be done on the kinds of institutional structures that will best address the needs of Polish women during the democratization process. This matter is extremely important because the experiences of other countries have indicated that organizing and local activism lead nowhere unless they become institutionalized. Second, research needs to consider the interrelations of the women's agenda and the policy-formation process during the transition period. What is the nature of women's involvement, and what is the context of the political process? How can Polish women counter the fact that often the process ignores the issues that are outside men's experience?

The evidence we have permits us to believe that while we are becoming more aware of the impact that democratization and the transition to market economies have on women, women are having almost negligible impact on these processes. Unfortunately, this situation is pervasive throughout the region, and Polish women's struggle is not unique. One can only hope that this recognition will mobilize even greater energies to build a better future in the new democratic Polish state.

References

Antolini, Denise. 1984. "Women in Local Government: An Overview." In *Political Women: Current Roles in State and Local Government,* ed. Janet A. Flammang, pp. 23–40. Beverly Hills, CA: Sage.

Bellows, Anne C. 1996. "Where Kitchen and Laboratory Meet: The 'Tested Food for Silesia' Program." In *Feminist Political Ecology: Global Issues and Local Experiences,* ed. Dianne Rocheleau, Barbara Thomas-Slayter, and Ester

Wangari, pp. 251–70. London and New York: Routledge.

Bishop, Brenda. 1990. "From Women's Rights to Feminist Politics: The Developing Struggle for Women's Liberation in Poland." *Monthly Review* 42 (November): 15–34.

Biuletyn Informacyjny: Miasto i Gmina Zelów [Informational newsletter: Town and municipality of Zelów]. 1992. May–June.

Biuro Studiów i Ekspertyz Kancelarii Sejmu (BSE). 1997. *Informacja o Sytuacji Kobiet w Polsce.* Warsaw.

Bystydzienski, Jill M. 1989. "Women and Socialism: A Comparative Study of Women in Poland and the USSR." *Signs* 14 (Spring): 668–84.

Carroll, Susan J., Debra L. Dodson, and Ruth B. Mandel. 1991. *The Impact of Women in Public Office: An Overview.* New Brunswick: Center for American Woman and Politics (CAWP), Eagleton Institute of Politics, Rutgers—The State University of New Jersey.

CBOS. 1997a. "Aspiracje Zawodowe Kobiet a Życie Rodzinne" [Career aspirations of women and the family life]. Report BS/12/12/97. Warsaw.

———. 1997b. "Udział Kobiet w Życiu Publicznym—Prawne Gwarancje Równości Płci" [Women's participation in public life—legal guarantees of sex equality]. BS/26/26/97. Warsaw.

Center for the American Woman and Politics. 1978. *Women in Public Office.* Metuchen, NJ: Scarecrow Press.

Clarke, Susan E., Lynn Staeheli, and Laura Brunell. 1995. "Women Redefining Local Politics." In *Theories of Urban Politics,* ed. David Judge, Gerry Stoker, and Harold Wolman, pp. 205–27. London and Thousand Oaks, CA: Sage Publications.

CRCEES. 1997. *Women's Advocacy and Lobbying: Quarterly Report.* New Brunswick: Rutgers University. June.

Eduards, Maud. L. 1994. "Women's Agency and Collective Action." *Women's Studies International Forum* 17, nos. 2 and 3: 179–84.

Einhorn, Barbara. 1992. "Concepts of Women's Rights" *WIDER Research for Action: Privatization and Democratization in Central and Eastern Europe and the Soviet Union: The Gender Dimension,* ed. Valentine M. Moghadam, pp. 59–73. World Institute for Development Economics Research of the United Nations University.

———. 1995. "Ironies of History: Citizenship Issues in the New Market Economies of East Central Europe." In *Women and Market Societies: Crisis and Opportunity,* ed. Barbara Einhorn and Ester Janes-Yeo, pp. 217–33. Sheltenham, UK: Aldershot, Edward Elgar.

Elster, Jon. 1992. "The Necessity and Impossibility of Simultaneous Economic and Political Reform." In *Philosophy of Social Choice,* ed. Piotr Płoszajski, pp. 291–308. Warsaw: IFiS PAN [Institute of Philosophy and Sociology, Polish Academy of Sciences].

Engelberg, Stephen. 1992. "Gloom and Economic Anxiety Overtake the Poles." *New York Times,* February 2.

Federation for Women and Planned Parenthood in Poland. 1992. *Annual Report.* Warsaw.

Foundation in Support of Local Democracy. 1992. "First Dialog: Improving Public Safety. Summary. Spring 1992." Bialystok. Mimeograph.

Funk, Nanette. 1993. "Feminism East and West." In *Gender Politics and Post-Communism: Reflections from Eastern Europe and Former Soviet Union,* ed. Nanette Funk and Magda Mueller, pp. 318–30. New York: Routledge.

———. and Magda Mueller, eds. 1993. *Gender Politics and Post-Communism: Reflections from Eastern Europe and Former Soviet Union.* New York: Routledge.

Fuszara, Małgorzata. 1991. "Legal Regulation of Abortion in Poland." *Signs* 17 (Autumn): 117–28.

———. 1993. "Women's Legal Rights in Poland in the Process of Transformation." *Beyond Law* 3, no. 8: 35–47.

———. 1994. "Market Economy and Consumer Rights: The Impact of Women's Everyday Lives and Employment." *Economic and Industrial Democracy* 15: 75–87.

———. 1997a. "The Activities of Family Courts in Poland." *International Journal of Law, Policy and the Family* 11: 86–102.

———. 1997b. "Wizerunek Kobiet w Społeczeństwie Demokratycznym." Address at the Joint Session of the Polish Parliament, Warsaw, March 8.

Gontarczyk-Wesoła, Ewa. 1997. "Women's Situation in the Process of Change in Poland." In *Ana's Land: Sisterhood in Eastern Europe,* ed. Tanya Renne, pp. 34–41. Boulder, CO: Westview Press.

Graham, Ann. 1997. *Citizens Participation in Small and Medium-Sized Polish Towns.* Unpublished Dissertation, Rutgers University.

———. and Joanna Regulska. 1997. "Expanding Political Space for Women in Poland: An Analysis of Three Communities." *Communist and Post-Communist Studies* 30, no. 1: 65–82.

Grobelna, Agnieszka, and Maria Łyszkowska-Cieślik. 1995. *Opinia Społeczna o Samorządzie Terytorialnym.* Warszawa: Profile.

Grzelak, Grzegorz. 1995. "Polityczne aspekty reformy państwa" [Political aspects of the state reform]. *Samorząd Terytorialny* 7–8: 93–95.

Jalušić, V. 1994. "Politics as a Whore: Women, Public Space and Antipolitics in Post-Socialism." Unpublished paper.

Jancar, Barbara W. 1985. "Women in the Opposition in Poland and Czechoslovakia in the 1970s." In *Women, State, and Party in Eastern Europe,* ed. Sharon L. Wolchik and Alfred G. Meyer, pp. 168–85. Durham, NC: Duke University Press.

Janowska, Zdzisława, Jolanta Martini-Fiwek, and Zbigniew Góral. 1992. "Female Unemployment in Poland." *Economic and Social Policy Series,* No. 18, May. Warsaw: Friedrich-Ebert Foundation.

Kelly, R.M. 1988. *Women and the Arizona Political Process.* Lanham, MD: University Press of America.

Kolaczek, Barbara. 1992. "Sytuacja kobiet na rynku pracy" [Situation of women on the job market]. *Życie Warszawy* 3315, no. 227, November 25.

Kronika Sejmowa [Sejm journal]. 1992. "Powstała grupa parlamentarna kobiet" [Parliamentary women's group created] vol. 53, no. 8, January 23–29.

Kulesza, Michał. 1995. "Samorząd Terytorialny w Rzeczypospolitej Polskiej—stan obecny i perspektywy" [Local Self-Government in the Republic of Poland—present status and the future]. *Samorząd Terytorialny* vol. 53, no. 5: 7–15.

Kuratowska, Zofia. 1991. "Present Situation of Women in Poland." Paper presented at the Regional Seminar on the Impact of Economic and Political Reform

on the Status of Women in Eastern Europe and the USSR, Vienna, April 8–12.
———. 1996. "Polish Civil Society Today and the Situation of Women." Unpublished paper.

Lake, Robert, and Joanna Regulska. 1990. "Political Decentralization and Capital Mobility in Planned and Market Societies: Local Autonomy in Poland and the United States." *Policy Studies Journal* 18 (Spring): 702–19.

Leven, Bozena. 1991. "The Welfare Effects on Women of Poland's Economic Reforms." *Journal of Economic Issues* 25 (June): 581–88.

Mason, David, Daniel Nelson, and Bohdan Szklarski. 1991. "Apathy and the Faith of Democracy: The Polish Struggle." *East European Politics and Societies* 5, no. 2: 205–33.

Moghadam, Valentine M., ed. 1992. *Privatization and Democratization in Central and Eastern Europe and the Soviet Union: The Gender Dimension.* Helsinki: World Institute for the Development for Economics Research, United Nations University.

Nelson, Daniel N. 1985. "Women in Local Communist Politics in Romania and Poland." In *Women, State, and Party in Eastern Europe,* ed. Sharon L. Wolchik and Alfred G. Meyer, pp. 151–67. Durham, NC: Duke University Press.

Nowakowska, Urszula. 1997. "The New Right and Fundamentalism." In *Ana's Land: Sisterhood in Eastern Europe,* ed. Tanya Renne, pp. 26–33. Boulder, CO: Westview Press.

Nowicka, Wanda. 1997. "Ban on Abortion in Poland. Why?" In *Ana's Land: Sisterhood in Eastern Europe,* ed. Tanya Renne, pp. 42–46. Boulder, CO: Westview Press.

Nowy Dziennik. 1992a. "Sondaże Opinii Publicznej" [Public opinion polls]. February 8/9.

———. 1992b. "Polacy na Dnie Pesymizmu" [Poles drowning in pessimism]. February 21.

———. 1992c. "Zmęczeni Demokracją" [Tired of democracy]. August 19.

Osiatyński, Wiktor. 1990. "Round Table Negotiations in Poland." Working Paper no. 1, Center for the Study of Constitutionalism in Eastern Europe, University of Chicago Law School.

Outshoorn, Joyce. 1996. "Teorie Demokracji i Przedstawicielstwa." In *Biuletyn, Centrum Europejskie Uniwersytetu Warszawskiego,* no. 3: 33–46.

Penn, Shana. 1994. "The National Secret." *Journal of Women's History* 5, no. 3: 55–69.

Przeworski, Adam. 1991. *Democracy and the Market.* New York: Cambridge University Press.

Rabska, Teresa. 1995. "Pozycja Samorządu Terytorialnego w Konstytucji" [Location of local self-government within the constitution]. *Samorząd Terytorialny* vol. 53, no. 5: 16–28.

Regulska, Joanna. 1992. "Women and Power in Poland: Hopes or Reality?" In *Women in International Perspective,* ed. Jill M. Bystydzienski, pp. 175–91. Bloomington: Indiana University Press.

———. 1993. "Local Government Reform in Central and Eastern Europe?" In *Local Government in the New Europe in the 1990's,* ed. Robert J. Bennett. London: Belhaven Press.

———. 1997a. "Decentralization or (Re)Centralization: Struggle for Political

Power in Poland." *Environment and Planning C: Government and Policy* 15, no. 2: 187–207.

———. 1997b. "Decentralization or Deconcentration: Struggle for Political Power in Poland." *International Journal of Public Administration* 20, no. 3: 643–80.

———. 1998a. "'The Political' and Its Meaning for Women: Transitional Politics in Poland." In *Theorizing Transition: The Political Economy of Change in Central and Eastern Europe,* ed. John Pickles and Adrian Smith, pp. 309–329. London and New York: Routledge.

———. 1998b. "Local Government Reform." In *Transition to Democracy in Poland,* ed. Richard F. Staar, pp. 113–132. New York: St. Martin's Press.

Renne, Tanya. 1997. *Ana's Land: Sisterhood in Eastern Europe.* Boulder, CO: Westview Press.

Reszke, Irena. 1991. *Nierówności płci w teoriach* [Gender discrimination in theories]. Warsaw: IFiS PAN [Institute of Philosophy and Sociology, Polish Academy of Sciences].

Sajo, Andras. 1990. "Round Tables in Hungary." Working Paper no. 2. Center for the Study of Constitutionalism in Eastern Europe, University of Chicago Law School.

Semprich, Zaneta. 1992. "Baby, ach te baby" [Women, oh, those women]. *Rzeczpospolita,* no. 171, July 22.

Shaul, Marnie S. 1982. "The Status of Women in Local Governments: An International Assessment." *Public Administration Review,* November/December, pp. 491–500.

Siemieńska, Renata. 1990. *Płeć, zawód, polityka* [Gender, occupation, politics]. Warsaw: Uniwersytet Warszawski.

———. 1992. "Unexpected by Women: Consequences of Economics and Political Changes in Poland." Paper delivered at the conference Women and the Transition from Authoritarian Rule in Latin America and Eastern Europe, Berkeley, December 3–4.

Šiklová, Jiřina. "Are Women in Middle and Eastern Europe Conservative?" Manuscript.

Simpson, Peggy. 1991. "No Liberation for Women." *Progressive* 55, no. 2: 20–24.

Solidarity Trade Union. 1991. "Declaration of the National Section of Women." January 23. Mimeographed.

Tarasiewicz, Malgorzata. 1991. "Women in Poland: Choices to Be Made." *Feminist Review,* no. 39 (Autumn): 182–86.

U.S. Agency for International Development. 1991. *Poland: Gender Issues in the Transition to a Market Economy.* Prepared by Coopers and Lybrand. Washington, DC.

Wadstein, Margareta. 1996. "Udział Kobiet w Rozwoju Demokracji w Krajach Nordyckich." in *Biuletyn,* op.cit., pp. 50–62.

Weschler, Joanna, and Dorothy G. Thomas. 1992. "Hidden Victims: Women in Post-Communist Poland." *News from Helsinki Watch* 4, no. 5, March 12.

Wolchik, Sharon L. 1992. "Central and Eastern Europe." In *Privatization and Democratization in Central and Eastern Europe and the Soviet Union: The Gender Dimension,* ed. Valentine M. Moghadam, pp. 50–58. Helsinki: World Institute for Development Economics Research, United Nations University.

5

Women and Politics in
Western Germany

Eva Kolinsky

Old and New Gender Divisions

The history of women in German politics starts with a paradox: the Social Democratic Party, which had been an early champion of equal rights, lost out after women were enfranchised in 1918, while the forces of political conservatism, which had been opposed to woman suffrage, secured the lion's share of votes. In the Weimar Republic, the left-right division of women's preferences favored the Catholic Center Party and other conservative forces and impeded the political consolidation of the Social Democrats as a governmental party.

In the Federal Republic, women's political preferences were transferred to the Christian Democratic Party (CDU) and its ally, the Christian Social Union (CSU).[1] Until the late 1960s these parties enjoyed the support of a secure majority of West German women, while the Social Democratic Party (SPD) lagged 11 to 25 percentage points behind in women's votes (Table 5.1).

The persistence of women's political conservatism was bound up with a more general persistence of socioeconomic factors in German politics.[2] It changed as traditional class divisions subsided[3] and were replaced by new groupings based on income, education, and social values.[4]

The new social mobility left its mark on electoral preferences after the 1960s. The boundary between left and right was less rigidly drawn than it had been in the past as new middle-class voters and the upwardly mobile switched camps. The gender gap between the

Table 5.1

Party Preferences of Female (F) and Male (M) Voters in German Elections, 1953–94 (in percent)

Year	CDU/CSU[a] F	CDU/CSU[a] M	SPD F	SPD M	CDU/CSU advantage/ disadvantage F	CDU/CSU advantage/ disadvantage M	FDP F	FDP M	GREENS[b] F	GREENS[b] M	PDS[c] F	PDS[c] M	Others F	Others M
1953	47	39	28	33	+19	+6	10	12	—	—	—	—	17	15
1957	54	45	29	35	+25	+10	7	9	—	—	—	—	12	10
1961	50	40	33	40	+17	0	12	14	—	—	—	—	6	5
1965	52	42	36	44	+16	−2	9	11	—	—	—	—	4	3
1969	51	41	40	46	+11	−5	5	6	—	—	—	—	8	4
1972	46	43	46	47	0	−4	8	9	—	—	—	—	1	1
1976	49	47	43	44	+6	+3	8	8	—	—	—	—	1	1
1980	44	44	44	43	0	+1	11	11	1	2	—	—	—	1
1983	49	48	39	38	+10	+10	6	7	5	6	—	—	—	—
1987	45	43	38	39	+7	+4	8	9	8	8	—	—	1	—
1990	45	43	34	34	+11	+9	11	11	5	5	3	3	3	3
1994	42	41	36	36	+6	+5	7	8	8	7	4	5	3	4

Sources: Compiled from data in Eva Kolinsky, *Women in Contemporary Germany* (Oxford: Berg, 1993); *Wirtschaft und Statistik*, no. 4, 1991, p. 257; and Forschungsgruppe Wahlen e.V., *Die Bundestagswahl 1994* (Mannheim, 1994), p. 18.

[a] The CDU maintains a political alliance with the Bavarian-based CSU.

[b] In 1990, the West German Greens and the East German Alliance '90 fought separate campaigns. While the western Greens failed to pass the 5 percent hurdle, the Bündnis 90 did in the new Länder and thus entered the Bundestag. Before the 1994 elections, the two Green parties had merged into one.

[c] The PDS is the successor party of the Socialist Unity Party of the GDR. It is essentially an East German political party. In the 1990 elections, it attracted 11 percent of female and 12 percent of male voters in the East but fewer than 2 percent in the West. In the 1994 elections, the PDS won the support of 19 percent female and 20 percent male voters in the East but remained around 1 percent in the West. The PDS entered the Bundestag because it obtained four direct mandates and thus was entitled to parliamentary representation.

CDU/CSU and the SPD, a hallmark of German politics since 1919, narrowed. In 1972 the SPD attracted as many women voters as the CDU. Later elections revealed that none of the political parties could rely on women's electoral support. German unification appears to have turned back the clock. In the former German Democratic Republic (GDR) the SPD fared badly among women voters, while the CDU enjoyed an advantage reminiscent of its popularity among West German women in the 1950s (Table 5.2), gaining 43 percent to the SPD's 24 percent. By 1994, the CDU had lost some of its appeal as the party of unification in the new *Länder,* while PDS, Greens and PDS extended their support generally and among female voters. The PDS in particular consolidated its position in the new *Länder* from 11 to 19 percent among women and from 12 to 20 percent among men. In Germany as a whole, the Greens were the only political party to increase their share of the women's vote in all age groups and to attract more votes from female than male voters.[5]

Generational Perspectives

The political preferences of German women born before 1945 differ greatly from those of women born after the war. Table 5.3 suggests that women born before 1945 have been predominantly conservative, regardless of their occupation or educational level. The only exceptions to this rule are blue-collar women, among whom the SPD has fared better. Among women born after 1945, by contrast, the CDU/CSU has lost ground. These women have not simply shifted to the SPD but have scattered among the parties. Well-educated women of the younger generation have been especially likely to support the Greens.

Contemporary party preferences are increasingly determined by perceived party accomplishment; that is, potential voters may support or reject a political party in accordance with the issues they consider essential and the policies they expect a party to support.[6] In the early 1970s, for instance, the SPD was widely perceived to be the political party that was committed to equal opportunity. In the mid-1980s, the programs supported by the Greens appealed strongly to women under the age of 40. In the 1990s none of the political parties can rely on such a constituency; all are under scrutiny from an increasingly mobile, volatile female electorate.

Table 5.2

Party Preferences of Female (F) and Male (M) Voters in German Elections, 1990, by Region (in percent)

Region	SPD F	SPD M	CDU F	CDU M	CSU F	CSU M	FDP F	FDP M	Greens F	Greens M	Alliance B90[a] F	Alliance B90[a] M	PDS F	PDS M	REP[b] F	REP[b] M	Other F	Other M
Schleswig-Holstein	39%	39%	44%	42%	—	—	11%	12%	4%	4%	—	—	—	1%	1%	2%	1%	—
Hamburg	44	40	36	34	—	—	11	12	6	8	—	—	1	2	1	3	1	1%
Lower Saxony	39	39	46	43	—	—	9	11	4	4	—	—	—	—	1	2	1	1
Bremen	42	42	32	31	—	—	13	13	8	7	—	—	1	1	1	4	3	2
N. Rhine-Westphalia	42	43	40	39	—	—	11	11	4	4	—	—	—	—	1	2	1	2
Hesse	39	38	42	40	—	—	10	11	6	5	—	—	—	—	1	3	2	5
Rhineland-Palatinate	35	37	48	45	—	—	10	11	4	4	—	—	—	—	1	5	2	2
Baden-Württemberg	29	30	49	45	—	—	11	12	5	5	—	—	—	—	2	7	3	3
Bavaria	27	28	—	—	54	50	8	8	5	5	—	—	—	—	4	—	3	3
Saar Region	52	53	39	36	—	—	5	6	2	2	—	—	—	—	1	1	1	2
Berlin	31	30	40	38	—	—	9	9	4	4	—	—	10	10	2	3	4	5
Mecklenburg—Hither Pomerania	26	25	40	36	—	—	10	9	—	—	7	7	15	19	1	3	2	2
Brandenburg	31	32	38	35	—	—	10	10	—	—	7	6	12	13	1	2	2	2
Saxony-Anhalt	24	26	40	37	—	—	20	19	—	—	6	5	9	10	—	2	1	1
Thuringia	22	23	47	42	—	—	15	15	—	—	6	5	8	9	1	—	2	1
Saxony	18	19	51	47	—	—	12	13	—	—	6	5	9	9	1	2	3	5
FRG	34	34	38	35	7	7	11	11	4	4	1	1	3	3	1	3	2	2
FRG[c]	36	37	36	34	7	8	11	11	5	5	—	—	—	—	2	3	2	3
FRG[d]	24	25	43	39	—	—	13	13	—	—	6	5	11	12	1	4	3	4

Source: Wirtschaft und Statistik, no. 4, 1991, p. 257.
[a]B90 stands for Bündnis 90, an electoral alliance of the New Forum and other citizens' movements
[b]REP = Republikanische Partei, a political party of the extreme right.
[c]Old *Länder*.
[d]New *Länder*.

Table 5.3

Party Preferences of German Women Voters Born Before and After 1945: 1990 by Social Status and Education (in percent)

Occupation/Education	CDU/CSU		SPD		FDP		Greens		Other	
	Pre-'45	Post-'45	Pre-'45	Post-'45	Pre-'45	Post-'45	Pre-'45	Post-'45	Pre-'45	Post-'45
Occupation										
All occupations	52%	32%	39%	44%	6%	9%	3%	16%	0%	0%
White collar/civil service:										
Low level	56	33	39	46	6	6	0	15	0	0
Mid-level	55	32	33	46	6	11	6	12	0	0
High level	47	29	22	35	22	6	9	29	0	0
Self-employed	70	33	21	20	7	27	3	20	0	0
Blue collar	47	30	50	52	1	5	2	14	0	0
Education										
Lower	52	31	42	52	4	7	2	10	0	0
Intermediate	54	39	34	32	6	7	6	22	0	0
Advanced	46	19	18	26	32	13	5	39	0	3

Source: Heinz Ulrich Brinkmann, "Zeigen Frauen ein besonderes Wahlverhalten?" *Frauenforschung,* no. 3, 1990, pp. 60–61.
Note: The percentage of women of all groups who voted for the neo-Nazi German National Democratic Party (NPD) was negligible.

The entry of the postwar generations into German politics influenced the recasting of traditional party agendas. It has been argued that the postwar generations could focus on the quality of their lives because the conditions of material survival were no longer an issue.[7] In West Germany increasing affluence brought improved access to education, training, and employment for women. While discrimination has not disappeared and women's opportunities in society continue to differ from those of men, increasing numbers of West German women are qualifying for good jobs and are going after them. In East Germany, as Chapter 6 of this volume makes clear, the perception of employment as a normal part of a woman's life has been and remains even more widespread.[8]

Taking Part in Politics

The new social participation of women lowered another gender barrier: the customary lag in women's participation in politics. Starting in the mid-1960s, young West German women expressed more interest in politics than women had traditionally done and began to play more visible roles in German politics as members of political groups, movements, and parties. The 1960s saw the emergence of the new women's movement when female activists broke away from the student movement, which had excluded them from its policy debates.[9] The social movements that have emerged since the early 1970s have received as much support from women as from men; women have been especially prominent in the networks of nonhierarchical action groups outside of parliamentary politics.[10]

The discourse on women's role and the emphasis on women's right to be in charge of their destinies—to choose abortion, for example, or to search for equality through employment instead of cultivating the traditional homemaking skills and subservience—gave women a new public voice and collective awareness. The mass protests against the criminalization of abortion engendered a multifaceted women's culture of meeting places, bookshops, safe houses, and refuges. These gathering places became focal points for women across the country and helped to revive the debate on women's opportunities that had been dormant since the immediate postwar years.

The new women's movement arrived at distinctive answers to questions about the chances and limits of equality. It regarded society and the organizational structures that dominated it as defined and controlled by men, tailored to male behavior and basically hostile to women. If women wanted to fulfill their own potential and live by their own preferences and strengths, they needed to break away and create nonhierarchical and noncompetitive environments, a language cleansed of sexism, based on female rather than male values. The underlying assumption of a fundamental male/female division of social action produced a women's movement that has remained and wishes to remain outside the conventional channels that constitute mainstream politics and set the agenda for equal opportunity.

Participating in Political Parties

The increased interest of German women in political participation in the 1970s was also evident at the more conventional level of party membership. Membership in a political party serves many purposes and may satisfy a range of individual aspirations. Within a democratic polity, however, its key function relates to the fact that political parties serve as reservoirs for the recruitment of the political elite. Party membership is always the first step toward selecting that elite or becoming a part of it. Members of legislatures from the local to the national level, government administrators, and many holders of public offices obtain their positions through their membership and active involvement in a political party.[11]

In the recast democracy of the Federal Republic, political parties remained relatively small in the 1950s and 1960s—about 2 percent of the electorate were members—and predominantly male. Only the SPD had a tradition of mass membership—close to 600,000 at the end of the 1960s. The CDU at the time numbered fewer than 300,000. Women constituted between 7 and 17 percent of the membership. In the 1970s, West German political parties began to grow. By the end of the decade, overall party membership had doubled; among women it had trebled. Membership grew most rapidly in the CDU and CSU. Together they topped the 1 million mark in the mid-1970s; the SPD welcomed its millionth member, a woman, in 1976.[12]

The 1970s set in motion a transformation of all political parties into mass organizations[13] in which women occupied a more visible place. From an average of 15 percent in 1970, women's share of membership in political parties in 1995 rose to 31 percent in the CDU, 34 percent in the

Table 5.4

Female Membership of German Political Parties, 1969–95 (in percent)

Year	CDU	CSU	SPD	FDP	Greens	PDS
1969	13	7	17	12	n/a	n/a
1976	20	12	21	19	n/a	n/a
1980	21	13	23	23	30	n/a
1983	22	14	25	24	33	n/a
1987	22	14	25	23	33	n/a
1991	26	15	27	30	33	49
1995	25	16	28	30	42	48

Sources: Compiled from data supplied by the *Bundesgeschäftsstellen* of the relevant parties. For 1991, see Frauenbericht for the CDU and Gleichstellungsbericht for SPD and FDP; for 1995, see Oscar W. Gabriel and Oskar Niedermayer, "Entwicklung und Sozialstruktur der Parteimitgliedschaften," in *Parteiendemokratie in Deutschland*, ed. Oscar W. Gabriel, Oskar Niedermayer, and Richard Stoess (Opladen: Westdeutscher Verlag, 1997) p. 296.

SPD, 30 percent in the Free Democratic Party (FDP), and 43 percent in the Greens (Table 5.4). The PDS included 48 percent female members.

Motivations for Party Membership

Broadly speaking, women who have joined political parties since the early 1970s have sought to play active roles in politics, to hold offices, and often to make politics their career. Many have also been active in citizens' groups and have retained links to the women's movement, but they have not shared the feminists' assumption that involvement in conventional organizations will always be on men's terms and work in men's favor.

In the first hour of political reconstruction, women of all parties hoped for a recast role: away from a focus on the women's wings of their respective parties and closer to the hub of power. However, the first twenty years of party organization after the war saw women confined to the women's track: the Frauenvereingung of the CDU, the Frauenunion of the CSU, or the forerunner of the Association of Social Democratic Women in the SPD. Women's affairs remained separate, a matter of women's congresses with a phalanx of women speakers in front of all-women audiences.

The younger generation of women who joined political parties after

Table 5.5

Stated Reasons for Joining a Political Party, by Gender (in percent)

"How did you become a party member? What was your motivation?"

Reason	Women (N = 197)	Men (N = 363)	Both genders (N = 560)
I decided to join on my own account	40	54	51
A friend/colleague who was a party member approached me	28	24	25
My spouse found it important that I became a member	15	1	4
I was approached by an officer-holder whom I knew	5	12	10
I was approached during a party meeting that I attended as a nonmember	2	2	2
I was won over as a member during an election campaign	2	*	1
I was won over as a member during a recruitment drive at election time	1	1	1
Other	7	7	7

Source: Beate Hoecker, *Frauen in der Politik* (Opladen: Westdeutscher Verlag, 1987), p. 178, citing data from a survey of party members in Bremen.

the early 1970s see their role differently. A perception of active party membership has been most evident in the SPD, where women, like men, stress that a primary reason for joining was a wish to make a political impact. The hope of holding a political office is just one aspect of such participation.[14] Twenty years earlier, a study of the SPD had shown that its members were largely passive, content to support the organization without straining to make a personal contribution.[15] CDU members in the 1960s and 1970s were particularly eager to hold an office in the party or through the party in parliamentary politics.[16] In the mid-1980s women tended to join the CDU in order to communicate with like-minded people and the SPD to influence policies (Table 5.5). The third most important reason for women to join their present political party was that their partner was also a member; for men, this reason came near the bottom of the list.

To the Free Democrats, an internal survey in the mid-1970s yielded the surprise finding that nearly one in three of their number was a woman and that many of these women were keen to play more active roles while their party offered them few opportunities to do so.[17]

Women's Place: Traditions and Adjustments

The formative experience of women party members in the 1970s was the gap between party traditions and the new political role women intended to play. In 1971, for instance, the young women who had joined the SPD insisted on removal of a protective clause that had reserved places for women on the party executive.[18] Determined to succeed on their own merits and confident of their ability to do so, the SPD women of 1971 were bitterly disappointed when just two of their number were elected to the party executive instead of the customary five.[19] The 1972 Bundestag elections produced a similar shock. A record number of women voted, and a record number supported the SPD. In the Bundestag, however, the number of women members fell to an all-time low, and the SPD elected fewer women than the rival CDU/CSU (Table 5.6).

The SPD

The 1970s were a decade of discontent for women in the SPD. The party had entered the postwar era with a paternalistic view of women in politics: their task was, above all, to instill socialist values in their children and thus consolidate the social and political fortunes of their party. A women's association did exist, but it was closely controlled by the party executive and had little scope for action. In the late 1960s, the party was interested mainly in enhancing its profile among voters, and the organizational basis for women in the party was discontinued. The new women's association, the Association for Social Democratic Women (ASF), which was founded in 1973, had been intended as an umbrella group for all female party members, at the beck and call of the party leadership. Instead, the ASF turned itself into an effective and vociferous pressure group for women's rights and opportunities in German society and also in their own party. The ASF spearheaded a protracted campaign for women's access to parliamentary seats and party offices. In 1977 it began to demand quotas; a 40 percent quota was finally written into the party statutes at the SPD congress in Münster in 1988.[20] Although the party

Table 5.6

Seats in the Bundestag Held by Women, 1949–94, by Party

Year	All parties		CDU/CSU		SPD		FDP		Greens		PDS		Other	
	N	%	N	%	N	%	N	%	N	%	N	%	N	%
1949	28	7	11	8	13	10	0	0	n/a[a]	n/a	n/a	n/a	4	5
1953	45	9	19	8	21	13	3	6	n/a	n/a	n/a	n/a	2	4
1957	48	9	22	8	22	12	3	7	n/a	n/a	n/a	n/a	0	0
1961	43	8	18	7	21	10	4	8	n/a	n/a	n/a	n/a	1	6
1965	36	7	15	6	19	9	2	7	n/a	n/a	n/a	n/a	—[b]	—
1969	34	7	14	6	18	8	2	5	n/a	n/a	n/a	n/a	—	—
1972	30	6	15	6	13	5	2	5	n/a	n/a	n/a	n/a	—	—
1976	38	7	19	8	15	7	4	8	n/a	n/a	n/a	n/a	—	—
1980	44	8	18	8	19	8	7	13	—	—	n/a	n/a	—	—
1983	51	10	17	7	21	10	3	12	10	36	n/a	n/a	—	—
1987	80	15	18	8	31	16	6	13	25	57	n/a	n/a	—	—
1990	135	20	44	13	64	27	16	20	3[c]	38	8	47	—	—
1994	177	26	41	14	85	34	8	17	29	59	13	43	—	—

Sources: Adapted from Eva Kolinsky, Women in Contemporary Germany (Oxford: Berg, 1993), p. 222; and Eva Kolinsky, "Women in the 1994 Elections," in Germans Divided, ed. Russell J. Dalton (Oxford: Berg, 1996).

[a]The symbol n/a denotes that political party did not yet exist.

[b]Denotes that party/parties failed to win parliamentary representation.

[c]In 1990, the West German Greens failed to win representation in the Bundestag while the East German Greens/Alliance 90 passed the 5 percent hurdle in the new Länder and thus constituted the only Green Bundestag representation between 1990 and 1994.

had instituted an equal opportunity commission under the chairman-ship of Willy Brandt and had repeatedly appealed to officeholders and decision makers to give women better chances, the gender balance in the SPD had fallen short of women's expectations.

The Greens

The Greens have been the catalysts for organizational adjustments. From the outset, women held prominent positions in the party leadership and in the Bundestag, and gained a public profile as main spokespersons on key policy issues such as ecology, defense, the economy, nuclear power, and fossil fuels, not just the traditional women's issues—family, health care, abortion, education. When the West German Greens were represented in the Bundestag in 1983 and 1987, theirs was the largest group of women members. From the vantage point of other parties, Green women had all the opportunities to make their mark in politics that were coveted and largely denied elsewhere. In fact, the Greens had introduced a women's quota in 1985, partly to satisfy the expectations of their women's group but also to demonstrate publicly that their party abided by its principles: the principle of gender equality, which figured prominently in the Green party program and policy agenda, figured as prominently in the organiza-tional reality of the party.[21]

The CDU

The Christian Democrats focused on women's opportunities in 1985 but for different reasons and with an altogether different outcome. As I mentioned earlier, the party had lost electoral ground among women of the postwar generations. When the CDU targeted women, it did so with the specific aim of restoring its electoral fortunes. In 1985 a "partnership" congress was organized to launch a new legislative pro-gram for women. Conservative policymakers at the time had under-stood that young German women could not be tempted back to the traditional roles of full-time homemaker and mother; they wanted to combine family roles with employment. If the conservatives' goals of preserving the family and halting the decline in the birthrate were to be achieved, women needed support in their two roles, not a prescription to choose one or the other.[22] The congress, attended by over 1,000 CDU women and an additional 500 invited guests—women from all walks of life and political backgrounds—was no more than a publicity gimmick. The legislative program struck a firmer note and included pension rights for childrearing, parental leave, and a job guarantee after a maternity leave.[23]

Adjustments of the gender balance within the organization were halfhearted by comparison. The so-called partnership principles of 1985 yielded few gains.[24] In 1987 the party congress in Mainz passed a resolution that the party should involve women in accordance with their share of the membership and report on the participation of women in the party; one year later, a similar statement of intent was issued on women's place in the CDU.[25]

Redress of the gender balance in the CDU was recommended, not required in the sense of a women's quota, and the effort has, as we later see, had a limited effect. Within the CDU-Frauenunion, the women's organization affiliated with the party, the younger generation wished for a more forceful effort to win party and parliamentary posts, while the older generation favored the traditional formula: women's political work should broaden the appeal of the party and reach into the community, rather than serve as a springboard for political careers.[26]

Some recent developments in the 1990s suggested that the CDU might move toward a firmer commitment to women's equality in politics. In Schleswig-Holstein, for instance, the CDU supported an SPD initiative to change the regional constitution in order to guarantee that an equal number of men and women are represented on important political committees. In the Rhineland-Palatinate, the regional CDU adopted a 30 percent quota for all levels of the party organization: "This means that the CDU in the Rhineland-Palatinate is the first regional CDU organization to react with quota regulations—albeit a should-be quota—to the stagnating number of women officeholders in the party and to the drastic decline of the CDU among women voters."[27]

The CSU

In the CSU, the Bavarian partner of the CDU, no comparable debate on women's participation has surfaced, but more women than in the past have been nominated for legislative and other political offices.

The FDP

The situation of the Free Democrats seems similar to that of the CDU: they reject formal quotas but declare their commitment to women's participation in line with their share of the membership at all levels of the party organization.[28] The post of equalization officer was created at the national headquarters to monitor and coordinate changes in the gender balance of the FDP and to compile an annual report. In 1993 the promotion of women in the party was due to conclude with a congress to take stock and determine future steps.[29]

In contrast to other German parties, the FDP does not have a women's association, although an Association of Liberal Women was founded in 1990 as an additional (nonparty) tier of liberal political activity and possibly as a pressure group to influence the party executive. More important has been the presence in the FDP of women eager to hold political office. In the mid-1970s these women had been the least satisfied with the opportunities their party offered them.[30] Today the party's policy of promoting women *(Frauenförderung)* has narrowed the gender gap, but not enough, it seems, to quell the sense of disadvantage. As the trial period for equal opportunity is drawing to a close, women in the FDP have begun to demand quotas. Irmgard Schwaetzer, a former business manager and treasurer of the FDP and nearly the successor of Hans-Dietrich Genscher as foreign minister in 1992 (she was denied the post by the machinations of the FDP parliamentary party), has been the driving force behind a renewed debate about quotas, this time with direct reference to the women's quota in the SPD.[31] At the 1991 congress of the FDP, however, an urgent request by the liberal women to discuss quotas was rejected because the party chairman did not regard the issue as urgent.[32]

Women in Politics: Contemporary Developments

On two counts, the introduction of prescribed or recommended women's quotas in German political parties has failed to achieve the expected results. There is no evidence that party preferences are determined by quotas or that political parties with female candidates can expect electoral gains. The gender factor does appear to have some effect among potential Green voters, and the party has gained support among women between the ages of 25 and 40, but none of the other parties can rely on a clear link between gender and choice. The Bavarian CSU, for instance, has always performed better among women than among men, but has barely modified its traditional reluctance to run women candidates. By the same token, there is no evidence that women vote for women candidates. In the new state of Brandenburg, for instance, women were placed too far down the electoral list to win a seat in the first all-German Bundestag in 1990, yet the CDU fared better among women voters there than in other regions where more women were nominated (see Table 5.2).[33]

The second gain that did not occur was in membership. Quotas or their equivalent were forced onto the political agenda by women whose motivation for active involvement in politics as a career was hampered by party cultures that had tended to direct women toward a separate women's association and allowed them limited participation in mainstream politics. Once the obstacles to participation were removed or lowered, it was argued, women would turn to political parties as members, activists, and potential politicians. This influx of women has failed to materialize. Generally speaking, membership in all political parties has been stagnant or on the decline. Among new members, no more than one in three is a woman. In the early 1970s and before quota-guaranteed opportunities, women accounted for 40 percent of new members. In the new *Länder,* many women have dropped out after a brief spell of activism in 1989–90, and fewer than 20 percent of new members are women.[34] The 1996 report on women in the CDU shows a decline of female membership in the new *Länder* since 1991 from 40 percent to 34 percent, although this level of female participation still reflects the quota regulation of the GDR era about the gender balance in party organizations and remains 10 percentage points higher than that in the old *Länder.*

Data for the SPD suggest that the majority of women members join the party when they are between 35 and 55 years old. Among the youngest cohort of members, men are more numerous than women. In 1991, 12 percent of male members and just 9 percent of female members were under the age of 21. In the CDU, both female and young members seem to be so scarce that the party organization of Lower Saxony adopted the guideline that a woman and a person under the age of 30 should always be among the first six persons to be nominated for party posts or parliamentary seats.[35] In 1991, 2,000 of the 9,000 CDU local party organizations had no more than one female member, and in 300 of them no members were under 40 years old.[36] The data provided by the party organizations seem to indicate a stagnant or declining membership in the western regions of Germany, a virtual standstill in the East, and major problems everywhere in efforts to recruit members between 16 and 25 years of age. The relative indifference toward party membership applies to both women and men. In the mid-1990s, just 2 percent of CDU and CSU members and 3 percent of SPD members were under 25 years old. In the conservative parties, well over 80 percent were over 40 years old. In the Social Democratic Party the 40–plus group constituted 75 percent of the membership.[37]

Recasting the Gender Balance: Party Cultures in Transition

Women who are members of political parties today enjoy unparalleled opportunities to hold party office, compete for parliamentary seats, and win government posts. With political parties the main institutional channels for recruiting the political elite, the introduction of women's quotas has broken down some of the obstacles that have faced women who wish to make politics their career. The contemporary emphasis on the participation of women and the ultimate goal of a gender balance in politics reduced one of the key obstacles women encountered in the past: prolonged periods of organizational activity and officeholding at the lower levels of a party before parliamentary seats or positions at the leadership level came within reach. This so-called *Ochsentour* has been characteristic of elite recruitment through political parties in Germany. The new salience of gender balance has modified the dominance of established party organizations and functionaries, for it opens unprecedented opportunities to newcomers to party politics. Now that a lengthy track record of organizational involvement has become less important to women who seek political opportunities, more women are in a position to build up organizational and political expertise in their party and in the legislatures. In this way women can become more closely linked to their party's policy perspective and should be able to develop the experience and expertise to qualify for high political offices. Quota regulations have broken the vicious circle of excluding women from the organizational career tracks parties can offer and then denying them access to political office because they lack organizational know-how.

The focus on achieving a gender balance in politics has begun to recast elite recruitment and has helped to recast the discourse on women and politics in Germany. "In those places where women's quotas are applied, women report positive developments: men try really hard, right down to linguistic detail. According to Heide Pfarr, the Berlin Senator for Federal Affairs ... debates have become more succinct: the gentlemen claim that the climate is more factual and less dominated by vanity, although men have been inclined to launch into big speeches. 'Every time a man has a relapse and begins to show off, a woman begins to laugh in a disbelieving way.'"[38] On the other hand, a quota continues to be vilified as the wrong means to achieve their end: "I am against quotas because I believe they devalue rather than advance women and women's aspirations, and make them into alibi-women."[39] Indeed, surveys of women candidates in regional and national elections in 1987 and 1990 showed that the majority of women hold strong reservations about quotas and would prefer a political environment where they could fulfill their political expectations without them. Yet as a means to an end that cannot be achieved through goodwill, pleading, or gentle persuasion, quotas have gained acceptance as "the lesser evil."[40]

Women have transformed the organizational basis of political power. In 1991, when the quota commitment began to take effect, women in the SPD were better represented than in the CDU or the FDP at all levels of officeholding. At the top levels of party leadership—the national executive, the party presidium, and the party council or federal committee—women in the SPD were pushing toward the 40 percent mark, while they had yet to reach 20 percent in the CDU. In the FDP the picture was more varied (Table 5.7). In September 1991, four of the thirteen elected members of the party presidium were women, but there were only six women among the thirty-four members of the federal executive. With the exception of the Greens, whose leadership team of three has included at least one woman, none of the political parties has been headed by a woman, nor has a woman occupied the chair of a parliamentary party, the hot seat of policymaking in Germany. Yet party congresses had a visible contingent of women in 1991: with women accounting for 42 percent of delegates, the SPD reached its quota target for the mid-1990s and was heading toward a gender balance. In the FDP, 21 percent of the delegates were women; in the CDU, just 17 percent: neither party attained its recommended quota of women.

The effectiveness of a prescribed quota and the relative weakness of a recommended one were also borne out by the differences among the parties in women's officeholding at other levels. In the regions that are now called the old *Bundesländer,* the SPD already more than fulfilled its target of 30 percent in 1990 and has since extended the organizational integration of women members as officeholders (Table 5.7). In the CDU, deficits in women's representation as officeholders have

Table 5.7

Women in CDU, SPD, and FDP since 1991: Membership and Officeholders (in percent)

Party Position/Office	CDU 1991	CDU 1996	SPD 1990	SPD 1996	FDP 1991	FDP 1997
Member	26	31	27	28	30	30
Party executive	18	33	36	42	18	18
Party presidium	18	25	38	39	31	20
Congress delegate	17	29	42	42	21	24
Regional executive						
Baden Württemberg	20	27	38	41	12	18
(Bavaria = CSU)	20	21	42	48	0	21
Berlin	22	14	33	41	31	38
Bremen	21	27	41	38	22	28
Hamburg	19	19	33	35	21	23
Hesse	19	35	41	44	21	20
Lower Saxony	30	32	45	48	26	39
North Rhine-Westphalia	16	35	47	42	18	35
Rhineland-Palatinate	33	32	35	43	17	17
Saar Region	20	28	45	45	22	36
Schleswig-Holstein	27	30	48	45	24	32
New Länder						
Brandenburg	34	31	27	40	23	17
Mecklenburg-Vorpommern	17	27	21	46	22	17
Saxony	17	23	23	38	24	8
Saxony-Anhalt	20	21	35	41	9	17
Thuringia	17	23	42	33	27	29

Sources: Frauenbericht der CDU, 1991, 1995; *Der Gleichstellungsbericht des Parteivorstandes der SPD*, 1991, 1995; *Frauenanteil in der F.D.P.*, 1991; *Mehr Chancen für Frauen in der F.D.P.* Bericht vorgelegt zum Bundesparteitag 1997. In each of the three parties, a report on the gender balance of officeholding is presented to party congress in order to monitor whether the prescribed or voluntary women's quota has been met. The women's reports are published with the conference papers by the head offices of the relevant party.

been reduced since the early 1990s in all regions, although gender disadvantages remain larger in the new *Länder* than in the old. Since unification, all parties in the new *Länder* suffered membership losses and often found it difficult to establish a party organization over and above the elective and parliamentary positions at the local and regional levels that they already hold. Among East Germans of both genders and all political persuasions, membership in a political party has yet to be accepted as an effective means of contributing to the political process. The participation of women in politics is just one dimension of a broader transformation of political culture. A delegate at the 1990 SPD congress in Mecklenburg-Vorpommern spoke aptly of "the chance to newly discover politics as an integral part of our lives, and especially for women."[41]

In the West, the increased participation of women has also been seen as a first step toward "change in the political culture of the political parties."[42] When the Green Party introduced quotas, the women who had advocated them had expected a change in policy styles and issues, a feminization of politics that would change the quality of political life. Because the Greens were unable to fill the many quota slots for parliamentary candidates and especially in the party organization with their own members, the majority of women who nominally represented the Greens had little or no affiliation with the party and tended to pursue their own political agendas. The original intention to project the voice of the new women's movement into politics miscarried as the movement's activists shunned the conventionality and hierarchical structure of mainstream political institutions while those who did take part were too factious to constitute a unified women's voice.[43]

In the SPD's Association of Social Democratic Women, which spearheaded the quota campaign, the hub of the debate was access to power and equal career opportunities for equally qualified and motivated women. The notion that women might bring particularly female qualities into politics had no official place in an approach that insisted on women of the same caliber as the men they would replace. In fact, the ASF had entered the debate on women's representation by challenging the assumption that the chancellor of the Federal Republic had to be a man, and by presenting to the press a complete women's cabinet-in-waiting. In several regional governments, women held ministerial office outside the traditional women's realms of health, youth, education, and, since the early 1980s, women.

Yet remnants of an organizational and political track for women separate from main-line politics remain. In the SPD, for instance, the majority of female salaried party officials are employed at the level of *Sachbearbeiter,* administrative assistant or secretary. All topics related to women are delegated to the specialists who deal with women: general policymaking and women's policymaking remain separate. Sometimes even activist women subscribe to stereotypes that have no place in the official view of women's role in politics. In 1989, for instance, Ursula Pausch-Gruber, chair of the ASF and a member of the SPD executive in Bavaria, castigated her regional party for nominating only eight women instead of the sixteen needed to meet the quota. Her comment underlines the salience of the women's quota as a lever to gain elite positions and the uncertainty about the way the case for women should be argued: "The Bavarian SPD has to . . . understand that not everyone who now holds a seat in parliament can be nominated again. The party has to understand in particular that it will be easier to achieve a credible policy of reform if there are women in the front line of the SPD, because women normally have a better understanding of everyday problems such as the housing shortage or the creation of a child-orientated society."[44]

Nearly a decade after the SPD committed itself to a women's quota, women have gained visibility in the party but not full equality. The 1994 election campaign, which should have been a celebration of the recast gender balance in the SPD and in German politics, confined women candidates to women's issues, while matters of economic, foreign, or security policy were the preserve of men when political statements in the media or other public pronouncements were called for.[45] In the CDU, women's failure to translate the promise of improved representation into nominations to winnable constituency seats or secure places on the electoral lists rekindled discontent among female activists and revived the quota debate in the party. The appointment of Claudia Nolte, an East German of the young generation, as minister for women can be seen as an attempt by the CDU to halt the decline in women's support in the *Länder* and gain new credibility among women under 30 years of age.

Outlook

Women have made uneven inroads in the competition for political positions, but all parties have expanded opportunities for women. At the governmental level, most women have been appointed to look after women's domains, such as women's ministries and equalization offices. Yet, some women have broken the gender barrier. At the regional level, women have served and are serving in the late 1990s as ministers in formerly male domains such as economic affairs or justice. For a time, Berlin even had an all-women regional government. In Schleswig Holstein, Heide Simonis (SPD), has been minister president for the better part of the decade. Inside the political parties, the increased participation of women may not have changed the party cultures, but it has provided women with greater influence and with a public voice to bring their priorities to bear on policies and on the composition of party and parliamentary elites.

The new prominence of women in West German politics is too recent and may be too strongly determined by existing party practices to affect the quagmire of local politics in the service of local business interests, as has recently been exposed in the case of the CDU.[46] In the wake of their quota commitments, the national executives of the CDU, SPD, and FDP played important roles as catalysts, creating opportunities for women in the national leadership and diminishing the role of local politics as the foundation for a political career. From this perspective, reducing the gender gap in party politics makes the social foundations of party politics more accountable and more democratic.

The push toward equal opportunities for men and women in German politics is but one aspect of a broader development. In the 1980s the SPD and the Greens prepared draft legislation to outlaw sex discrimination. In 1991 the federal government ruled against women's quotas in the public sector.[47] North Rhine-Westphalia and Hamburg, two SPD-led regions, had already agreed on a 50 percent quota in their public service sector, while the federal minister for women, Angela Merkel, called for quota regulations to improve women's access to vocational training and employment.[48]

Dissenting voices have been raised, however. The minister of education, Rainer Ortlieb (FDP), specifically rejected quotas for women in training and employment;[49] a similar rebuff came from the economics minister, who declared that "quotas in professional life adversely affect the work atmosphere and curtail achievement."[50] Yet clearly the debate about women's quotas has spilled over from the political parties to the society at large. Frauenförderung has been adopted widely in the private and public sectors, although a debate on the issue in the Bundestag attracted only a few members, most of them women.[51] In 1990 the German unification treaty pledged to extend opportunities for women. Women in all political parties have interpreted this pledge as a first step toward gender balance in German society. Drawing on Article 3 of the Basic Law and its promise of equality for men and women, the new legislation is designed to ensure that the state devises and implements suitable measures to transform the constitutional promise of 1949 into social and political reality half a century later. Today, all political parties—not merely the Greens and the SPD—are preparing antidiscrimination legislation to reduce inequalities and optimize women's opportunities to realize their potential in education, at work, and by combining family and employment roles. Without the new numerical strength of women in German politics, such a momentous change would not even be discussed; with them, it may even succeed.

Notes

1. For empirical data see Joachim Hofmann-Göttig, *Emanzipation mit dem Stimmzettel: 70 Jahre Frauenwahlrecht in Deutschland* (Bonn: Neue Gesellschaft, 1986); also Eva Kolinsky, "Party Change and Women's Representation in Unified Germany," in *Gender and Party Politics,* ed. J. Lovenduski and P. Norris (London: Sage, 1993).

2. Stein Rokkan and Seymour Lipset, eds., *Party Systems and Voter Alignments: Cross-National Perspectives* (New York: Free Press, 1967).

3. Helmut Schelsky, "Die Bedeutung des Klassenbegriffs für die Analyse unserer Gesellschaft," in *Auf der Suche nach der Wirklichkeit,* pp. 352–88 (Cologne/Düsseldorf: Diederichs, 1964). See also Ralf Dahrendorf, *Democracy and Society in Germany* (London: Weidenfeld & Nicholson, 1967).

4. For example, Stefan Hradil, *Sozialstrukturanalyse in einer fortgeschrittenen Gesellschaft* (Opladen: Leske & Budrich, 1987); Bernhard Schäfers, *Gesellschaftlicher Wandel in Deutschland: Ein Studienbuch zur Sozialstruktur und Sozialgeschichte der Bundesrepublik,* 2nd rev. ed. (Stuttgart: Enke, 1990).

5. Eva Kolinsky, "Women in the 1994 Federal Elections," in *Germans Divided,* ed. Russell Dalton (Oxford: Berg 1996).

6. See Russell J. Dalton, "The German Voter: Dealignment or Realignment?" in *Developments in West German Politics,* ed. Gordon Smith et al., pp. 99–121 (London: Macmillan, 1989).

7. Ronald Inglehart, *The Silent Revolution* (Princeton, NJ: Princeton Univer-

sity Press, 1977); empirical data in Jens Alber, "Continuity and Change in German Social Structure: Why Bonn Is Not Weimar," in *Social and Political Structures in West Germany: From Authoritarian to Postindustrial Democracy,* ed. Ursula Hoffmann-Lange, pp. 15–42 (Boulder, CO: Westview, 1991).

8. For detailed analysis see Eva Kolinsky, *Women in Contemporary Germany* (Oxford: Berg, 1992), and "Women in Germany: The East-West Gender Divide," in *Developments in German Politics,* ed. Gordon Smith, W.E. Paterson, Stephen Padgett, and Peter H. Merkl, 2nd rev. ed. (Basingstoke: Macmillan, 1992).

9. See Rob Burns and Wilfried von der Will, *Protest and Democracy in West Germany* (Basingstoke: Macmillan, 1988); Roland Roth and Diether Rucht, eds., *Neue soziale Bewegungen in der Bundesrepublik Deutschland* (Bonn: Bundeszentrale für Politische Bildung, 1987); Joachim Raschke, *Soziale Bewegungen* (Frankfurt/Main: Campus, 1985).

10. Dietrich Herzog et al., "Bürgerinitiativen" (unpublished report, Free University of Berlin, 1978).

11. Dietrich Herzog et al., *Abgeordnete und Bürger* (Opladen: Westdeutscher Verlag, 1990). Also Heino Kaack and Reinhold Roth, *Handbuch des deutschen Parteiensystems* (Opladen: Leske & Budrich, 1980), 1: 81–100; Richard Stöss, ed., *Parteienhandbuch* (Opladen: Westdeutscher Verlag, 1983).

12. See Eva Kolinsky, "Party Organisation and Political Culture: The SPD and the Second 'Fräuleinwunder,' " in *Political Culture in France and Germany: A Contemporary Perspective,* ed. John Gaffney and Eva Kolinsky, pp. 207–38 (London: Routledge & Kegan Paul, 1991).

13. Alf Mintzel, "Auf der Suche nach der Wirklichkeit der Großparteien in der Bundesrepublik Deutschland," *Passauer Papiere zur Sozialwissenschaft* 5 (1990); Heinrich Oberreuter and Alf Mintzel, *Parteien in der Bundesrepublik Deutschland* (Munich: Olzog, 1990).

14. Beate Hoecker, *Frauen in der Politik* (Opladen: Leske & Budrich, 1987), p. 178.

15. Nils Diederichs, "Zur Mitgliederstruktur von CDU und SPD," in *Parteiensystem in der Legitimationskrise,* ed. Jürgen Dittberner and Rolf Ebbinghausen (Opladen: Westdeutscher Verlag, 1973) p. 52; also Armin Meyer, "Parteiaktivitäten und Einstellungen von CDU und SPD Mitgliedern," in ibid., p. 67.

16. Wolfgang Falke, *Die Integration von Parteimitgliedern: Eine empirische Studie zur Teilnahme und Kommunikation der Mitglieder in der Organisation der CDU 1971–1977* (Berlin: Duncker & Humboldt, 1982).

17. Institut für Kommunikationsforschung, "Situationsanalyse zur Ermittlung der Voraussetzungen für methodische Öffentlichkeitsarbeit innerhalb der Mitgliederstrukur der FDP" (unpublished report, 1977); see also Eva Kolinsky, *Parties, Opposition and Society in West Germany* (London: Croom Helm, 1984), pp. 101–21.

18. Gabriele Bremme, *Die politische Rolle der Frau in Deutschland* (Göttingen: Vandenhoeck & Ruprecht, 1956); Mechthild Fülles, *Frauen in Partei und Parlament* (Cologne: Wissenschaft und Politik, 1969).

19. Kolinsky, "Party Organisation and Political Culture," p. 226.

20. The quota was to be implemented in stages; by 1994, 40 percent of all party offices were to be held by women; by 1998, the gender balance of SPD

parliamentary parties was to have been recast. By the year 2013, the quota is to be abolished and equal participation established as the norm, rather than the exception, in the political life of the SPD.

21. Eva Kolinsky, "Women in the Green Party," in *The Greens in West Germany*, ed. Kolinsky, pp. 189–222 (Oxford: Berg, 1989).

22. Heiner Geißler, ed., *Abschied von der Männergesellschaft* (Frankfurt/Main: Ullstein, 1986).

23. Conservative opposition to the new liberalism was considerable, but in German politics its initial impact and public success were greatly assisted by Rita Süßmuth, minister for women, youth, family, and health and since 1988 president of the Bundestag. The CDU is by no means unanimous in embracing the pragmatic accommodation of the nontraditional lifestyles and expectations of the postwar generation of women. A strong faction in the party, notably including the Catholic activists, advocate an aggressive return to a society in which women's primary roles are housewife and mother.

24. "Leitsätze der CDU für eine neue Partnerschaft zwischen Mann und Frau (Essener Leitsätze)," in Geißler, *Abschied von der Männergesellschaft*, pp. 192–214.

25. Resolution C3. Passed at the thirty-fourth federal congress of the CDU, October 7–8, 1986 in Mainz, requiring the party executive to work with the women's association and introduce suitable measures to attain the recommended representation of women; resolution passed at the thirty-sixth federal congress of the CDU, June 13–15, 1988 in Wiesbaden, requiring all levels of the party organization to implement the guidelines on women's representation and the party executive to prepare and publish a report on the representation of women in the CDU. All three resolutions (Essen, Mainz, Wiesbaden) are contained in a special brochure Frauen in der Union, edited by Rita Süßmuth, the chair of the Frauenunion.

26. Interviews by the author with Otti Geschka, secretary of state for equal opportunities in Hesse, April 11, 1988, with Rothraud Hock of the Women's Association in Rhineland Palatinate and Eliva Bickel, a CDU member of the Landtag, Rhineland Palatinate on April 12, 1988.

27. *Süddeutsche Zeitung*, March 5, 1990.

28. Frauenförderplan der F.D.P. (Plan for the Promotion of Women) Resolution of the party executive, April 6, 1987. Published in *Fdk (Freidemokratische Korrespondenz)* no. 89, April 7, 1987.

29. Interview by the author with Heidrun Tampe, the Equal Opportunities officer at the party headquarters in Bonn, March 31, 1992.

30. Kommunikationsstudie der FDP.

31. *Express*, October 31, 1991.

32. *dpa*, November 1, 1991.

33. In the German Bundestag, half the members of parliament are elected for a constituency, the other half via regionally compiled party lists. The nomination process is separate for the two types of candidacy, although constituency candidates can also compete for a place on the regional list. On that list, places are numbered from one upward with diminishing electoral chances. Nomination for each place is fought separately. The number of successful list candidacies depends on the overall share of the vote won by a political party, and the number of constituency seats it has secured. The overall number of parliamentary seats held

by a party is determined by the percentage of the national vote.

34. Data from Frau Görres, Geschäftsführerin der CDU Leipzig, interview May 11, 1992; also Christina Krestschmar, parliamentary business manager of the SPD, City council of Leipzig, May 8, 1992. Data provided by the SPD Bundesgeschäftsstelle in 1992.

35. Landesverband der CDU Niedersachsen, September 28, 1990. File 2/290/17 Konrad Adenauer Foundation Archive, St. Augustin.

36. Information provided by Hermann Gröhe, chairman of the Junge Union, the youth organization of the CDU. See *dpa* October 24, 1991. Konrad Adenauer Foundation Archive, File 2/290/17.

37. Oscar W. Gabriel and Oskar Niedermayer, "Entwicklung und Sozialstruktur der Parteimitgliedschaften," in *Parteiendemokratie in Deutschland,* ed. Oscar W. Gabriel, Oskar Niedermayer and Richard Stoess, pp. 294–95 (Opladen: Westdeutscher Verlag, 1997).

38. "Zufrieden mit der Quotenfrau," in *Süddeutsche Zeitung,* September 9, 1989.

39. Count Lambsdorff, Chairman of the FDP, quoted in *Express,* October 31, 1991.

40. Eva Kolinsky, "Women's Quotas in West Germany," in *West European Politics* 14, no. 1 (January 1991): 56–72. The author also conducted postal surveys of women candidates in German elections (regional and national) in 1988 and 1992, with funding support from the Nuffield Foundation.

41. Arndt Noack, a congressional delegate, quoted in *Protokoll des Parteitages* der SPD vol. 27–28. Bonn, September 1990, p. 27.

42. Traute Walter, a congressional delegate for Hamburg at the 1988 congress in Münster, saw the quota as a challenge and an innovator: "It requires a capacity for dialogue inside and outside the party. It requires that we improve our social competence as people and grow above ourselves in character. It is important that we also change the political culture inside the party." *Protokoll* vol. 1, Bonn 1988, p. 104.

43. Kolinsky, "Women in the Green Party."

44. *Süddeutsche Zeitung,* December 9, 1989.

45. For a detailed discussion see Kolinsky, "Women in the 1994 Election," in *Germans Divided.*

46. "Cliquen, Kartelle, Seilschaften," in *Der Spiegel* 6, 1992 reports main findings of a study by Erwin and Ute Scheuch, the publication of which has been stopped by the CDU.

47. *dpa,* May 15, 1991.

48. *dpa,* April 25, 1991.

49. *dpa,* March 9, 1991.

50. Helmut Haussmann, FDP; he also stressed that any guarantee of employment would disadvantage small- and medium-sized businesses. *dpa,* April 3, 1990.

51. The debate had been called by women members from all parties to prepare new legislation which would incorporate women's quotas in all areas of society, a demand first voiced by the Greens in their antidiscrimination initiative of 1986. *dpa,* November 10, 1991.

6

Women in the Politics of Eastern Germany

The Dilemmas of Unification

Marilyn Rueschemeyer

The problems facing the two Germanies after the first euphoria of unification were overwhelming. They threatened the long-embedded democratic civic culture of West Germany, they disrupted the social and economic life of the former German Democratic Republic (GDR), and they even affected the process of European integration. But it is not at all an exaggeration to suggest that women have suffered more than anyone else in these transitions and that as a group East German women have had the most difficulty reestablishing themselves in the new, united Germany.

East Germany differed in many ways from other East European communist societies. It was set apart by its industrial development, by its particular historical formation, and by its Protestant background. Significant, too, was East Germany's political and economic interweaving with West Germany long before unification took place. The supports from the Federal Republic of Germany (FRG), the manifold contractual relations, but also the tensions and the competition between the two German states affected the very nature of the unification process. The issues involved in these past relationships and the process of unifying the two German countries form the core of the current political discussion and debate in Germany. And they also have an impact on the way women engage in politics and on the issues that are of concern to them.

Women in the Two German States Before Unification

Before unification, women both in the West and in the East had serious complaints about the lack of equality between men and women and about the inadequacy of the attention paid by the state and the work-place—and by the men they lived with—to several important issues. But the situation of women in the two Germanies before the recent transformations differed dramatically.

By the time unification took place, nearly 90 percent of all East German women eligible for employment were studying or were in the labor force. Women contributed 40 percent to the family income.[1] Seventy percent of all women had completed an apprenticeship or more advanced vocational training, and women 40 years or younger had achieved the same level of education as men. Women constituted about half of all college and university students.[2]

The GDR had a liberal abortion code, which became legal in 1972. It allowed abortion during the first three months of pregnancy.

Day care for children was comprehensive. Over 85 percent of children between the ages of 1 and 3 were in day-care centers, and nearly 90 percent of those between 3 and 6 were in kindergarten.[3] Other supports for working parents included a guarantee of forty days per year of paid time off from work to care for sick children 14 years old or younger, and after childbirth a parental leave was granted until the child was a year old, at 75 to 90 percent of net pay with a guarantee of return to the job at the same level of employment.[4] In the last years of the GDR, this leave could also be taken by the spouse or the grandmother.

These supports were especially important for single parents, mostly mothers. These women had preferential access, before their married colleagues, to an apartment and to child care when they resumed their work outside the home. Naturally, these provisions did not alleviate problems of loneliness or the burdens of child care, nor did they eliminate all financial strain. But they provided a solid basis on which single parents could build normal lives.[5]

During and after World War II the population of able-bodied male workers was so depleted that women's labor was needed in both Germanies. But the two German states later developed very different policies with respect to incorporating women into the labor force. In the East, in order to encourage women to take jobs, the Soviet military administration established regulations entitling women to equal pay for equal work; and the new constitution established in 1949 decreed formal gender equality in all areas of social life. These policies and constitutional guarantees were supported by activists under the influence of the earlier ideas and writings of socialist women and feminists. A shortage of labor continued to be a problem throughout the life of the GDR. Many skilled and professional workers emigrated to the West before the Berlin Wall went up in 1961; and in any case the economic system based on central planning generated a chronic labor shortage.

West Germany did not suffer long from a shortage of labor. It first had to accommodate 8 million refugees from German territories that became part of Poland and Russia; 2 million moved from East to West Germany before the Wall was built; and from the 1960s onward millions of "guest workers" migrated from southern Europe and Turkey to find work in West Germany. These contrasting experiences form an important background to the differences in the status of women in East and West Germany.

West Germany, too, incorporated an equal rights provision in the Fundamental Law of 1949, the constitution of the FRG. Despite this provision, however, traditional gender roles were quickly reestablished. The issues involved in their enduring strength even after the experience of women's participation in the labor force, and economic responsibility during the war, are complicated.[6] One problem was the tension between the principle of gender equality and the principle of freedom of contract between employer and worker, also guaranteed by the constitution. There was a great deal of discussion in the FRG about how much the state should interfere in society. If the state's role was to set general norms, rather than to legislate behavior in the private sphere, and if freedom of contract between employer and worker remained a primary goal, it is not surprising that West Germany encountered difficulty in implementing equal rights for men and women. Politicians and the churches promulgated a return to "normalcy," and for a long time most women accepted their roles as homemakers or supplementary earners. After the war, of course, many women were left without a male breadwinner and thus had to work outside the home. And over the years, the share of women in the labor force increased considerably. During the 1950s and 1960s many women who worked in factories and offices were dismissed when they married, but by 1985, 45 percent of West German women were in the labor force. That figure has now increased to approximately 50 percent—still low in comparison with the figure for the former GDR. Women in Western Germany contribute only 18 percent of family income. But nearly 40 percent of West German university students are women.[7]

By the mid-1980s, working women in West Germany had a total of fourteen weeks' maternity leave, with a stipend and employer's supplement that together were equivalent to their wage or salary. From the fifteenth to the thirty-second week they received a small stipend but no employer's supplement. Only 3 percent of children under the age of 3 were in public day-care centers. We do not known how many West German families can afford private child care or have the help of relatives. Before unification, a mother could take five paid days a year to care for a sick child of 8 years or younger.

These limited supports and family policies, especially with respect to children under the age of 3, made it difficult for women to enter the labor force and establish themselves in a career. Public provisions were far less extensive than the supports for families in East Germany, where work was institutionalized, and they remained even below the level of supports offered to families in many West European countries.

Although women in the GDR entered previously male occupations in large numbers in both Germanies, they tended to cluster in specific areas (see Table 6.1). And even in the GDR, with its emphasis on promoting women's participation in the labor force, socialization at school encouraged gender segregation there and in leisure activities.

In both Germanies the percentage of women in the highest executive positions remained low, less than 4 percent, and women held few professorships. At present, women hold only between 3 and 5 percent of the most senior university positions.[8] Their participation in the middle levels of management was higher in East Germany, though still limited; about a third of these positions were filled by women.[9]

Although there were considerable differences between the two German states, in general the higher the positions, the lower the percentage of women; this was their situation at work, in the union, and in the government in the mid-1980s. Women accounted for a third of the members of the GDR parliament; but as late as 1985, of the twelve members of the Secretariat of the Socialist Unity (communist) Party, only one was a woman. Of the twenty-five members and candidates in the Politburo, only two, both candidates, were women.

This was one of the unresolved issues that came under increasing criticism in the 1980s. The members of parliament in the official Democratic Women's Federation could discuss women's problems and did bring up matters of importance to women, but they did so within the framework of party policy on women's issues; they were never able to challenge the continuing patriarchal underpinnings of the system and

Table 6.1

Proportion of German Women Employed and of Jobs Held by Women, by Economic Sector, 1970–85 (in percent)

Economic Sector	Women as Percentage of Persons Employed				Percentage of Jobs Held by Women			
	1970	1980	1984	1985	1970	1980	1984	1985
Industry	42.5	43.3	41.9	41.7	32.3	33.0	32.1	32.1
Crafts	40.1	38.0	37.4	37.2	4.3	2.4	2.3	2.3
Construction	13.3	16.2	16.3	16.5	1.9	2.3	2.3	2.3
Agriculture and forestry	45.8	41.5	39.4	39.1	12.2	8.9	8.6	8.6
Transportation	25.5	27.4	27.0	26.9	3.0	3.2	3.2	3.2
Post and telephone	68.8	70.0	69.3	69.1	2.5	2.3	2.2	2.2
Retail trade	69.2	72.8	72.8	72.6	15.8	15.8	15.0	15.0
Other productive branches	53.7	55.1	55.0	56.1	2.6	3.5	3.4	3.3
Nonproductive branches	70.2	72.9	73.2	73.1	25.4	29.3	30.9	31.1
All sectors	48.3	49.9	49.4	49.3	100.0	99.9	100.0	100.1

Source: Statistiches Taschenbuch 1986, p. 37 (data as of September 30); Hildegard Nickel, "Sex-Role Socialization in Relationships as a Function of the Division of Labor: A Sociological Explanation for the Reproduction of Gender Differences," in *The Quality of Life in the German Democratic Republic: Changes and Developments in a State Socialist Society*, ed. Marilyn Rueschemeyer and Christiane Lemke (New York: M.E. Sharpe, 1989), p. 53.

the effects of these assumptions on hiring, work organization, and personal life.

The Transition Period

Women in the GDR became increasingly involved in political activities on a wide variety of levels before unification took place. Some participated actively in their professional associations. Earlier, many retreated in frustration to the private sphere; that they then were willing to stand for election seems clearly related to their assessment that some possibilities for new initiatives were opening up.[10] Some feminist groups, broadly defined, and feminist research projects were started. In the transition period after the fall of 1989, an independent women's movement was formed, a coalition of groups from all over the GDR encompassing a variety of perspectives, including socialist women's initiatives as well as Christian groups.[11] They were included in the round tables where democratic political negotiation and control of administrative action took place before the elections in March 1990. The round tables formed as coalitions in opposition to the old leadership, or they replaced it completely.

The possibility that women might influence policy at that time of transition was variously assessed, but their participation in the Independent Women's Movement and the round tables proved difficult to translate into a political base in the emerging new party structure.

Overall, women had great difficulty in participating effectively in political life after 1989. It is easy to take these difficulties for granted. The life experiences of women in the former GDR of course varied in accordance with their level of education, their occupational skills, and the opportunities they had in the old regime; but my findings, which have been confirmed by studies done by both East German and Western researchers after 1989, clearly indicate that many women developed a sense of self and a set of life expectations that have been strongly influenced by their incorporation into the work force. Their ideas may have differed from official notions of family and work life, but they had powerful effects nonetheless. This is important to keep in mind when we explore their relatively small role in politics in the new Germany during the early transformation years and some of the changes that have taken place since that time.

Table 6.2

Composition of East German Labor Force, May 1992

	Number (thousands)	Percent
Employed in East Germany (est.)	5,400	58.5
Employed in West Germany, commuting (est.)	540	5.9
Employed in part-time government-subsidized job	437	4.7
Employed in short-term government-subsidized job (ABM)	405	4.4
Unemployed	1,149	12.5
In early retirement	301	3.3
On prepension transition pay	481	5.2
In retraining program	510	5.5
Total	9,223	100.0

Source: Der Spiegel, no. 28, 1992, p. 87.
Note: "East Germany" refers to the five new states of the FRG and the eastern part of Berlin.

East German Women in Unified Germany

Certainly women have every reason to engage in shaping the political future of Germany. Aside from the most important reason—that by participating in the political process they have at least a possibility of shaping the conditions that will affect their lives for a long time to come—several burning issues have to be addressed immediately. Women of the former GDR face a future that is potentially devastating for their participation in the labor force. With unification, unemployment rose dramatically. In 1992, the second year of unity, the unemployment rate in the new German states, if one also counts people in short-term employment (which is often very short), in retraining programs, and in early retirement, came close to 40 percent (see Table 6.2).

Of the 9.6 million employed citizens of the former GDR, some 49 percent were women. Since unification, the proportion of employed women has sunk to one-third of all persons employed in the five new German states. At the end of June 1992, 63.6 percent of the unemployed in Eastern Germany were women; there were 2 million unemployed women if the "hidden unemployed" in training programs and early retirement are included. A large number of the unemployed were single parents. In 1994, that percentage of unemployed women had increased to 66.9 percent. Although unemployment generally has been reduced, the changes have been to the disadvantage of women. Among the unemployed in 1994, male long-term unemployment was 24 percent compared to 40 percent for females.[12]

Women had been strongly represented in public administration and in such industries as textiles and clothing, electronics, chemistry, and plastics, branches of employment that have been adversely affected by unification. In the centrally controlled economy, better-educated women often filled administrative positions that have been abolished, and they were overrepresented in cultural institutions, publishing houses, and other such organizations where jobs are eliminated. Women over the age of 50 have practically no chance to obtain work.[13] There had been several reports that increasing numbers of young women are choosing to be sterilized. Women fear for their future if they have children; many women who ask for sterilization explain their decision by reference to the poor prospects for employment for mothers.[14] The many women who have been given jobs through *Arbeitsbeschaffungsmassnahmen* (ABM)—public grants to create jobs—have temporary work for a year or two. Some of these positions will turn into regular jobs, but many others will simply disappear. Furthermore, these ABM grants, as well as short work subsidized by the government and retraining programs, are being reduced (see Table 6.3).

Furthermore, fewer young women than men are placed in apprenticeship programs, yet it is through apprenticeships that young people gain access to promising occupational opportunities.[15] Women do participate in retraining programs along with men, but given the present state of the economy in Eastern Germany, they may not easily find work after their training is completed. Furthermore, studies indicate that women's jobs are less likely than men's to involve travel. That was also the case in the GDR, and it has limited women's opportunities; the jobs of many of their male colleagues now regularly take them to other parts of the country, especially to West Germany.[16]

Immediately after unification, there was a lot of public discussion—on the radio, on television, and in the press—about the possibility that East German women could now stay home with their children. Indeed, women do not speak with one voice on this issue. Some conservative

Table 6.3

Unemployment, Part-Time Work, Short-Term Work, and Retraining; Five New States and East Berlin, 1991–95

Year	Unemployed N (thousands)	Unemployed % of Workforce[c]	Short-term Work[a] N (thousands)	Short-term Work[a] % of Workforce[c]	Public Employment Program ("ABM") N (thousands)	Public Employment Program ("ABM") % of Workforce[c]	Retraining[b] N (thousands)
1991	913 (58% female)	10.3	1,616	18.2	183 (36% female)	2.1	892
1993	1,149 (64% female)	15.8	181	2.5	260 (47% female)	3.6	294
1995	1,047 (63% female)	14.9	71	1.0	206 (65% female)	2.9	257

Source: Statistisches Bundesamt, *Statistisches Jahrbuch 1996,* partly recalculated.

[a] In contrast to part-time work, short-term work involves a partial loss of employed work time.

[b] This column indicates the sum of all entries into occupational continued education. Since continued education may be combined with unemployment, short-term work, or work in public employment programs, and since such retraining may involve periods shorter than a year, no rate is calculated.

[c] Number of unemployed, in short-term work and in public employment programs respectively, as a percentage of all members of the labor force.

constituencies in the West favor a traditional division of labor in the family, and some women in the East are eager to be with their children. Yet studies have shown that very few women in the new German states want to stay at home all day long. They indicate that although most women want to reduce their hours of employment and nearly half want to be at home with the children until they reach the age of 3, most women want—and need—to continue their occupational lives.[17]

That goal is difficult to achieve. As we have seen, women have been let go in far greater numbers than men. At home they are saddled with many more responsibilities than their husbands. Many single mothers have lost their jobs, and to lose a job is to lose not only income but valued associations with colleagues. Homelessness is increasing among both women and men. But even women who are not in such dire straits express frustration with their new situation.[18] Furthermore, the closing of day-care centers for children under the age of 3 is likely to continue when so many women are at home because they have lost their jobs; and how is a woman to search for a job if she has no one to care for her child? When East Germans were asked in 1991 which institutions of the former GDR should be preserved, 95 percent mentioned child-care facilities; only 1 percent wanted them abolished.[19]

Abortion is one of the most contentious issues East German women continue to face. Potentially it could have become a catalyst for the mass political involvement of East German women. Abortion was legal in the GDR during the first three months of pregnancy, as we have seen, and contraceptives were distributed free of charge. Article 218 of West Germany's penal code outlawed abortion unless the woman met certain criteria.[20] An abortion law for both the East and the West was to be created by the end of 1992. An agreement allowing abortion after counseling during the first three months of pregnancy had been reached in parliament but was reversed by the Federal Constitutional Court in the spring of 1993. In 1995 the new regulations allowed abortion without punishment during the first three months of pregnancy, preceded by regulated counseling.[21] The debate on abortion regulations not only brought opposing constituencies in Germany to the fore but revealed both the difficulties women experience in their efforts to influence major party decisions and the very strong pressures for unity within the parties.[22]

With unification the West German party system became entrenched in the former GDR. The Christian Democrats (CDU/CSU) and the

Free Democrats (FDR) coopted the apparatus of the corresponding "bloc parties" that had been satellites of the communist Socialist Unity Party in the GDR. The Social Democratic Party (SPD) was thus the only party with mass appeal that had no organization in the East, and it has found it difficult to develop one.

In the first election, the East handed a major victory to the CDU/CSU and the FDP and also gave seats in the Bundestag, the federal parliament, to members of the Party of Democratic Socialism (PDS, the reformed Communist Party), the Greens, and the Alliance 90/Green coalition, an East-West alliance of environmental activists in the transition period. In the federal elections of 1994, the CDU maintained its lead but lost votes in four of the new German states; in Brandenburg, the SPD became the strongest party. The PDS achieved gains in all five eastern states and Berlin; its support in the west remains negligible.

In the local and state elections in 1994, the CDU remained the leading party in most places, but both the social democrats and reformed communists received increased support. The PDS became the third strongest party in eastern Germany.

How did women fare in these early elections? Observers of East European political developments since the end of communism have witnessed a dramatic reduction in the percentage of women in national parliaments. Though the parliaments of the old regimes had much less power than other political institutions and though women were barely represented within those more powerful political units, we note that the representation of women in most East European parliaments during the communist period ranged from about a fifth to a third of the total membership. Since 1989 this percentage has generally declined substantially. In the German Bundestag, however, women held 20.7 percent of the seats in 1990 and 26.3 percent in 1994. This development is probably attributable to changes in the politics of West Germany that resulted in increased attention to women's concerns.

Transformations in Western Germany

Although West Germany has a much more conservative history with respect to women than the former GDR, it has taken dramatic strides in the past twenty years, and these changes have had a strong effect on the political parties of the Federal Republic. Since these developments are discussed in detail in Eva Kolinsky's chapter, I mention only briefly the ones I consider most significant.

In reaction to the restrictions on women at work, in politics, and in the private sphere, feminist groups of many kinds emerged in the 1970s. Many of the women involved had associations with similar groups in Western Europe and the United States. West German women were also aware of a number of public support systems in East Germany, such as the generous maternity leave policy, even if they did not look to East German society as a model for them. Gradually the linkages between feminist groups and some of the political parties became stronger.

The linkages were particularly strong among members of the Greens, but they greatly increased also in the more established and powerful Social Democratic Party. Women began to exert pressures for greater representation in party offices and in administrative positions. Although members of feminist groups felt generally more at home with the less structured and less bureaucratic Greens, the Social Democratic women involved in the women's organization of the party (*Arbeitsgemeinschaft Sozialdemokratischer Frauen,* or ASF) espoused some of the feminists' aims and were influenced by feminist critiques of the existing power structure. Actually, many of these ideas had penetrated far beyond the feminist groups, and so women active in the Social Democratic Party were also responding to a constituency that itself was being transformed. The Christian Democrats had an established women's organization (the Frauen Union), but the steps they took to ensure equality for women within the party apparatus and in elective offices at local and state levels took them in a different direction from those taken by the SPD and the Greens.

The introduction of a quota system in at least some of the parties was an important achievement for women, and for democratic participation more generally. The goal of the Social Democrats is to have 40 percent of all party offices and 50 percent of public administrative posts occupied by women by the year 2000.[23]

Of the members of the CDU/CSU caucus in the 1990 Bundestag, 13 percent were women. The CDU/CSU based its goal for women's participation on membership in the party, but had no quota plan for elective and party positions in 1994.[24] At the party's annual conference in 1996, however, delegates agreed to reserve a minimum of one-third of party offices and parliament seats for women in the next five years though the enforcement regulations are limited. In 1990, women represented 19 percent of the Bundestag members of the Free Democrats (FDP)[25] and half of the delegates of the transformed communist party (PDS); there were three women and five men in the Bundestag delegation of the Alliance 90/Green coalition.[26] In the 1994 parliament, women constituted slightly over a third of the SPD caucus, compared to 43 percent of the PDS, 59 percent of the Greens/B90, 19 percent of the FDP, and 14 percent of the CDU, indicating a major difference between the parties to the left of center and the parties to the right.

The Reluctance of East German Women to Become Involved in Politics

How can we understand the hesitation of East German women to become active in public life? The enthusiasm of the transition period has waned, and women who were involved in the Independent Women's Movement, in the round tables, and in research on women's issues have reduced their participation considerably, both in women's groups and in the political sphere.

There are many reasons for this decline in women's activism. The first is obviously the time and effort women now spend getting settled in a society whose institutions are unfamiliar to them. They have to negotiate a new medical system, a new insurance system, a changing education system. They are primarily responsible for everything that happens in the household. Jobs are oriented to the people who are assumed to be the primary breadwinners, and in such a poor employment climate, it is increasingly expected that men will receive the available jobs. Certainly West German managers have these expectations, and there have been complaints of similar attitudes on the part of East German managers.

Many women, however, are highly motivated to reestablish themselves in their occupations, and if they see any opportunities, they will devote any free time and energy to preparing themselves for work. Interestingly, a number of local initiatives have been taken. Rostock, for example, has a center where women can leave their children if they want to search for employment or if they are employed at irregular hours. The city also prepared two houses for single parents in the center of town, rather than in the suburbs. The rationale is that a home in town center would allow single parents, mostly women, easier access to services and shops, including—especially important—organizations that help people find employment.[27]

Some of the issues involving discrimination at work are handled through equal opportunity, and women's affairs offices set up in all communities with a population of 10,000 or more. The head of one such office described how older women were being fired only weeks before they were eligible for retirement. In a few instances they were able to persuade the people responsible to allow the women to keep their jobs for that limited time.[28] But as important as these offices are and as diverse as the work they do is, they cannot provide an institutionalized impact on the political process, cannot substitute for political influence and coalition building to introduce legislation to prevent these kinds of actions and to initiate regulations against discrimination.[29] The women's affairs offices are asked not to be political; the head of one such office complained that the expectation was unreasonable if they were to take any stand at all on proposals that would affect women. One such topic was abortion, one of the most heatedly debated issues since unification of the two Germanies.

Past experience has shaped women's attitudes toward participation in political life. In the former GDR, the state formulated policy on women's issues and interpreted these policies and goals for the public as well. Most people considered the official women's organization irrelevant. It was largely an ineffective organization and its transformed successor association suffered a dramatic loss of membership. Most women were not only dissatisfied with politics as it had been carried out then but thought it was a waste of time to become involved in political activities. Only in the late 1980s did an increasing number of women become involved in public life, when they believed they could actually have an effect on what was happening in their society.

In the new Germany, many women (and men as well) are—after a surge of hope—again disillusioned with politics. This development is partly a consequence of the very serious social and economic problems encountered; partly it derives from democratic ideals grounded in the experience of autocratic rule but untested by reality.

Women blame the major parties, especially the ruling CDU, for many of their difficulties, for the way privatization is carried out, for the high unemployment rate, for rising prices and the reductions of subsidies. Together, the social democrats and reformed communists received proportionately more votes in 1994 among East German women than they did among women in the west (see Table 6.4). Some people are uncomfortable with the power exerted by the parties in

Table 6.4

Electoral Support for SPD and PDS in Selected Groups; Federal Elections, 1994

	East Germany			West Germany		
	SPD	PDS	Together	SPD	PDS	Together
Women, aged						
18–34	35.2	19.1	54.3	43.1	1.2	44.3
35–59	32.6	15.3	47.9	38.7	0.9	39.6
60 and older	30.0	12.1	42.1	37.6	0.2	37.8
Men, aged						
18–34	30.8	18.8	49.6	39.1	1.8	40.9
35–59	35.0	16.1	51.1	40.4	0.5	40.9
60 and older	32.9	16.2	49.1	35.6	0.1	35.7
Farmers	21.0	16.5	37.5	12.4	1.7	14.1
Workers	36.1	13.4	49.5	53.7	0.9	54.6
White Collar	32.6	18.8	51.4	39.6	0.8	40.4
Self-employed	21.0	15.0	36.0	18.6	1.0	19.6

Source: Marilyn Rueschemeyer, "The Social Democratic Party in Eastern Germany: Political Participation in the Former DGR after Unification," in *Participation and Democracy East and West: Comparisons and Interpretations*, ed. Dietrich Rueschemeyer, Marilyn Rueschemeyer, and Björn Wittrock (Armonk, NY: M.E. Sharpe, 1998). Recalculated from *Focus, Wahl-Spezial*, October 18, 1994, pp. 24, 26, 27.

control and the influence they have on local politics. Others who had initially been active complain of party intrigues, are disappointed in the competition, and are uncertain how to affect the process. Their ideas of democracy from below may be naive, but they represent what many people hoped for after the end of the GDR. Most, once again, feel that it is not worth their while to become involved.[30]

Feminism in East and West Germany

East German women interested in the broad issues of feminism, those who were critical of some of the thinking that led to the official GDR policy on women, and those who were committed to remaining in the labor force and maintaining state support for child care might have been attracted to the West German feminist network. Some women, especially those with international contacts, did indeed become increasingly involved in feminist groups, but others soon became disillusioned with "Western" feminism. When East German women attended meetings, they were upset to learn that their Western counterparts claimed exclusive knowledge of what feminism was and who the real feminists were. West German feminists looked down on the family-and-child orientation of East German women and criticized their lack of sophistication in regard to women's issues. Many East German women were of the opinion that despite the problems they had experienced in the GDR, they had enjoyed a better position in the family and in the society as a whole than their West German counterparts.[31]

West German feminists were and are concerned with somewhat different issues from those that engage many East German women. At the same time, the Independent Women's Movement in the East had lost many of its members and was divided on major issues.

One of its prominent members, Christina Schenk, formerly a physicist at the Academy of Sciences, became a member of the Bundestag. Although affiliated with Alliance 90 at the time, Schenk disagreed with the Alliance's policies concerning women and thought of running as an independent on the Green list. Since then, of course, the two parties have merged. When I interviewed her in 1992, Schenk expressed uncertainty about whether it was possible to accomplish substantial change in the Bundestag because of the "patriarchal nature of West Germany and the pressures exerted by the party on its members to support the majority vote." She is now affiliated with the PDS. Schenk strongly criticized the compromises on the abortion issue, such as the requirement of counseling.[32]

The differences in orientation between women's groups in East and West are rooted in their experiences in the two German states. In the GDR, the state set policy on women's issues, and it did so to a considerable extent for economic and political reasons of its own. The women's association, though providing education on a variety of issues, was a relatively docile mass organization. In the West, the women's movement played an important political role. It modified a long-established social policy that had strong conservative features. The West German women's movement thus operates in a country dominated politically by social policy concerns on the one hand and relatively conservative conceptions of gender roles on the other. "Progressive" ideas about women's issues and gender relations are often at odds with the forces that push for social initiatives in the conservative coalition. An additional complicating factor is that, aside from the unions, many women's organizations in the West are largely middle-class and upper-middle-class groups.

The critical women's issues in the new German states are the social and economic issues of working women, and that group includes a very large number of working-class women. At the same time, women's organizations in Eastern Germany are at best in an embryonic state.

Some Observations on Unions in the East

The unions that the West German union organizations sponsored in the new German states could potentially provide women with powerful resources for achieving equity at the workplace. The Metal Workers' Union, for example, succeeded in obtaining an agreement on a series of wage increases in the metal industry so that in a few years wages in the East should be equal to wages paid in the West. This success was important for the strength of the union in the West as well, and industrialists and others claim that it will aggravate unemployment. Whatever the judgment in terms of public policy, this wage agreement surely demonstrates the power of unions.

The unions are in a position to address many problems, and indeed they have attempted to do so. Especially important for both women and men is the provision of legal counsel and representation. The labor law of the Federal Republic is new in Eastern Germany, and it offers an important counterpart to the equally new impact of market forces on employment opportunities and work conditions. The Federation of German Trade Unions reported that infringements of the labor laws are common in Eastern Germany; as early as 1991 2,000 legal proceedings were being initiated every month.[33]

One union district administrator fears that women will continue to be reluctant to become involved in union affairs. Similar fears were also expressed by other women. Some female employees reported that they have received veiled threats about attendance at union meetings. A district leader claimed that women in her district committee were taking vacation days to attend union meetings because they feared that otherwise they would be fired or given fewer hours of work.[34]

Efforts have been made by individual unions and by the Federation of German Trade Unions to address issues of special concern to women. Some union offices in the East attempt to maintain the old proportion of women in the enterprises and to grant public ABM jobs to women in proportion to their percentage among the unemployed. The results of such efforts are mixed. In November 1991, in the early period of transition, women metalworkers (IG Metall) held a conference with West German union delegates, who were in the majority because the West has more states than the East. Despite tensions aroused by some issues, the West German unionists were responsive to the concerns of their East German colleagues. One difference revolved around acceptance of the night shift. Since the East German women clearly feared losing their jobs if they were not allowed to continue working at night, a compromise was found to allow night work to continue during a transition period. Another issue discussed in the Federation of German Trade Unions was employers' support for daycare centers and kindergartens; some enterprises indicated interest in the possibility of providing such facilities. The women want that support but believe the kindergartens should be managed by the community so that employers cannot use them as a means to control their women employees. One union functionary in the East hoped to be able to use some of the techniques and mechanisms that the old regime devised to promote women's labor in her new work in the union, but now "for the real development of women themselves."[35]

Women have not been strongly represented in union leadership. In fact, aside from a few spectacular successes, such as Monika Wulf-Mathies's victory in the election for the presidency of the large Public Employees and Transport Workers' Union, and the election in 1997 of Dr. Eva-Maria Stange, an East German mathematics and physics teacher, to the presidency of the Union for Education and Research (Gewerkschaft für Erziehung und Wissenschaft [GEW]), overall they are poorly represented.

The Postal Workers' Union has introduced a quota system for women on boards and committees in proportion to their membership in the union. That move is significant in the West and even more so in the East, where 70 percent of postal employees are women. The Public Employees' Union also introduced a quota for women. By June 1992 two East German women had been elected to the board.

In the fall of 1992 the board of the League of German Unions pronounced that women should have priority in the state and economy until such time as they are no longer underrepresented. Ursula Engelen-Kefer, then deputy head, explained this women's offensive as a response to the inability of women to compete with men in a tight labor market and demanded an equality clause in the constitution. Aside from the high unemployment rate of women in the East, she noted that women receive a small number of public works positions and that the increasing part-time employment of women in the East results in a loss of social benefits. Like political parties, unions pursue multiple goals and priorities.[36] We still do not know the long-term impact of the actions being initiated for women.

Women in Eastern Germany have some experience in being active at the workplace. Research on the GDR indicates that although the union was closely linked to the management of the enterprises, low-level workers attempted to moderate the impact of work demands and to have some input on their own work environment.[37] The results varied in accordance with such factors as occupation and the success of the work collective. But it is probably fair to say that people at this level of the union structure, including many women, did gain some important organizational experience. How much they will be able to accomplish in the present difficult period of economic upheaval remains an open question.

Political Parties in the Eastern Context

The political parties have not succeeded in establishing grassroots organizations in the East. In fact, more than a few people who earlier joined political parties have dropped their memberships. The difficulty has to do in part with the fact that parties either had to develop an organization from scratch (as in the case of the Social Democrats) or had to rely on established organizations that were now discredited (CDU, FDP, PDS). Developing an organization from scratch proved to be the harder route. In a population of nearly 66 million in the West and somewhat over 15 million in the East, the membership in the five "new" states is quite low, except for two of the earlier established parties, the PDS and the CDU. With approximately 100,000 members, the PDS is the largest party; the CDU has just under 80,000 members; the SPD, only 27,725; the FDP, approximately 25,000; and the Alliance 90/Greens, 3,000.[38] The Party of Democratic Socialism (PDS) does maintain a strong local network in many communities and has a women's organization, the Linkesozialistische Arbeitsgemeinschaft, though its activities, too, have weakened in some states.

The attempt to establish an Eastern movement combining left and right approaches to protection of the interests of citizens of the former GDR initiated by prominent intellectuals and politicians was, despite its difficulties, a dramatic manifestation of the frustration that many people felt. So was the success of the restructured Communist Party in the Eastern states. That the major parties overall are seen as not addressing the real needs of German citizens is a warning that should not be ignored.

Some expectations of Eastern women have in fact been addressed by Western politicians, especially when they coincide with political demands made in the West.[39] Aside from the recent attempts to liberalize abortion regulations, policy initiatives of this kind include an increase in the number of days off allowed to care for a sick family member, from five to ten (for single mothers, to twenty),[40] and the raising of the age of a sick child for whom such leave is granted to 12; the goal of a kindergarten place for all children by 1999; and a parental leave (up to three years, with a set support for the first six months which then varies according to income). These changes were made in response to agitation in Eastern Germany at the loss of such benefits.

Not all women in Western Germany are sympathetic to the many new initiatives that are being proposed. Furthermore, even with the support of many women and even with the relatively strong presence of women in some of the parties, the proposals have to be voted on within the party, and the outcome is not at all a foregone conclusion. They then may be further compromised in the effort to get them through the Bundestag. But even if the proposed regulations become law, they may become another excuse for not hiring women if strong legal measures against such discrimination are not passed.[41]

It is probably fair to say that since the dominant parties were formed and developed in the former Federal Republic, they have their roots in a West German context and even now respond primarily to the needs expressed by their old and larger constituencies in the West. Furthermore, the very fact that several categories of women in the East, especially unemployed single mothers, are worse off in many respects than they were before increases their political weakness instead of strengthening the expression of their interests.

Perspectives within the parties differ significantly between the East and the West. As we have seen, that situation led to attempts to create a movement that would give voice to Easterners' concerns. We have also noted the differences in perspective of women in the two Germanies. The consequences in the Social Democratic Party have been interesting. The SPD, which has responded to a number of political and social demands of women, is oriented primarily to its West German members. After years of distant relations with feminist groups, the women's section of the party incorporated some of their concerns in the Social Democratic agenda. They did so in part in response to the success of the Greens, who took a strong stand on issues of concern to feminists, including homosexuality, the use of language to maintain traditional gender relations, and the politics of the private sphere. As we have seen, their East German counterparts are generally much more concerned about employment opportunities, abortion rights, and continuation of the social supports they had in the GDR. Ironically, the absorption of feminist issues into the agenda of the Social Democrats separated their members to some extent from their East German colleagues. Few women in the East join and attend meetings of the women's group of the SPD (or any other party). They therefore influence policies to a lesser extent than their West German counterparts, even if they have representation in the federal and state legislatures. However, women's representation at all levels of government is stronger among parties of the left than parties of the right. Aside from the above-mentioned percentage of female deputies in the parliament, women hold 22 percent of the ministerial positions in East German state governments; yet this proportion is 30 percent of SPD-held positions in contrast to 11 percent of CDU-held positions (see Table 6.5). The increase in the Eastern states was due to the greater success of the SPD in the federal elections. We find the same pattern in Western Germany.

The Christian Democratic coalition is less supportive of women's integration in the work force than the SPD. Perhaps this is the reason that the party has demonstrated little concern for social policy issues that are of great interest to women, even though there are deputies from the West and from the East who are interested in these issues.

The desperate need for child care is a good example. Only 3 percent of West German children under the age of 3 is in public child-care facilities. The support for public child care varies from place to place; but when one realizes that West Berlin's 9 percent is factored in to achieve the overall figure of 3 percent, the dimensions of the lack of support elsewhere become clear. Dr. Hanna Renate Laurien, former president of the Berlin parliament and a member of the CDU, was critical of the child care provided by the former GDR, which served over 85 percent of children

Table 6.5

Male and Female Ministers of the Five New German States and Berlin, by Party, 1990 and 1995 (in percent)

State	CDU		SPD		FDP		Alliance 90-Greens		No party affiliation		Total	
	90	95	90	95	90	95	90	95	90	95	90	95
Berlin												
Women	0	0	50	67	—	—	—	—	—	0	20	25
Men	100	100	50	33	—	—	—	—	—	100	80	75
Brandenburg												
Women	—	—	17	20	0	—	50	—	0	33	18	25
Men	—	—	83	80	100	—	50	—	100	67	82	75
Mecklenburg-Vorpommern												
Women	29	24	—	25	0	—	—	—	—	—	22	22
Men	71	80	—	75	100	—	—	—	—	—	78	78
Saxony												
Women	11	11	—	—	—	—	—	—	—	0	11	8
Men	89	89	—	—	—	—	—	—	—	100	89	92
Saxony-Anhalt												
Women	13	—	—	22	0	—	—	100	—	—	8	30
Men	87	—	—	78	100	—	—	0	—	—	92	70
Thuringia												
Women	13	17	—	25	0	—	—	—	—	—	9	20
Men	87	83	—	75	100	—	—	—	—	—	91	80
All six states												
Women	15	11	33	30	0	—	50	100	0	20	10	22
Men	85	89	67	70	100	—	50	0	100	80	90	78

Source: Calculated from Albert Oeckl, ed., *Taschenbuch des öffentlichen Lebens* (Bonn: Festland, 1991 and 1996).

under the age of 3. She suggested that in other industrial societies, 12 percent of these children were in state facilities and that Germany should not be placing a higher percentage in day care. Her position was that only children in need should be in day care at that age, and she stressed the importance of according as high a value to women who choose to stay at home as to women who choose to work outside the home.[42] Aside from matters of ideology and disagreements about how a child is best socialized, it is difficult to decide which children really need day care. Certainly more than 12 percent of women have to work.

A committee of the Bundestag is concerned with problems of child care and single parents, but state-provided child care for children under the age of 3 is certainly not a major policy goal of the dominant parties. To argue that women can stay home and thereby save the state the bother and expense of child care is to duck the issue, because many women cannot afford to remain at home and because many women would not choose to do so. Moreover, in the absence of regulations to ensure that a woman who wishes to stay home until her child reaches kindergarten age can have her job back, the woman who drops out of work for such a long period may find herself permanently excluded from meaningful employment.

Germany is a social welfare state that provides its citizens with a variety of important social supports, and churches and other organizations step in to address some of the major needs of people in difficulty. The strong support for social policy legislation, however, does not automatically coincide with a commitment to gender equality at work, in the home, or in the political sphere. In both the old German states and the new, opinions on these issues vary. But with unification, the ability of a large segment of the population in the East to realize some of its most important goals is being threatened. Expectations of combining work and family life and of participating in the public sphere are so far unrealized, and the prospects for the future are not good. Political pressures to address some of the most distressing issues are an important first step, but they are no substitute for political self-determination. True, democracy involves negotiation and compromise, winners and losers. But the stage on which future democratic developments will be played out is being set now. Bringing women into the political process, where they have a real chance to influence the direction their own lives will take, is a crucial condition for democracy. It is certainly crucial for the lives of the women of the former GDR.

Notes

I am very grateful to the International Research and Exchanges Board for supporting my stay in Rostock and Berlin in the summer of 1992. I also thank Gretchen Iversen, who helped me gather some of the material for this chapter, and the GDR Studies Association of the United States for funding her work on this project.

1. Peter Voigt, University of Rostock.

2. For a more detailed description of women in East and West Germany, see Marilyn Rueschemeyer and Hanna Schissler, "Women in the Two Germanies," *German Studies Review,* DAAD Special Issue 1990, pp. 71–85.

3. In the 1950s and 1960s, the state supports for working parents were meager; by the 1970s, most children were in day-care centers subsidized by the state and by the various enterprises.

4. Women with two or more children received an additional extension and could remain at home for eighteen months. These benefits did not guarantee easy integration into occupational life after the leave ended. A few of the women I interviewed expressed fear of falling behind their colleagues during this period, and were tense upon their immediate return to work. See Marilyn Rueschemeyer, *Professional Work and Marriage: An East-West Comparison* (London: Macmillan 1981; and New York: St. Martin's Press).

5. Before unification, a third of the children born in the GDR were born to single parents; after unification, both the number of children born and the number of marriages in the eastern part of Germany decreased.

6. See Rueschemeyer and Schissler, "Women in the Two Germanies."

7. Women study languages, literature, and education but are increasingly to be found also in medicine and law. Nearly three-quarters of West German women employed are in the service sector. See Rueschemeyer and Schissler, "Women in the Two Germanies."

8. Professorial rank makes a critical difference. In 1992, women represented only 5.4 percent of C3 professorships, equivalent to associate professor, and 2.3 percent of C4 or full professorships. See *Die Zeit,* May 1, 1992, p. 46. In 1996, *The Week in Germany* (March 8, 1996, p. 6) noted that on average, out of every forty professors, only one is a woman. With half of Germany's professors retiring in the next ten years, the German Women Academics' Union (DHB) will push to correct the imbalance.

9. Gerd Meyer, "Frauen in den Machthierarchien in den DDR," *Deutschland Archiv* no. 3 (1986): 294–311.

10. See my article "State Patronage in the German Democratic Republic: Artistic and Political Change in a State Socialist Society," *Journal of Arts/Management Law* 20 (Winter 1991): 31–55, for an analysis of developments in one professional association.

11. Brigitte Weichert and Helmut Hoepfner, "Frauen in Politik und Gesellschaft," in *Frauen-Report '90,* ed. Gunnar Winkler, pp. 199–227 (Berlin: Wirtschaft, 1990).

12. Hildegard Maria Nickel, "Frauen im Umbruch der Gesellschaft," *Aus Politik und zeitgeschichte* (Bonn: Bundeszentrale für politische Bildung, September 1995), p. 27.

13. A Rostock study showed that three-quarters of the women and two-thirds of the men between the ages of 55 and 65 had retired unwillingly (lecture by Peter Voigt, University of Rostock, summer 1992). See also G. Gylen et al., *Arbeiten und Leben in Rostock seit der Wende* (Rostock: Progress-Institut für Wirtschaftsforschung [PIW] and Büro für Strukturforschung, July 1992).

14. The head of a school I interviewed mentioned that her son-in-law, who is 35 and the father of four children, was refused permission for sterilization because of his age, but he was told that his wife could undergo the procedure. In 1992 the Federal Labor Court in Kassel ruled that an employer may not ask a potential employee if she is pregnant; and if a woman says she is not pregnant before accepting a job but in fact is, the lie is not cause for dismissal. See *The Week in Germany,* October 30, 1992, p. 6. It was only in 1996 that births in east Germany increased by 11.5 percent after a six-year decline. Ibid., February 21, 1997, p. 8.

15. To take one early example, according to the head of an equality office in Rostock, at the end of the school year in May 1992, 3,116 students applied for apprenticeships and 776 received them. Of 1,470 young men who applied, 507 were successful; of 1,646 young women who applied, only 134 were successful. Regine Hildebrandt, a prominent member of the Social Democratic Party and minister for social policy, labor, families, and women in the state of Brandenburg, succeeded in arranging enough financial help for employers so that 70 percent of the young people who applied for apprenticeships received them—the highest percentage in the new German states, according to her office. But the lack of sufficient apprenticeships remains a problem. In 1996, the Employment and Occupational Research Institute reported that young women made up under 3 percent of all apprentices in traditionally male trades in western Germany and 1.5 percent in the east. *The Week in Germany,* September 13, 1996, p. 5.

16. Only 21 percent of the 500,000 East Germans whose work involves travel are women. See Vera Gaserow, "Die neue Landflucht," *Wochenpost,* no. 27 (June 25, 1992): 5.

17. Discussion with the sociologist Hildegard Nickel. In an often cited early poll by the Institute for Applied Social Research, Bad Godesberg, conducted in the fall of 1990, only 3 percent of 1,432 women between the ages of 16 and 60 in the new states described "housewife" as a "dream job." Fifty-eight percent thought that mothers with careers were "just as good" mothers as those who stayed at home. A recent study indicated that more women (39 percent) were ready to work part-time than men (27 percent). Income and perceived fragility at work were among the differences found; 44 percent of women who had finished high school, university, or vocational training were ready to work part-time, compared to somewhat less than a third with eight to ten years of schooling. *Berliner Zeitung,* no. 74 (March 30, 1997): 41.

18. Studies have investigated the psychological effects of unemployment. In the Rostock sample, for example, 47 percent of the women compared to 9 percent of the men reported doubts about their abilities as a result of unemployment; 76 percent of the women and 51 percent of the men said it got on their nerves to spend so much time at home; and 37 percent of the women and to 21 percent of the men reported frequent depression (Gylen et al., *Arbeiten und Leben in Rostock,* p. 66). These findings may relate to other factors, such as a willingness to

express difficulties, the likelihood of finding work again, and the different responsibilities assumed by women and men in the household.

19. See Thomas Gensicke, "Mentalitätsentwicklungen im Osten Deutschland seit den 70er Jahren," *Speyerer Forschungsberichte,* no. 109 (Speyer: Forschungsinstitut für Öffentliche Verwaltung, 1992), p. 40.

20. The criteria include the health of mother and baby as well as social and criminal considerations.

21. Recently, there have been fights in some states about the nature of the counseling sessions. These have been especially intense in Brandenburg, where the SPD has more power than in other eastern states. Caritas, the Catholic Charity Association, has been warned about possible withdrawal of funds if the organization continues to push its antiabortion stance in these sessions.

22. According to an active member of the SPD women's organization (ASF), women have a much more difficult time in the CDU than in the SPD: "Many are more radical than it seems, but they represent the party line in public."

23. The SPD also has introduced a speaker's list in its party convention, ensuring men and women equal opportunity to address the audience.

24. See the discussion on regionalism and the CDU in Chapter 5.

25. The goal here is women's representation in proportion to their share of membership.

26. At the beginning, Alliance 90 did not have a quota system despite the fact that half the delegates in some of the local governments were women. In Prenzlauer Berg, a district in East Berlin, a men's list and a women's list were prepared to ensure that every other person elected to the Alliance 90 delegation would be a woman.

27. Andreas Schubert, director of city development in Rostock, attempts to respond to the needs of various social groups in his planning. See my article "Participation and Democracy: Observations of Residential Communities of the Former GDR in Transition," *Urban Studies* 30, no. 3 (April 1993): 495–506.

28. In one incident, the head of a women's affairs office had to work to persuade an employer to keep a woman on for one more week so that she could retire at 55 and receive her pension.

29. Political clout is important. Sometimes these offices do succeed in having a degree of political impact at the local level. Again in Rostock, where a women's committee of parliament members had difficulty persuading their own party to take on certain issues, a women's initiative composed of union, church, political, and other groups, organized by the women's affairs office, gathers regularly to press for their own interests. This particular association has been consulted by the municipality on a number of occasions.

30. Slightly over a quarter of East Germans did not vote in either the 1990 or 1994 federal elections.

31. One local community leader in the East mentioned that there were no women in the equivalent position in their West German partner city. She interpreted this difference as an indication that women were more accepted in the public sphere in the East than in the West.

32. Interview with Schenk, 1992.

33. Ursula Engelen-Kefer, deputy director of the League of German Unions, noted this large number of cases; the East German courts at that time were not yet

fully functioning. See *The Week in Germany,* April 26, 1991, p. 5. It has been suggested that Eastern employers employ tactics that are not technically illegal, pressuring women to leave voluntarily. They may also be forced out of jobs after a maternity leave by being given unpleasant or especially difficult tasks. Ibid., March 3, 1995, p. 7.

34. Interview with union district leader, 1992.

35. Interview with union functionary, 1992.

36. The pursuit of multiple goals is further complicated by diverse interests in various segments of the membership. Indeed, the German unions have to be, and are, most responsive to their major constituency, their members in Western Germany. Some Eastern workers who joined unions immediately because they feared unemployment have dropped their membership.

37. Marilyn Rueschemeyer and Bradley Scharf, "Labor Unions in the German Democratic Republic," in *Trade Unions in Communist States,* ed. Alex Pravda and Blair Ruble, pp. 53–84 (London and Boston: Allen & Unwin, 1986).

38. Hieko Gothe, Ulla Kuz, Gero Neugebauer, et al., *Organisation, Politik und Vernetzung der Parteien auf Kriesebene in den fünf neuen Bundesländern* (Berlin: Freie Universität, February 1996), p. 41. As Chapter 5 indicated, 20 percent of the new members in the East were women.

39. There is a very small feminist party, Die Frauen, in Germany that is able to afford one paid position, the federal secretary. Aside from financial difficulties and differences among members regarding a number of issues, there is a debate about whether to run their own candidates in the 1998 elections or support oppositional candidates in an effort to defeat the coalition.

40. If other children in the family are also ill, this leave can be extended to twenty-five days (fifty for single parents).

41. In the summer of 1992, women in the SPD, responding to the high unemployment rate among women, also proposed a change in the Fundamental Law to guarantee equal conditions for women in all social spheres.

42. Interview with Dr. Laurien, 1992. Women who may wish to work were not included in her considerations. One manifestation of the value accorded full-time homemakers, Laurien suggested, would be a credit given toward the pensions of women who stay at home to care for children.

7

Women and the Politics of Transition in the Czech and Slovak Republics

Sharon L. Wolchik

In the Czech and Slovak republics, as in other postcommunist states, the end of communist rule has had contradictory results for women's relation to the political realm. On the one hand, the end of the Communist Party's monopoly of power and the repluralization of politics have opened new opportunities for women, as well as for men, to participate in politics, to articulate their political preferences, and to organize with others who share similar policy perspectives to pressure political leaders to be more responsive to their needs. On the other hand, the backlash against the notion of women's equality and the new freedom of advocates of more traditional roles for women to articulate their views publicly have been reflected in a marginalization of women from politics. The magnitude and number of tasks that must be completed as part of the transition to democratic rule and the market, coupled with the tensions that produced the split between Czechs and Slovaks, have also served to put women's issues on the back burner for most policymakers and citizens.[1]

Women and Politics in the Communist Period

Women's roles changed in important ways after the institution of a communist system in Czechoslovakia. The most noticeable changes were in the areas of education and employment. Women's access to education increased, and sizable groups of women entered the labor force. In both these areas, significant inequalities remained. Although girls and young women entered technical education programs in greater numbers, most chose or were channeled into areas that traditionally were seen as appropriate for women or into areas that became feminized, such as medicine. Gender-related differences in education in turn were reflected in the high degree of occupational segregation that continued to exist in the labor force. Although the range of occupations available to women was far broader than it had been earlier, most women were concentrated in low-priority branches of the labor force that had lower-than-average wage structures. Women were also excluded, by and large, from important managerial positions in the economy.[2]

As numerous observers have noted, changes in women's education levels and employment patterns were not reflected in any real increase in women's exercise of political power during the communist period. As in other communist countries, women in Czechoslovakia were exposed to more political information than they had been previously, and particularly in rural areas, they were drawn into membership in a national political community. As the 99 percent turnout figures common for elections during the communist period attest, both women and men voted in the manipulated, single-slate elections. They also participated in mobilized demonstrations on major holidays and in other regime-organized events.

Women were also well represented among the symbolic governmental elites at all levels. But they were seldom found in positions of real power in the Communist Party hierarchy. As in several other communist countries, the proportions of women in the party and among its leaders were greatest in the period before and immediately after the establishment of a communist system.[3] Women's representation decreased, however, as the Stalinist system was consolidated. Women's political influence was further limited by the fact that the few women who did reach elite positions differed significantly from their male counterparts in social background and previous career experiences.[4]

To some extent, these patterns reflected the limited role women played in the direct exercise of political power throughout Czechoslovakia's history. Women supported the national movements that developed in the Czech Lands and in Slovakia in the nineteenth and early twentieth centuries and were active in a variety of communal organizations. They were enfranchised in 1919, soon after the creation of the Czechoslovak Republic, and made important contributions as individuals to the life of the country during the interwar period. Despite the fact that the education levels of women were equivalent to those of women in other developed European states at the time and despite the lack of religious traditions that prescribed a markedly subordinate role for women, as in the Balkans, women played a small role in the leadership of political parties, and few were elected to government offices. Nonetheless, in contrast to the situation that developed after 1948, when the Communist Party had firmly established its power, women were active in a variety of charitable, social, women's, and partisan organizations during the interwar period. Those who chose to do so also were able to use the mass media to air complaints and raise issues of interest to women.[5]

These opportunities were eliminated after 1948. The organization of political life and the official value system that communist leaders adopted had a profound influence on women's political roles. The Communist Party's monopoly of political power and women's lower level of representation among party members and leaders ensured that women had very little access to the policy-making process. Women's reluctance to accept promotions to more responsible jobs or political functions, attributable in large part to the burden of family responsibilities, also limited the channels that women could use to get issues of interest to them onto the political agenda. Prohibition of independent organizations also meant that women, as well as men, had few if any possibilities to meet with others to articulate and define their interests.[6]

Women played a more important role in the activities of Charter 77 and other dissident organizations before the change of regime. Although women were a minority among the signatories of the charter, one of the spokespersons of the organization was generally a woman. And although the charter did not pay very much attention to women's issues, charter documents did support women's right to work. Women intellectuals were also involved in the networks of nonconformists that developed in Slovakia toward the end of the communist period, including the group that developed around environmental issues and provided the nucleus for the development of Public Against Violence.[7] They also took party in the pilgrimages and other demonstrations by Catholic activists. Young women also emerged as founders and leaders of several of the new dissident organizations that emerged in Czechoslovakia in the last few years of communist rule. Given the risks involved in these activities, however, and the perception that ordinary citizens had little if any influence on political decisions, many women confined their political activities to the minimum required and turned their attention to other issues.

There was similarly little change in the actual division of labor within the home during the communist period. Despite the fact that most women worked outside the home, women continued to bear primary responsibility for the running of the household and care of children. This uneven pattern of change in women's roles can be traced to the fact that the elite's commitment to women's equality was largely instrumental. Women's equality was incorporated in Marxist-Leninist ideology and in the country's constitution, but women's equality was a low-priority goal, and changes in women's roles were influenced to a much greater extent by their relation to higher-priority policies. In the early communist period, the highest priority was accorded to rapid industrialization and the mobilization of all labor reserves. While some effort was made early in the communist period to integrate women into national political life and to enact measures that would ease women's household burdens, these efforts soon faded as the Stalinist system was consolidated. From the mid-1960s on, policies toward women were influenced primarily by efforts to raise the birthrate.[8]

Patterns of Women's Political Participation in the Postcommunist Period

As in other countries in which the collapse of the communist system came about as the result of mass demonstrations, rather than through more extended negotiations between dissidents and Communist Party leaders,[9] women in Czechoslovakia were actively involved in the events that came to be termed the "Velvet Revolution." Women students and dissidents in both the Czech Lands and Slovakia were soon joined by thousands of other women in the mass protests that followed the police attack on peaceful student demonstrators on November 17, 1989. Women intellectuals and professionals, including those active in Charter 77, were involved in the creation of the Civic Forum and the Public Against Violence. Young women also played important roles in organizing the strikes in November. As in other countries in the region, women undermined support for the communist system in less direct ways too, by their roles in shaping and transmitting values within the family.

Despite the role that women played in the events that brought about the end of communist rule, however, women were soon marginalized politically. As in other postcommunist states, this trend has been particularly evident at the level of political elites.[10] Rita Klímová, a former dissident activist, and Jana Ryšlinková served as spokespersons for the Civic Forum in the days of the revolution. Several women were appointed to high political office in the early postcommunist period. Dissident writer Eda Kriseová and former gymnast Věra Čáslavská, for example, served as top advisers to President Havel. Rita Klímová was appointed Czechoslovakia's ambassador to the United States. Attorney Dagmar Burešová, who had defended dissidents during the communist period, chaired the Czech National Council.

But these women are the exceptions. Very few women were nominated or elected to top positions in the government. There was only one woman among the twenty-one persons who held ministerial rank in the interim government formed at the federal level after the collapse of the communist system, and none in the government of Slovakia. Women held two of the ministries in the Czech government during this period, those of Justice and of Trade and Tourism.[11] Women were similarly scarce in the governments formed as a result of the June 1990 parliamentary elections: one woman was appointed to a cabinet post in Slovakia (the Ministry of Labor) and one in the Czech Lands (Trade and Tourism).

There are also very few women in leadership roles in the new political movements and parties that have emerged as the repluralization of politics has proceeded in the Czech and Slovak republics. Although women continued to be involved in the work of the Civic Forum, few served on the Council of the Forum or in leading positions in regional- or local-level organizations. Soňa Szomolányiová, a sociologist and activist, was the sole woman in the leadership of Public Against Violence. With Iveta Radičová, who served as spokeswoman, she was also one of the few women to play a major role in the Civic Democratic Union, the right-of-center political party that emerged from Public Against Violence after the split with the supporters of Vladimír Mečiar. Petra Buzková, a 31–year-old lawyer, is vice-chair of the Social Democratic Party and currently enjoys a high level of trust.

Women are also underrepresented in the new legislative elites formed as a result of democratic elections. In a pattern common to the region as a whole, the percentage of women in the federal and republic legislatures decreased sharply after the fall of communism. Women's representation among members of the federal legislature, which ranged from approximately 23 to 26 percent in the last decade and a half of communist rule, dropped to 10.7 percent (32 of 300) after the June 1990 elections.[12] Women accounted for 13.5 percent of deputies to the

Czech National Council and 9.3 percent of deputies to the Slovak National Council elected at that time.[13] Women's proportion of deputies dropped to 8.7 percent among those elected to the Federal Assembly (26 of 300) and to 10 percent among those elected to the Czech National Council (20 of 200) in June 1992. Women's representation among members of the Slovak National Council increased slightly, to 11.5 percent (23 of 200), as a result of that election.[14]

Women's representation in the lower house of the Czech parliament increased to 15 percent (30 of 200 deputies) as the result of the June 1996 elections. Women accounted for 11.1 percent (9 of 81) of the members of the country's newly established upper house, the Senate.[15] In Slovakia, women's representation in parliament increased to 14 percent after the September 1994 elections.[16]

There were no women in the Czech government formed after the 1996 elections. On January 6, 1997, Vlasta Parkanová became minister of justice after the resignation of Jan Kalvoda. Three women were members of the Slovak government formed in 1994: Katerina Tothová, Deputy Prime Minister; Eva Slavkovská, Minister of Education and Sciences; and Olga Keltošová, Minister of Labor, Social Affairs, and Family. Zdenka Kramplová, a 39–year-old graduate of an agricultural academy who ran the Office of the Slovak government from 1994 until her appointment, was named Foreign Minister of Slovakia in June 1997.

As in other countries, women are best represented in local-level councils, where they accounted for 16 to 21 percent of deputies in 1990.[17] Women accounted for 17.9 percent of local council members in 1994 in the Czech Lands and from 10 to 30 percent of local council members in Slovakia in 1994.[18]

The decline in the number of women deputies since 1989 does not represent such a great loss of political influence as it might suggest, for most of the women chosen to occupy these positions during the communist period were there largely for symbolic purposes. Although there were fewer of them, the women deputies elected in 1990 were comparable in education to the men elected at that time and were drawn from comparable occupations.[19] Fifteen of the twenty women elected to the Federal Assembly in 1990 on whom information is available, for example, had university or other postsecondary educations. Five of these women were physicians and three were lawyers. All twenty-nine of the women deputies and senators in the Czech parliament in 1996 for whom information is available have a higher education. Seven of these have law degrees; five have medical degrees; and four have Ph.D.s.

Thus, although they account for a smaller number of leaders than women did under communism, women elected to parliament since 1989 have had backgrounds that give them a greater chance than their predecessors in the communist era to be influential. Nevertheless, women's limited representation in these elites is significant because it means that issues of particular concern to women are less likely to reach the political agenda than they might if more women held public office at these levels. It also means that women leaders face many barriers in defining and articulating women's interests.

The political attitudes and participation of men and women in politics at the mass level also differ. Women display less interest than men in politics and in running for political office, and their political attitudes and preferences differ as well.

As the very high turnout in the first free election after the end of communism indicates, both women and men were eager to use the opportunity to vote in 1990. The relatively high turnout (86 percent) for the second postcommunist parliamentary elections, held in June 1992, suggests that gender-related differences in voting in those elections were not great. The results of these elections, then, indicate that the tendency for gender-related differences in lower-level political activities such as voting to decrease in the United States and many West European countries in recent decades is also evident in the Czechlands and Slovakia.[20]

Several preliminary studies, however, document Czech and Slovak women's lower levels of interest in politics and knowledge of or confidence in their own political judgments. A 1990 study of women's political attitudes based on an analysis of readers of *Vlasta,* the major women's magazine, a case study of 263 women, and a content analysis of letters sent to *Vlasta* found that more than 80 percent of the women surveyed indicated that they certainly planned to vote in the June 1990 parliamentary elections. A majority of the women surveyed, however, were not involved in any political party, civic association, or interest group. Women who were active tended to be involved in the Civic Forum or the Communist Party. The women studied saw public issues as falling into two groups. Most women thought that women should be active primarily on issues that related to the family, the rights of women in society, the elderly and the ill, the environment, education, the peace movement, and culture. They were far less likely to think that women should be active in regard to the second group of issues, which included economic policies, citizens' initiatives, internal and external politics, entrepreneurial activities, nationality questions, church affairs, and religion. Women displayed most interest in issues related to the family and to the defense of women's rights. As the authors note, however, women rejected the idea of feminism and were not interested in the development of a feminist movement.[21]

The numerous public opinion polls conducted since the end of the communist system have found relatively few significant differences in the political values or attitudes of men and women toward the effort to create a democratic political system, individual political leaders, or the general principles of economic reform. Women have been more pessimistic about the future, however, and more concerned about losing their jobs and about the impact of economic reforms on the living standard.[22] A study conducted in June 1991 confirmed these differences, as gender was one of the factors that most strongly accounted for differences in attitudes toward unemployment. Slightly over 30 percent of women but only 18.8 percent of the men surveyed were afraid they would lose their jobs.[23] A study of popular attitudes toward political and economic issues conducted by the Institute for Social Analysis of Comenius University in July 1991 found similarly few significant gender differences. Men and women identified unemployment, the functioning of the economy, the living standard, and social welfare as the most important problems of Slovakia. Women were somewhat more likely to emphasize issues related to the living standard and social welfare, as well as unemployment, while men focused more on economic problems and gave more importance to nationality relations. Women were also less likely than men to support rapid economic reform. Although the authors of the study found no significant differences in partisan preferences, women were somewhat more likely than men to trust political and social institutions. One of the primary differences evident in this survey was women's far greater tendency to be undecided or to be unsure of their views.[24]

The picture that emerges from these studies, then, supports the view one gets from the mass media and from talks with women activists and citizens concerning women's attitudes toward the political system and their own roles in it. As was true during the communist period, politics is seen as foreign and of little immediate interest to many women in the new political system.[25]

Women's Organizations

Although voting is most women's sole political activity, some women have taken advantage of the new possibilities to organize independent women's groups. Hurt by its past subordination to the Communist Party and by the negative stand its leaders took in regard to the student demonstrations in November 1989, the official women's organization, the Union of Czechoslovak Women, separated into Czech and Slovak organizations, which continue to function. Leaders of these organizations argue that they are continuing to work for women's rights in the context of the new democratic framework.[26] They have also sponsored initiatives designed to coordinate the actions of the multitude of new women's groups that have formed since 1989. These actions, including an attempt to organize a national congress of women, have not been very successful. Although the organizations still have substantial memberships, many women share the view articulated by activists and leaders of some of the new organizations that these groups do not represent the real interests of women. Many also criticize the successors to the old women's unions for the "old style" of their work and actions.[27] In the words of one activist, "The leaders of these organizations were not women, but men."[28]

Other groups have formed independently of the old women's unions. Among them are a variety of Christian groups, such as the Union of Mothers, the Prague Mothers, and Convent žen, as well as the Union of Women Entrepreneurs and other professional groups. Women have also created numerous voluntary associations and charitable organizations.[29] As in other postcommunist countries, new feminist groups have also formed since 1989. Women intellectuals gathered around the sociologist and activist Jiřina Šiklová have established a center for gender studies in Prague, which continues to organize lectures on women's issues at several Czech universities, as well as other activities for women.

Slovak women have also formed a number of new groups. Some of these are affiliated with political parties. Others consist of business and professional women or women intellectuals. In 1995, with funding from a European Union assistance program called PHARE, Slovak women also began to organize a new mass women's organization, the Association of Slovak Women, independent of the old unified women's organization. Women intellectuals in the Czech Republic and Slovakia also cooperate in producing *Aspekt,* a very high quality feminist journal in Bratislava. These groups and initiatives play an important role in raising popular awareness of gender issues. But most of them, particularly those with an explicitly feminist orientation, are small, have few resources, and operate only in urban areas.[30]

Many of the new women's groups do not call for greater gender equality but in fact are explicitly devoted to fostering women's domestic roles. Most deny that they are feminist; many deny that they are political at all. As numerous activists and analysts have noted, many people continue to see "feminism" as a dirty word in these countries, as most citizens associate the term with radical, man-hating activists.[31] Some women activists, including representatives of New Humanity and the Helsinki Citizens' Assembly, see themselves as supporters of "sane feminism," or a form of feminism that does not imply antagonism to the family or to men. Many activists stress the need for women to develop a type of feminism that will reflect the specific needs and experiences of Czech and Slovak women.

The leaders and activists of many of the groups that explicitly reject the feminist label are also actively working to bring about changes that will benefit women. Women activists in Slovakia, for example, created a Society for Planned Parenthood, which attempts, among its other functions, to influence government legislation on reproductive rights. Women's groups in Prague, primarily Christian in orientation, banded together to form a coordinating committee to lay claim to public resources and serve as a source of information for women's groups.[32] Some of the women associated with this effort and with New Humanity have also been active in efforts to work with women parliamentarians. Several women's groups have attempted to influence the government's legislation in regard to abortion, in both pro-life and pro-choice directions. Other groups have organized lecture courses for women on the impact of the economic changes and new entrepreneurial possibilities for women. But these groups are generally small and have few if any links to political parties or leaders. They thus have had little influence on the making of public policy.[33]

The re-creation of democratic political institutions and the repluralization of political life that have followed the end of communist rule in these republics, then, have not eliminated gender differences in politics. The experiences of women here, as in the other postcommunist states, demonstrate that the creation of democratic institutions does not of necessity mean equal access to the policy-making process or an equal chance of political participation for all citizens. As in more established liberal democratic systems, women continue to play a limited role in politics, with the result that issues of special concern to women are unlikely to be addressed adequately by political decision makers. Part of the explanation for the current pattern of women's political involvement is to be found in the legacy of the communist period. The nature of the economic and political transition that is taking place and the characteristics of the political systems that have emerged also have an important impact on women's political roles.[34]

The Communist Legacy

To some extent, the political marginalization of women is a continuation of trends that developed during the communist period. As in other areas of life, the legacy of forty years of communist rule is proving to be more difficult to eradicate than most people imagined in the heady days of late 1989 and early 1990. Women's political behavior and attitudes in the postcommunist period continue to be shaped in important ways by the impact of the approach to women's issues and policies adopted during the communist period.

Women's current attitudes toward politics, here as elsewhere in Central and Eastern Europe, have been influenced, first of all, by a widespread reaction to the uneven pattern of gender-role change produced during the communist period. In contrast to the situation in the United States and many European countries that were not communist, the goal of women's equality was not chosen by women themselves but was imposed from above by political leaders. Faced with the state's appropriation of women's equality and forced to live daily with the contradictions that the uneven pattern of gender-role change created for women and their families, many women, as well as men, reacted by rejecting the goal of gender equality itself.[35]

These attitudes, which are reflected in the mass media and in conversations with leaders and ordinary citizens, are particularly evident in regard to women's economic roles. There appears to be widespread agreement, for example, that the levels of women's employment that existed under communism were too high and should be reduced. Many experts and officials also emphasize the need for women to be able to choose whether to work or to stay home.[36] Such attitudes were clearly expressed during the June 1990 election campaign. Most candidates questioned during a television debate, for example, agreed that levels of women's employment were too high. One individual, who represented the extreme end of the spectrum, argued that all women with children under the age of 10 should be barred from the labor force.[37]

The results of a survey conducted in Slovakia in early 1991 provide some idea of the popularity of such views. Only 8 percent of all respondents and 12 percent of women in the prime childbearing years (18 to 39) believed that women should be employed just as men are. A further 18 percent of all respondents and 20 percent of women thought that women should be employed only part-time. Forty-seven percent of all respondents and 52 percent of women believed that women should first of all care for their children and family, but should also be able to take jobs outside the home if they wanted to. Over one-quarter of the total sample but only 15 percent of the women surveyed believed that women should devote themselves solely to the care of home and children while men supported the family economically.[38]

These attitudes, which are often coupled with an emphasis on the primacy of women's domestic roles, are similar to those that emerged during the last two decades of the communist period, when concern over the low birthrate led to the adoption of pronatalist policies. Although most women continued to work outside the home, the model of the ideal socialist woman changed, and propaganda campaigns aimed at women emphasized the contribution women's maternal roles made to socialist society. The call for women to return to the home also echoes the arguments made during the reform period of the 1960s, when numerous economic officials and managers claimed that it was not efficient economically for women with small children to be employed.[39]

The ongoing economic and political crises of the last decades of communist rule reinforced a desire to return to more traditional gender roles. Preoccupied with declining economic performance and growing political disaffection, political leaders in Czechoslovakia as elsewhere gave very little attention to issues related to gender equality. Economic and political crisis also increased the economic importance of the family and reinforced the tendency to focus on private concerns.[40] With the elimination of censorship and the repluralization of politics, such attitudes can now be expressed openly. The Catholic church and other religious organizations that support traditional roles for women are also able to be active in politics today.

As I have argued earlier in regard to the region as a whole, many individuals hold similar attitudes concerning women's political roles.[41] Many former dissidents and other political leaders appear to see politics as not quite appropriate for women. Evident in the notion that politics is too dirty for women, that women have more important things to do; and that women's political involvement should wait until the critical issues that face the country are resolved, such attitudes are also reflected in survey research. A study of public attitudes toward women in public life conducted in late October and early November 1991 by the Institute for Public Opinion Research in Prague, for example, found that opinion was divided as to whether women were sufficiently represented in public life. Forty-two percent of respondents believed they were not; 38 percent believed they were; and 20 percent did not know. Women were more likely than men to regard their representation as inadequate (49 percent, compared to 34 percent). Although two-thirds of those questioned believed it was useful for women to be active in public life, a third said it was not. Substantially more women (69 percent) than men (52 percent) thought women's involvement was useful.

Opinion among those who supported the idea of women's involvement in politics was nearly evenly divided between those who believed that women should be active primarily in social, health, charitable, and other volunteer organizations (23 percent) and those who believed that women should be involved in all areas that men were, because they were equal (22 percent). Both men and women identified either the need to care for family and children or lack of free time as the primary reason why women were less involved, but women were more likely than men to cite lack of time. More men than women were among the 18 percent of respondents who argued that women do not belong in politics, have no possibility of becoming involved, or are not elected as the primary reason for women's low participation. Although relatively few women believed that men kept women out of politics, more than twice as many women as men thought so.[42]

The results of a survey of the adult population of Slovakia conducted in early 1991 provide further information about popular views of women's political roles. While a majority of all respondents and of a subgroup of women in the prime childbearing ages (18–39) believed that women were insufficiently represented in the government of the Slovak Republic and at the federal level, nearly a third of the total sample and 21 percent of young women disagreed. Similar proportions (44 and 49 percent) believed that women were inadequately represented in the Slovak National Council and Federal Assembly; slightly larger proportions (33 and 25 percent) of respondents disagreed. Young women and all respondents were more satisfied with women's representation in local-level organizations (44 percent and 38 percent), but approximately a third of both groups were dissatisfied. From 21 to 27 percent of respondents were unable to make a judgment about women's representation at all levels. As in the case of attitudes toward women's employment, views concerning women's political representation varied by education and the political orientations of respondents. Those with higher and secondary education were most critical, as were those who preferred the Democratic Left, Slovak National, and Green parties.[43]

The results of a study of political values in 1991 also shed some light on the extent to which women feel disadvantaged by their gender. Thirty-two percent of respondents in the Czech Lands and 41 percent in Slovakia indicated that they sometimes felt themselves to be the victims of injustice because of their gender.[44] Although we do not know how many of these respondents were women, it seems safe to assume that most of the people who experience such disadvantages are women. These sentiments, however, as well as more general dissatisfaction with the course of political and economic affairs, have yet to propel women to organize in large numbers to promote their interests or pressure political leaders.

The organization of political life during the communist period and the forced mobilization of women during that time have also had an impact on women's political roles. The activities of the official women's organizations, for example, and the willingness of the leaders of those organizations to support the regime have fueled the backlash against women's political involvement and the goal of gender equality. Although leaders of these organizations discussed problematic aspects of women's roles more openly in the last decades of communist rule, most women appear to have seen the official women's groups as out of touch with the concerns of ordinary women.[45] Leaders of these organizations became the butts of private ridicule. Their activities helped to discredit the idea of women politicians and contributed to the sense that "the idea of women politicians is somehow funny."[46]

Women's forced mobilization during the communist period also has had an impact on their willingness to be involved in politics now. Women's presumed responsibility for the running of the household and care of children let many women get by with lower levels of political activism than men in comparable positions.[47] Most women, however, had to go through the motions of being politically active to some extent. Now that political activity is voluntary, many women appear to prefer to focus on other aspects of life. As a former woman dissident replied when asked why women were not more active politically, "Why should women ruin their lives? There are more important things to do now."[48]

The Impact of the Transition

The legacy of the communist period and the reaction against the pattern of gender-role change produced during that period provide part of the explanation for women's limited interest in political affairs in the postcommunist Czech and Slovak republics. But other elements of the current situation also contribute to it.

One of the most important of these is the nature of transition politics. As the breakup of the federal state illustrated, the political systems in the two republics are still in flux. Free elections held in 1990 legitimated the new federal government formed soon after the end of communist rule. Czechoslovakia's new leaders also made considerable progress in revising the country's legal codes and creating the legal basis for a democratic state. Nonetheless, as the inability of political leaders to agree on a new constitution, the outcome of the June 1992 election, and the eventual breakup of the federation demonstrated, the political situation was far from stable. Popular disaffection with government institutions and leaders increased dramatically, and political preferences remained volatile.[49]

The absence of a stable party system also influences women's political roles. As in Poland and several other postcommunist states, the good showing of the umbrella organizations that led the revolution, Civic Forum and Public Against Violence, in the first postcommunist elections raised the possibility that a new, nonpartisan form of politics based on social movements might develop in Czechoslovakia. Since there is some indication that women were more strongly drawn than men to nonpartisan political movements, the continuation of such politics might have been beneficial to women. Development of a form of politics based on nontraditional political organizations might also have created greater opportunities for a redefinition of politics and more space in the political arenas for issues of greatest concern to women.[50]

Interest in joining political parties continued to be low among all groups of the population in 1991 and 1992. But with the breakup of Civic Forum and Public Against Violence in 1991, the nonpartisan politics of the early postcommunist period was replaced by the development of more structured political parties. The poor electoral showing of Civic Movement, the heir to the nonpartisan tradition of Civic Forum, may have been due in part to its center-left orientation. But it may also reflect a rejection of nonpartisan politics.[51] If, as some analysts argue, women's concept of the political is more diffuse than men's and if women are indeed more comfortable with nonpartisan politics, this shift may well be accompanied by a further decline in women's active participation in politics.

The need to rely on party organizations for nomination and election will continue to limit women's access to political positions.[52] Few parties have given any real attention to nominating women candidates or have given thought to the obstacles that prevent women from being more visible in political leadership. The main exception to this pattern, the Party of Women and Mothers, formed in 1990, did not do well at the polls.[53] The weakness of many of the political parties that have emerged since 1989 also poses obstacles to the election of women candidates. Because most of them have few resources in terms of either finances or members, the advantages that might accrue to women by virtue of the system of proportional representation that both the new Czech and Slovak republics continue to use may be vitiated by the inability of many political parties to deliver the vote for their candidates.

The importance of "personalities," or individuals with high profiles, in political contests is another factor that limits women's political representation. Given the absence of strong political parties with well-developed local organizations, election to public office has tended to depend to a great extent on the degree to which a candidate is already known to the public. Because few women emerged in leadership roles in the revolution, few received the extensive media coverage that male leaders did. The impact of this factor was particularly noticeable in the elections of June 1990, given the short time that had elapsed since the end of the old system and the fact that many of the new political parties had been in existence for only a few months. Opinion polls conducted in 1991 and 1992, which demonstrated a degree of stability in the partisan preferences of citizens over time, suggest that personal recognition may have been less important in the June 1992 elections. Yet the difference between the predicted and actual results for individual parties suggests that this element still played a role in voters' decisions.

Lack of data prevents assessment of the extent to which women were hurt by the tendency to rely on the local equivalent of "personalities," or local-level notables, in local elections. Nevertheless, the fact that few women occupy positions of leadership even in those occupations and professions in which they predominate suggests that this factor may have worked against women at the local level.

Finally, women's relationship to politics and the way women's issues are considered are also influenced in important ways by the transitions from communist to democratic rule and from one republic to two. The magnitude of the economic, political, and other tasks that face the republics' leaders as they deal with the legacy of forty years of communist rule in all aspects of life are too well known to need enumeration. These tasks and the need to deal with the economic, political, and other consequences of the breakup of the federation clearly have occupied much of the attention of Czech and Slovak leaders. The changes that have occurred since 1989 also have had a major impact on ordinary citizens in both countries. As the results of public opinion polls demonstrate, many Czechs and Slovaks supported the end of communist rule and some of the changes that have followed. Many of the changes, however, particularly those that have been enacted as part of the effort to re-create a market economy, have increased the hardship of everyday life for many groups and reduced the resources available to deal with pressing economic and social issues. Although the reintroduction of a market economy may well lead to improvement in the standard of living in the long run, in the short term the end of subsidies, liberalization of prices, and structural changes involved in economic reform have reduced the standard of living and increased the economic pressure felt by most families.[54] By early 1993, the economy of the Czech Republic began to recover; however, the shift to a needs-based social welfare system threatened to increase hardship for many. The difficulties the Czech economy faced in early 1997 presaged further cuts in government programs. Although the Slovak economy experienced a high rate of growth after 1993, unemployment continued to hover at about 13 percent, and the economic situation of many families in Slovakia is likely to be very difficult for some time to come.

The end of strict control of information and the downgrading of the role of the police and security forces have also led to the reemergence in stark form of old social problems, such as prostitution, pornography, drug abuse, alcoholism, and child and spouse abuse, and to the appearance of new social problems.[55] Other conflicts, including the ethnic tensions that led to the breakup of the state, which could not be aired openly earlier, also became important public issues.

As in other postcommunist countries, then, there has been a great deal of uncertainty and change in almost all aspects of life. The process of being in transition is in itself an important feature of public and private life at present, quite apart from the kinds of institutions or policies that will emerge.[56]

The impact of these changes on women's political roles is twofold. First, the magnitude of the problems the countries' new leaders face has an impact on the way women's issues are perceived. As in earlier historical periods, the current leaders, who are beset by critical problems in many areas, as well as many ordinary citizens, appear to view an explicit focus on women's needs as a luxury they cannot afford at present.[57] Some leaders, including those attentive to women's concerns, argue that it is first necessary to ensure a stable democratic system. Rita Klímová, Czechoslovakia's ambassador to the United States, noted in 1990 that "feminism is a flower on democracy."[58] The intense competition for scarce government resources that characterizes current political life also bodes ill for the maintenance or extension of some social programs that benefit women.[59]

In addition to deflecting elite attention from women's issues, the transition also carries psychological costs for individuals and families. Though many women, as well as men, have welcomed the new opportunities and freedoms that the collapse of communism has brought, the need to adjust to change in everything from the organization of retail trade to expectations at the workplace creates its own stresses. Although there has been little systematic study of how individuals are adjusting to the burden of living in such times or the impact of pervasive change and uncertainty on women's political roles, such costs may influence women's interest in and ability to be involved in politics both directly and indirectly. Lack of certainty about the competence and procedures of governmental or other political bodies and the bewildering and changing array of political parties and political choices offered voters and activists today undoubtedly increase the costs of becoming politically involved, for example.

Women also bear a disproportionate share of the burden of the economic transition.[60] In addition to the stress created by unemployment, new demands at the workplace, and increased competition, women face new difficulties in obtaining what they need to run their households and take care of their families. Women's tasks in this regard became more difficult in part because the ways of getting by that developed during the communist period had to be changed to one degree or another. As several women leaders have noted, the need to comparison-shop and the increased prices of basic consumer goods also complicated women's lives in recent years.[61] Just as in the period before 1989, then, time constraints and the burden of family responsibilities also undoubtedly help to explain women's limited political involvement in politics. Given women's responsibility for managing the emotional work of the family, women may also be hesitant to take on additional commitments in the political realm in a situation in which other family members are also likely to be experiencing stress. Equally important, voters and party leaders who decide who will be nominated for political office are also likely to see women as unsuitable in these circumstances.

Future Possibilities

Current developments in the Czech and Slovak republics point in opposite directions in regard to the levels and kind of political involvement of women we are likely to see in the near future.[62] The trends we have seen and the experiences of women in other parts of the world during the period of transition from authoritarian rule are not encouraging with respect to prospects for women's participation in the new democratic system in these republics. Women's limited role in the exercise of political power either as political leaders or as members of interest groups is particularly worrisome because the perceptions of who is a legitimate political actor and definitions of what are legitimate political issues that develop during the early period of the transition to democracy have an impact on the nature and accessibility of political life once political structures and institutions solidify. In many Latin American countries, the fluidity of the early stage of the transition from authoritarian rule created greater scope for new groups, including women's organizations, to participate in politics in a meaningful way. The experience of these groups, however, whose influence declined as the political situation normalized, demonstrates the obstacles women face in translating any power they obtain during the opening of the political game into political clout when politics once again becomes routinized.[63] Given the trends we have seen, women in the Czech and Slovak republics, as well as elsewhere in the region, will start from a lower base as the political situation normalizes.

The economic hardships and dislocations that have accompanied the move to a market economy and the climate of uncertainty will persist for some time to come. Both of these features of the current situation will in all likelihood reinforce the notion that politics is inappropriate for women. Together with the increased demands they pose on women's time, they may deflect women from taking steps to pressure political leaders to deal with the issues of greatest concern to women. They will also, in all likelihood, contribute to the sense on the part of political leaders that there are more urgent issues than must be solved before attention can be given to women's issues. The breakup of the Czech and Slovak federation reinforced this sense. Although the common state of Czechs and Slovaks ended through negotiation rather than the violence that has torn apart what was Yugoslavia, both the Czech Lands and Slovakia experienced short-term disruptions.

There are also, however, several aspects of the current situation that could lead to greater interest in politics and higher levels of activism by women. First among them are economic factors. The impact of more experience with a capitalist economy, including increased pressures to perform better and adopt new work habits, greater competition, and higher unemployment rates, may motivate more women to use the political opportunities available to them to protect their interests. Such actions will be particularly likely if, as seems to be happening, the rejection of the old, communist-sponsored version of gender equality and the relegitimation of traditional attitudes toward women and the family result in more open discrimination against women workers and higher levels of sexual harassment at the workplace. Young, highly educated women also face greater difficulties than their male schoolmates in finding employment suited to their qualifications and interests in the current economic and political climate than earlier cohorts did.[64] The motives these developments may create for women to organize, articulate, and defend their interests will be reinforced by the cuts in social services and social welfare provisions and the increased costs of such services that efforts to cut government budgets have already begun to bring.

Other, more political factors may also help to mobilize women. As noted earlier, some women supported environmental groups and took part in protests concerning environmental issues during the communist period. In 1990 a group of young Czech mothers pushed their babies in carriages down Prague's main street to protest the environmental damage and the contamination of the food supply by toxic chemicals. Challenges to women's reproductive rights may also mobilize women. Numerous public opinion polls indicate that most women, as well as a majority of men, oppose the banning of abortion.[65] The bill submitted by the Slovak government in March 1992, which would have made abortion all but impossible for most women to obtain by increasing the price, greatly failed to mobilize Slovak women, however, because it was clear the Jan Čarnogursky's government would lose the June 1992 election.

These cases give credibility to the view that women can best be mobilized by perceived threats to their ability to care for their families and by direct challenges to their own rights. As Jane Jaquette has argued in the case of Latin American women,[66] Czech and Slovak women may be most likely to enter the political realm when they perceive the connection between political issues and their roles at home.

The activities of many of the women's groups that have formed in the Czech and Slovak republics may also support this development. As discussed above, most deny that they are feminist or have any interest in politics at all. Yet many of these groups have sponsored actions that in fact are designed to improve women's qualifications, increase their knowledge of the political and economic situation, or put pressure on public officials to resolve issues of special concern to women. By providing a space where women can meet to articulate and share their concerns, the new women's groups may foster recognition of common interests and the development of feminist consciousness or greater political activism. They may also lead women to take more formal, organized action in their own behalf.

Notes

1. As I have written at some length about the impact of the political changes since 1989 on the way issues of special concern to women get onto the political agenda and are dealt with by policymakers, I treat this aspect of women's relation to the political system only very briefly. See Sharon L. Wolchik, "Women's Issues in Czechoslovakia in the Communist and Post-Communist Periods," in *Women and Politics Worldwide,* ed. Barbara Nelson and Najma Chowdhury (New Haven: Yale University Press, 1994); and *Czechoslovakia in Transition* (London: Pinter, 1991), ch. 3.

2. See Marie Čermáková, "Sociální postavení ženy v československé společnosti," in *Každodennost' ženského sveta: Problémy a prístupy* (Bratislava: Slovenská sociologická spoločnost' pri SAV, 1991); Hana Navarová, "Co dal socialismus ženám?" in Marie Čermáková, Irena Hradecká, and Hana Navarová, *K postavení žen v socialistické společnosti;* and Jiřina Šiklová, "Are Women in Middle and Eastern Europe Conservative?"; Hana Navarová, "Impact of the Economic and Political Changes in Czechoslovakia"; and Barbara Jancar, "Women under Communism." See also *Women and Politics,* ed. Jane Jaquette (New York: Wiley, 1974): Hilda Scott, *Does Socialism Liberate Women?* (Boston: Beacon Press, 1974); Alena Heitlinger, *Women and State Socialism: Sex Inequality in the Soviet Union and Czechoslovakia* (Montreal: McGill–Queen's University Press, 1979); and the following works by Sharon Wolchik: "The Status of Women in a Socialist Order: Czechoslovakia, 1948–1978," *Slavic Review* 38 (December 1979); "Ideology and Equality: The Status of Women in Eastern and Western Europe," *Comparative Political Studies* 13 (January 1981); "Demography, Political Reform, and Women's Issues in Czechoslovakia," in *Women, Power and Political Systems,* ed. Margherita Rendel, pp. 135–50 (London: Croom Helm, 1981); "Women and the State in Eastern Europe and the Soviet Union," in *Women, the State, and Development,* ed. Sue Ellen Charlton, Jana Everett, and Kathleen Staudt, pp. 435–65 (Albany: SUNY Press, 1989); "Central and Eastern Europe," in *Privatization and Democratization in Central and Eastern Europe and the Soviet Union: The Gender Dimension,* ed. Valentine M. Moghadam (Helsinki: World Institute for Development Economics Research, United Nations University, 1992).

3. See Wolchik, "Status of Women," pp. 594–95; "Ideology and Equality," pp. 460–62; and "Women and the State," pp. 50–51, for a discussion of these trends in Czechoslovakia. For information about similar trends in other communist countries, see Gail W. Lapidus, *Women in Soviet Society: Equality, Development, and Social Change* (Berkeley: University of California Press, 1978), ch. 6; Barbara W. Jancar, *Women under Communism* (Baltimore: Johns Hopkins University Press, 1978), ch. 5; and Wolchik, "Eastern Europe," in *The Politics of the Second Electorate: Women and Public Participation,* ed. Jane Lovenduski and Jill Hills (London: Routledge & Kegan Paul, 1981).

4. See Wolchik, "Status of Women"; Heitlinger, *Women and State Socialism.* See Marie Čermáková and Hana Navarová, "Women and Elections '90" ("Ženy a volby '90"), manuscript, 1990; and Wolchik, *Czechoslovakia in Transition,* ch. 4, for more recent data.

5. For further discussion, see Bruce M. Garver, "Women in the First Czechoslovak Republic," in *Women, State, and Party in Eastern Europe,* ed. Sharon L. Wolchik and Alfred G. Meyer, pp. 64–81 (Durham, NC: Duke University Press, 1985); and Karen J. Freeze, "Medical Education for Women in Austria: A Study in the Politics of the Czech Women's Movement in the 1890s," in ibid.; and Wolchik, "The Precommunist Legacy, Economic Development, Social Transformation, and Women's Roles in Eastern Europe," in ibid.; "Elite Strategy Toward Women in Czechoslovakia: Liberation or Mobilization?" *Studies in Comparative Communism* 14 (Summer/Autumn 1981): 127–29; and "Women in the Czech Lands," in *Women's Studies Encyclopedia,* ed. Helen Turney (Westport, CT: Greenwood Press, 1989).

6. See Wolchik, "Status of Women"; Scott, *Does Socialism Liberate Women?* and Heitlinger, *Women and State Socialism,* chs. 13–18, for discussions of the temporary increase in such opportunities in 1968.

7. See Barbara Jancar, "Women in the Opposition in Poland and Czechoslovakia in the 1970s," in Wolchik and Meyer, *Women, State, and Party;* and Sharon Wolchik, "Women and the Collapse of Communism in Central and Eastern Europe," paper presented at the World Congress of Slavic Studies, Harrogate, England, July 25, 1990.

8. See Wolchik, "Status of Women," "Elite Strategy," and "Women and the State"; Scott, *Does Socialism Liberate Women?* and Heitlinger, *Women and State Socialism.*

9. See Wolchik, "Women and the Collapse of Communism," for a discussion of the impact of the method by which the communist system fell on women's participation in the process.

10. See ibid.; Wolchik, "Women in the Transition to Democracy in Central and Eastern Europe," paper presented at the annual meeting of the American Political Science Association, San Francisco, September 1990; Šiklová, "Are Women in Middle and Eastern Europe Conservative?"; Čermáková and Navarová, "Ženy a volby '90"; and the following papers presented at the Research Conference on Gender and Restructuring: *Perestroika,* the Revolutions, and Women, World Institute for Development Economics Research, United Nations University, Helsinki, September 2–3, 1991; Barbara Einhorn, "Democratization and Women's Movements in East Central Europe: Concepts of Women's Rights"; Dobrinka Kostova, "The Transition to Democracy in Bulgaria: Challenges and Risks for Women"; Marilyn Rueschemeyer, "German Unification and the Status of Women"; and Anastasia Posadskaya, "Changes in Gender Discourses and Politics."

11. From information in Foreign Broadcast Information Service, *Daily Report,* EEU-90–071, April 12, 1990, pp. 30–31.

12. Wolchik, "Status of Women"; "Women and Politics: The East European Experience," in Lovenduski and Hills, *Politics of the Second Electorate;* and "Women and the State"; "Volby 1990," *Hospodářské noviny,* June 14, 1990.

13. See Čermáková and Navarová, "Ženy a volby '90"; and *Kdo je kdo v ČSFR* (Prague: Nakladatelsto kdo je kdo, 1991).

14. Information from the Federal Statistical Office, Prague, June 1992.

15. Český Statistický° Úřad, "Welcome to the Election Server of Central Electoral Commission." Http://www.volby.cz/_ASCII_/volhome/anglic1.htm 05/31/97.

16. EU Net Slovakia, "Elections 94." Http://www.eunet.sk/slovakia/elections-94/parl-members 05/06/97).

17. Čermáková et al., *K postávení žen*, p. 17.

18. Marie Čermáková, "Process of Developing Pro-Women Policies in the Czech Republic" (unpublished manuscript), p. 21, and *Naše Slova*, March 1997.

19. See Sharon L. Wolchik, "Men and Women in Parliamentary Elites in Czechoslovakia." Manuscript.

20. See Wolchik, "Ideology and Equality," for references to studies that illustrate these trends.

21. Čermáková and Navarová, "Ženy a volby '90," pp. 7, 12, 31–35, 57.

22. See Marek Boguszak, Ivan Gabal, and Vladimír Rak, *Československo-leden 1990* (Prague: Skupina pro nezávislou sociální analzu, January 1990); and *Československo-listopad 1990* (Prague: Skupina pro nezávislou sociální analzu, November 1990).

23. As reported in Jiří Večerník, "Nezaměstnanost: Obavy značně diferencované," *Data & Fakta* no. 1 (September 1991) 1–2.

24. Zora Bútorová et al., *Slovensko-Júl 1991* (Bratislava: Ústav pre sociálnu analzu Univerzity Komenského, 1991), p. 32.

25. See Wolchik, "Central and Eastern Europe," for an earlier discussion of this point.

26. Interview Dr. Zdenka Hajná, Prague, March 1992.

27. Interview with Eda Kriseová, March 1992; interview with Dr. Maria Stefanovová, Bratislava, March 1992. See also Čermaková and Navarová, "Ženy a volby '90."

28. Interview, March 1990.

29. See Plávková, "Women's Views on the Past and the Future of Women's Organizations," in *Contemporary Problems of Women and Family: Youth and Upbringing* (Bratislava, 1990); and *Sociológia* 23, nos. 1–2 (1991): 85–97, for information from a recent study of women's organizations in Slovakia.

30. Interview with Martina Holubová, Prague, March 1992; interview with Jiřina Vrábková, Helsinki Citizens' Assembly, March 1992. See also Čermaková and Navarová, "Ženy a volby '90."

31. Interview with Eda Kriseová, March 1992; interview with Jiřina Šiklová, March 1992; see also Marie Čermáková, Etela Farkašová, and Zuzana Kiczková, "Feministická filozofia: Problémy, perspektívy," in *Každodennost' ženského sveta: Problémy a prístupy* (Bratislava: Slovenská sociologická spoločnost' pri SAV, sekcia ženy a rodiny, 1991), pp. 39–49.

32. Interview with Martina Holubová, March 1991, Prague.

33. See Wolchik, "Women's Issues," for further discussion.

34. See Wolchik, "Central and Eastern Europe," for an earlier discussion of the impact of these factors on the region as a whole.

35. For earlier discussions of the importance of these factors, see Renata Siemieńska, "Women and Social Movements in Poland," *Women & Politics* 6 (Winter 1986): 5–36; and Wolchik, "Women and the State."

36. Interview with Jitka Havlová, March 1990; interview with Jiřina Šiklová, Prague, March 1992; interview with Dr. Maria Stefanovová, Ministry of Labor and Social Affairs of the Slovak Republic, Bratislava, March 1992; interview with Jan Sedláček, Czech Ministry of Labor and Social Affairs, Prague, March 1992;

see Sharon L. Wolchik, "Women and Work in Communist and Post-Communist Czechoslovakia," in *Women's Lives and Women's Work in Modernizing and Industrial Countries,* ed. Hilda Kahne and Janet Giele (Boulder, CO: Westview Press, 1992).

37. Czechoslovak television, June 1990.

38. "Verejnost' SR o postavení žien v súčasnej spoločnosti," *Ústav pre vskum verejnej mienky pri SSÚ [ÚVVM],* 1991, p. 4.

39. See Heitlinger, *Women and State Socialism;* Scott, *Does Socialism Liberate Women?,* ch. 17; Wolchik, "Demography, Political Reform, and Women's Issues," and "Elite Strategy."

40. Wolchik, "Women and the State"; Jancar, "Women in the Opposition." See Siemieńska, "Women and Social Movements," for a similar argument in the Polish case.

41. Wolchik, "Central and Eastern Europe."

42. See "Názory na zapojení žen do veřejného života," *ÚVVM,* November 1991, and "Ženy ve veřejném životě," *ÚVVM,* 1991; pp. 2–3.

43. "Verejnost' SR o postavení žien v súčasnej spoločnosti," *ÚVVM,* 1991, pp. 5–6.

44. Jadwiga Sanderova, "Proč asi většina na Slovensku mlčí?" *Data & Fakta* no. 6 (January 1992): 5.

45. Interviews, Prague and Bratislava, March and June 1990, March 1992.

46. Interview with Dáša Havlová, Prague, March 1990. See Čermaková and Navarová, "Ženy a volby '90," p. 47, for another analysis of the impact of this factor.

47. See Wolchik, "Women and the State."

48. Interview with Helena Klimová, Prague, June 1992.

49. See Wolchik, *Czechoslovakia in Transition.* Valerie Bunce and Maria Csanadi, "A Systematic Analysis of a Non-System: Post-Communism in Eastern Europe" (manuscript, 1992), discuss the chaos in current institutional and political life in Hungary. This tendency has also been documented in studies of other societies in transition from authoritarian to democratic rule.

50. See Jane S. Jaquette, *The Women's Movement in Latin America: Feminism and the Transition to Democracy* (Boston: Unwin Hyman, 1989); and Sonia E. Alvarez, "Gender Politics in Brazil's Transition from Authoritarian Rule: Implications for Comparative Analysis," paper presented at the annual meeting of the American Political Science Association, San Francisco, August 30–September 2, 1990, for discussions of the greater space available to women's groups in Latin America in the early postrevolutionary period.

51. Wolchik, *Czechoslovakia in Transition,* discusses the process of political differentiation as it occurred in Czechoslovakia in the early postcommunist period.

52. See Marie Čermáková, et al., *K postavení žen,* in Čermáková, for a discussion of this factor.

53. See Alena Valterová, "Úvahy o ekonomické reformě," *Žena '91,* no. 2 (1991) for the views of one of the leaders of this party.

54. See Wolchik, "Ethnic Issues in Post-Communist Czechoslovakia," paper presented at the conference Nationality and Ethnicity in Eastern Europe, Center for European Studies, Harvard University, December 4–6, 1991.

55. "Ženy české proti zkáze . . . a pornografii," *Lidové noviny,* May 28, 1991, and

the sources cited in Alena Heitlinger, "Women's Roles in Contemporary Czechoslovakia" (manuscript), 1991, discuss some of these issues as they affect women.

56. See Bunce and Csanadi, "Systematic Analysis"; and Wolchik, "Women in Central and Eastern Europe."

57. See Martha Bohacevsky-Chomiak, "Ukranian Feminism in Interwar Poland," in Wolchik and Meyer, *Women, State, and Party,* pp. 82–97; Freeze, "Medical Education"; and Garver, "Women in the First Czechoslovak Republic," for discussions of this tendency in earlier historical periods.

58. Irena Ziková, at Conference on Women in Leadership in Eastern Europe, Hunter College, New York, June 1990.

59. See Heitlinger, "Women's Roles," and Wolchik, "Women's Issues," for discussions of this issue. See Jiřina Vrábková, "Young Women's Priorities and Visions for the Year 2000" (manuscript), for an activist's views on the subject.

60. Sharon Wolchik, "Gender Issues during Transition," in *East-Central European Economies in Transition.* Study Papers submitted to the Joint Economic Committee, Congress of the United States, November 1994 (Washington, DC: Government Printing Office, 1994; also available from M.E. Sharpe).

61. Interview with Dagmar Burešová and Eda Kriseová, March 1991, Prague.

62. See Wolchik, "Women and the Politics of Transition," for an earlier discussion of these factors in the region as a whole.

63. See Jaquette, *Women's Movement in Latin America;* and Alvarez, "Gender Politics."

64. See Navarová, "Co dal socialismus ženám?"

65. See, for example, the results of surveys reported in "Názory občanu na interrupci," *ÚVVM,* 1991.

66. Jaquette, *Women's Movement in Latin America.*

Hungary

8

The Political Woman?
Women in Politics in Hungary

Eva Fodor

Men are making their own history in Hungary. They have transformed the single-party system and become top party officials; they have privatized firms and bought their shares; they are passing laws by the hundreds in parliament, laying the foundations for a new type of society. My concern, however, is the masses of women who play supporting roles in these processes and the few who have been able to enter the new arena of public life.

A Woman's Work

For the past twenty years, Ilona, a 38–year-old semiskilled worker, has been working in the same workshop of the same factory on the outskirts of Budapest. Every day she gets up at four o'clock in the morning, prepares breakfast for her family, and catches the factory bus to work. At 5:45 she takes her place among twenty or so other women and sets to work packaging medicine. At two o'clock she catches the bus back home, goes hunting for bargains at the local food market, returns home, and starts her second shift. She makes some preserves, cleans the house, takes care of the animals, and tends the garden, goes through the bills in the mailbox, worries about the new sneakers her kids need for the soccer team, and starts dinner. She has two children in school who need help with their homework; her youngest son has to be picked up at the nursery school. Her husband returns from his second job or a chat with his friends about six, and she serves dinner. She does the washing up, gets the children organized, puts them to bed, and collapses. Occasionally she catches a glimpse of the news on television and sometimes the beginning of the feature film of the day, but she is usually asleep by nine.[1]

Ilona is a classic example of the "emancipated female laborer" of the state-socialist era. From the end of the 1940s masses of women without much education—women who had done piecework at home, farm women, homemakers—began to join the labor force as the pace of forced industrialization created a severe labor shortage, and the Communist Party concocted the ideals of the "double wage-earner family" and the "wage-earner woman." By the end of the 1980s about 80 percent of women of working age were active wage earners; only 3 percent of them worked part-time. Less than 7 percent remained at home as "dependents."[2]

The most prominent characteristic of blue-collar women such as Ilona, who at the end of the 1980s constituted about 58 percent of all economically active women,[3] is that they are severely lacking in skills. Approximately 75 percent of blue-collar women but only 41 percent of blue-collar men are unskilled or semiskilled. Thus only about 25 percent of these women are skilled workers, whereas nearly 60 percent of men have skills. This is one of the reasons why blue-collar women earn about 65 to 80 percent of men's wages (the exact wage differential depends also on such factors as the branch of industry, the number of hours worked at night, and so on).[4]

This gender gap in the qualifications and education of the wage-earning population applies only to vocational and—to a declining degree—postsecondary training. More women than men have finished primary school and have graduated from an academic high school; both institutions provide a general education but no skills. More men than women have received vocational training or have earned university degrees. The gender gap in primary and secondary schooling has hardly changed in the past few decades, so we see why Hungary has a vast pool of semiskilled and unskilled female laborers.[5] The gender disparity among the university educated has narrowed, however, and 1990 data reveal that the proportion of women with degrees in the 20–34 age bracket now exceeds that of men.[6] At the graduate level, however, the proportion of women is much lower: in 1981 only about 12 percent of all Hungarians who had a first-level graduate degree and a mere 6 percent of those who had higher degrees were women.[7]

Even if women choose to attend a vocational school there is only a handful of fields they are likely to consider—health services, nursery teaching, trade, office work, various jobs in the textile and clothing industries. More than 80 percent of the students in schools that provide training for these jobs are women. Segregation by gender is also prominent in higher education. Women constitute some 90 percent of all students in tertiary-level health-care training and all teaching occupations. This is the usual pattern observed in developed societies, but in Hungary women outnumber men in schools of medicine, dentistry, and law as well.[8] Although at first the Socialist Workers' (communist) Party campaigned against gender segregation and displayed numerous posters depicting women driving tractors and working in mines, these efforts had little positive influence in the long run. The feminization of some traditionally male-dominated occupations (medicine, law, education, printing) re-created gender segregation of a different sort and resulted in a drop in the wage and prestige levels of these professions.

The pool of white-collar workers consists mainly of women who have attended academic, rather than vocational, high schools. These schools qualify their graduates to apply to universities or vocational colleges, but hardly more than a third are accepted each year. The majority thus have to start work at low-level white-collar, mostly clerical jobs. Women, as we would expect, are more likely to stay in these "mommy-track" secretarial jobs than to move on to managerial-level positions. At the end of the 1980s about 13 percent of all white-collar women but 43 percent of all white-collar men worked in management positions. This record is an improvement over that of previous decades, but it reveals that women are disadvantaged when they aim for leadership positions. At the same time, there are hardly any men in the lowest category of clerical work, but almost a third of all white-collar women are there (see Table 8.1).[9]

The same picture seen from another perspective reveals further differences. In 1980 about 75 percent of all managers were men, only a fourth women. As we go higher in the hierarchy, the proportion of women declines further. In 1980 only 7 percent of all chief executive officers (CEOs) and other top executives were women. Interestingly, segregation can be observed here as well: women were likely to be heads of personnel and social welfare departments or institutions, jobs seen as more "appropriate" for women. The women CEOs were more likely to work for smaller companies and cooperatives. The proportion of women in institutions that the Communist Party considered of primary importance (that is, the biggest or strategically most important

Table 8.1

Percentage of Hungarian Men and Women in Blue-Collar and White-Collar Jobs, 1986–88

	Women	Men
Blue-collar jobs[a]		
Skilled	25	59
Semiskilled	51	30
Unskilled	24	11
All blue-collar jobs	100	100
White-collar jobs[b]		
Managerial	13	42
Mid-level, professional	58	54
Low-level, clerical	29	4
All white-collar jobs	100	100

Source: Nők a mai magyar tà rsadalomban [Women in present-day Hungarian society] (Budapest: KSH, 1989); *A nők helyzete a munkahelyen ès a csal àdban* [The situation of women in the workplace and in the family] (Budapest: KSH, 1988).

[a]1988.
[b]1986.

ones) was about 4 percent in 1980. Though reliable data for later periods are not readily available, by the beginning of the 1990s this proportion seems not to have changed significantly.[10]

On average, white-collar women earn about 66 percent of men's salaries. The gap varies, however, according to the level of the job in the hierarchy. Women in high-level management positions earn about 78 to 85 percent of men's earnings; the figure falls to 65 percent in low-level jobs.[11]

Work outside the house was not a matter of choice for women in Hungary; it was both a duty prescribed by the state's ideology and a necessity, because the family could not survive on a single income. Even part-time work was not ideologically acceptable or economically feasible. For this reason, "work for wages" had a very different meaning for East European women than for their middle-class West European contemporaries: it had none of the implications of liberation or independence; it was seen more as a new burden imposed by the communist system. This is not to say that some or most women (even some of those who had to enter the labor force for the first time in

1949 after twenty years or more as homemakers) did not actually come to enjoy their work and the company of other women in their workplaces. But work that one cannot leave does not have the same meaning as work that one has chosen and can choose to abandon.

At the same time, the household was still women's responsibility. Therefore, most women, from unskilled assembly-line workers to state secretaries, started a second shift at home after their official work day was over. Hungary became the country of "beautiful girls and exhausted women." Women spent about six hours a day on household work, three times more than men, and were exclusively responsible for such chores as cooking, dishwashing, and sewing.[12]

Since the mid-1960s Hungary has provided very generously for the parents of small children. The most important one of these provisions is the set of policies for child-care leave introduced in 1967, which allow mothers to stay at home for three years with their newborn babies and receive about 75 percent of their pay for the first year and a fixed amount thereafter. The law was amended in 1985 to cover fathers as well. The parent's job is guaranteed at the termination of the leave, and she or he cannot then be laid off for a specified period. By the end of the 1980s almost all women who had babies took advantage of these policies, so at any given time about 8 to 10 percent of all wage-earning women were not, in fact, in the labor force. As one might expect, few fathers availed themselves of the opportunity for child-care leave.

After a brief period in the 1950s when it was strictly prohibited, abortion was cheap and legal in Hungary. Although women who sought abortion had to consult formally with a committee, permission was very rarely denied. The number of abortions is high in Hungary in comparison with international statistics (and even with those of other countries where abortion is legal) largely because most Hungarians lack information on sexual matters, even though contraceptives (not the most modern ones, but effective) have been freely available and cheap since the mid-1960s.

Women in Politics Before 1989

Women in National Politics

At the beginning of the communist era women were not only expected to play an active role in the production of communist commodities and the reproduction of the communist personality, they were also required to take part in communist politics. For most people political participation meant passive attendance at meetings and demonstrations to support the party and an occasional course at a party school. About 10 percent of the population were members of the ruling Communist Party.

About 30 percent of party members were women, but membership, though it provided certain benefits, did not entail real political influence. In the prosperous late 1970s, under Janos Kadar, none of the secretaries of the Central Committee of the party were women. About 18 percent of the members of the Politburo and 8 to 13 percent of the Central Committee members were women; later this figure climbed to 17 percent.[13] By this time, when qualifications as well as political loyalty were important in the selection of top party executives, an unspecified (though certainly low) quota for women was in place. Though a few women were in fact installed in the central leadership, they never became part of the old boys' network, never were included in the hunting trips or the poker games where group loyalty was consolidated and information exchanged. No similar informal mechanism for exchange of information ever developed among the few women in top positions.[14]

Party leadership positions were closely connected to high posts in government, in the trade unions, and in parliament, which were the other possible arenas of public activity for women. In the last state-socialist government the secretaries of the department of Health Issues and Light Industry were women, and usually one or two women were allowed in the cabinet all through the period, responsible mainly for the strategically less important "feminine" sectors.

The quota system was very much in force for the nominations for parliamentary representatives, and as a result the proportion of women in parliament rose from about 3 percent in 1945 to over 30 percent in 1980.[15] As a sign of democratization in 1985 two candidates were nominated by the Communist Party and statistics demonstrated that women tended to lose when they ran against men. As a result, after the elections of 1985, the last held under the state-socialist system, women's representation dropped to 21 percent.

The pyramid system of women's participation in politics is best seen in the contest of the trade unions. By the end of the 1970s more than half (55 percent) of union leaders at the lowest level were women, but as the importance of the position grew, the number of female officeholders declined. At the top level another unwritten but strictly adhered-to rule specified that one (and only one) of the five secretaries of the National Council of Trade Unions had to be a woman, and she was to be responsible for health and social welfare issues.[16]

On Women's Organizations

In the first decade of the twentieth century feminism started to gain ground in Hungary. Books and journals were published,[17] and the role of women in public life was a widely debated issue in the cafés that turn-of-the-century intellectuals liked to frequent. Feminist organizations of many orientations, from radical suffragist groups that aimed to change women's role in society to more conservative Christian groups that concentrated mainly on charitable activities, were part of the urban intellectual and political scene. Such organizations appealed mainly to educated urban women, some of them wives of well-known politicians or wealthy aristocrats. Village women had an organizational tradition of a different sort: often in conjunction with church activities they gathered to exchange secrets, make pasta, sing folk songs, or teach each other to read and write.

Several of these organizations survived World War II, and although the left-wing political influence was strong, they managed to maintain a relatively nonpolitical character for a while, taking part in the reconstruction of the country, in the reunification of families, and in adult education. The Democratic Association of Hungarian Women (MNDSz), established in 1945, was at first a multiparty (though certainly left-oriented) umbrella organization that maintained links with several smaller groups in and outside the capital, with churches, and with the women's sections of various parties.[18] At the beginning many of its leaders and sympathizers were wives of the top officials of the leading parties; one was the president's wife. In the elections of 1947 the Christian Women's Party (with strong links to the Christian Democratic Party) won four seats in parliament. This colorful political scene soon disappeared as the left-wing parties' influence grew. In 1949 the Communist Party gained power and banned most civil associations, including religious and secular women's organizations. The MNDSz managed to survive by surrendering to the party and becoming the conveyor of its doctrines. By 1955, however, the communist leadership decided that women were now emancipated and thus needed no separate organization. The MNDSz was collapsed into the National Patriotic Front, a nonorganization supposedly representing the public interest.

The revolution of 1956 was not devoid of antifeminist tendencies; one of its slogans was "Enough of the rule of uneducated peasant women!" ("Elég a fejkendős Mariskák alispánságából!").[19] We will encounter this phenomenon again in the "revolution" of 1989, in a much more pervasive form.

After 1956 a new women's organization, the National Council of Hungarian Women, was established, which in various shapes and forms survived until 1989. The Communist Party claimed that this organization represented the interests of all Hungarian women, and developed a spectacular bureaucracy that was managed on the principle of "democratic centralism." In actual fact, the Council was little more than a (quite insignificant) party organ and, like other party organs, it had little knowledge about the genuine interests or opinions of its presumed constituency. Toward the end of the 1970s, like most other party organs, it was allowed some freedom of action as long as it stayed within more or less broadly defined limits. The Council developed a circle of experts who did extensive research on issues concerning women and of interest to the Communist Party (labor force statistics, the position of women in the political and occupational hierarchy, population policy, and so on). It could and did lobby for or against certain decisions affecting women, basing their arguments on their experts' opinions. Any effect they had depended less on the weight of the organization than on the reputations of the experts.[20] The leader of the Council was a member of the Central Committee, but the organization itself had limited influence and power within the party leadership, and to the general public it was little more than a joke.

The public was not aware of the expertise of some of the Council's members and saw none of the bargaining that went on behind closed doors, for example when the Economic Committee proposed in 1988 that women's participation in the labor force be reduced.[21] Ordinary citizens saw only the facade of the spectacular Budapest villa the Council and its numerous employees occupied and heard the public speeches loudly proclaiming the current party line and expressing no concern for the women they purportedly represented.

Efforts were made to organize grassroots women's sections in the National Trade Union. The idea was accepted in principle, but the male majority in the central leadership effectively prevented all practical action that would have involved the sharing of power and resources.[22]

In sum, the official women's movement and the women's sections of the trade unions with their thousands of members were quasi organizations in the grip of a handful of experts and party officials who were fighting their own (often worthy) battles without looking for any real mass support, in fact consciously suppressing grassroots organizations. Public support might have threatened their positions as experts and could have turned the party hard-liners, with their fear of mass movements, against them. Deprived of space for political action, the women's civil organizations that had boomed before and even after World War II died a painful death and were not replaced until the beginning of the 1990s, when only vague memories of women's political activism remained.

The Communist Party and Its Policies Concerning Women

The main tenets of Engelsian-communist ideology held that women's participation in the labor force would automatically bring about their emancipation; that is, their equal status at the workplace and elsewhere. It posited the lack of women's uninterrupted and general inclusion in the labor force as the cause of women's subordination in other areas of life. Thus, when it came to improving the lot of women, the party leadership and the National Council of Hungarian Women concentrated most of their efforts on raising the participation rates of women in the labor force and in education, on bettering their position in the occupational hierarchy, and on improving their political training. This effort is obvious in all their documents, where the issue of the quantity and quality of women's labor force participation is always the first problem to be discussed and all others are subordinated to it. The Central Committee's key document on policies in regard to women, "On the Political, Economic, and Social Conditions of Women," prepared in 1970, devotes thirteen pages to issues concerning the "wage-earner" women, emphasizing the need for full equality at the workplace and decrying the prejudice that hinders women's participation in politics and in leadership. In three pages at the end of the document it touches lightly on women in the family.[23] This pattern is observable in all the documents concerning women produced by the Council and by the party over the forty years of their existence. It shows up in the speeches of party officials at the opening ceremonies of the Council's congresses, and in the daily press. We are thus led to conclude that the emancipation project was restricted to the workplace and that it involved other areas of life only to the extent that they contributed to or hindered women's participation in the labor force. (Whether the Communist Party genuinely wished the emancipation of women at the workplace is another matter; we have seen its record.)

But the daily need to "reproduce the labor power" of wage earners and the upbringing of the next generation remained tasks that could not be disregarded. It was obvious that women's traditional role in the household was an obstacle to their participation in the labor force. So the communist leadership resolved to "socialize" all household duties: it would provide day-care centers for children, cheap canteens and frozen or precooked dinners for families, apartments with modern household appliances, cheap laundry services. Note that this revolutionary idea was never intended to transform the responsibilities of men in the household. The word "husband" is conspicuous by its absence from the few pages on households in the 1970 document. The responsibilities of the wage-earning woman's husband are taken over by the all-powerful state as provider of all necessary services.

By the beginning of the 1970s it had become obvious that the socialization of household chores was a far too expensive way of solving the problem of reproduction. At the same time the pace of industrialization changed from extensive to intensive, so a constantly expanding labor force was no longer required. An additional problem surfaced: a decline in the birthrate created a negative rate of reproduction and evoked age-old worries that Hungarians were about to disappear from the face of the earth.

Thus, around the time when the American and Western European feminist movements were gathering strength, stimulating the movement of women into the labor force, Hungary introduced child-care leave so that women could resume their traditional roles as full-time mothers and homemakers for a few years after their children were born. This move also represented a subtle means for the state to intervene in the private sphere, in the lives of the families.

Child-care leave and the other family-oriented policies that were introduced, such as leave to care for a sick child, were immensely popular, not only because they eased the burdens of young mothers, but also because traditional beliefs did not die out in the first few decades of state socialism; people viewed these measures as a return to the natural state of affairs. There is no conclusive evidence to show the effect of the child-care years on women's careers, but it seems likely that they made employers cautious about hiring, training, and promoting young women: they assumed that they would leave within a couple of years to have babies. The child-care policies did nothing to halt the fall of the birthrate in the long run, but they did reinforce the traditional reproductive role of women. They also created a massive "reserve army of labor" (the 10 percent of all women of working age who are on child-care leave at any given time), whose significance women who intend to return to work nowadays are beginning to understand.

The introduction of child-care policies did not mean that the original idea of emancipation was abandoned. But the fact that those policies were substituted for the socialization of household chores, for the creation of the infrastructure to support a two-earner household, meant that for women with older children the party buzzword "emancipation" evoked images of the double burden: they were left alone to juggle work and daily family responsibilities, their only help was low-quality services that were hard to acquire and increasingly high priced.

Changes Since the Transition

Are women the losers in the transition? This question is often asked by social scientists (usually outside the countries undergoing the transition). Let us see.

Guaranteed full-time employment disappeared with the fall of the state-socialist economic system. With the closing or privatization of state-owned firms and factories, a large number of workers are being laid off, and hardly any new jobs are being created. Women have always been at a disadvantage when the economy collapses, in Western European countries as well as in the former state-socialist societies, because of their lower level of "human capital," their household responsibilities, and the traditional views on gender roles. Hungary is an exception to this often-observed rule. Although unemployment is strikingly high and has been increasing since 1989, women are less likely to be unemployed than men. In the summer of 1992 women accounted for 41 percent of the unemployed and 48 percent of all active wage earners. The unemployment rate was 7.7 percent for women, 10.5 percent for men. Close examination reveals that this difference is due mainly to the fact that unskilled women are underrepresented among the unemployed population. Strong gender segregation by industry may have been advantageous for women in this situation: closings and privatization were more prevalent in the heavy industries, where women are less likely to be employed.[24]

Aggregate statistics, however, may be showing only one side of the coin: scattered evidence (interviews with employment office workers, help-wanted ads in the daily papers) suggests that young women with children are disadvantaged when they look for work because private companies require flexible schedules and full commitment to the job, and they provide no special social benefits for women. According to current estimates, about 10 percent of the people receiving unemployment benefits are actually working illegally, and men may be over-represented among this population.

Unemployment may be less of a threat to women at the moment, but the cutbacks in the financing of social services certainly increase women's burdens. Poverty has grown rapidly since 1989. Families that used to be able to eat out occasionally, go away for a few weeks' vacation each year, use frozen or canned food, buy clothing in department stores, and use laundry services find themselves struggling to pay for the basic necessities. Women make up for the missing forints by preparing all meals at home, canning, preserving, darning socks, turning shirt collars, doing the laundry (while their husbands may be working at their second or third jobs). The new welfare policies are far from adequate to make up for the disadvantages created, and since women remain responsible for the children and the household, these measures have a more distressing and direct effect on them than on men.

The new employment and social security legislation passed by parliament also brought changes that potentially disadvantage women. The major concern and still a matter of debate is the action to raise the retirement age for women. During the state-socialist era women retired at 55, five years earlier than men. A large number of companies are in financial difficulties and are seeking relief from contributions to the social security fund, which has been significantly depleted. Since women live longer than men on average, they receive pensions for a longer period, which the social security fund, it is claimed, cannot afford to pay. Women's organizations maintain that most of the cost of the transition is being borne by older women, who cannot retire because of the country's economic difficulties.

Another employment-related issue is the fact that the job of a woman who returns to work after child-care leave is protected for only thirty days, which in essence means that young mothers are not likely to get their jobs back. At the same time, more and more women are forced to take child-care leave whether they want to or not because about 30 percent of nursery schools (for children under 3) have closed up for lack of community and company financing. Closings are predicted to proliferate, and soon kindergartens (for children between 3 and 6) are expected to have the same fate. A suggested alternative is extension of the child-care leave for three more years. If this proposal were adopted, it would amount to indirect exclusion from the work force of all but the declining number of mothers who could find jobs and afford to pay for private child care.

A proposal for a law against sexual harassment, inspired by Anita Hill's testimony before the U.S. Senate when it held hearings to determine the fitness of Clarence Thomas for a seat on the Supreme Court, was introduced by the Alliance of Free Democrats (SzDSz), a liberal opposition party, to an uncomprehending parliament. A small survey, however, shows that men and women alike find sexual harassment an important and painful issue, and interestingly men find it more of a problem than women. Thirty-five percent of women but 48 percent of men thought the new employment regulations should include penalties for such behavior, though only about one-fifth of all respondents claimed that sexual harassment was a problem at their own workplaces.[25] Apparently the members of the Hungarian parliament were among the other four-fifths of the population, for they refused even to discuss the matter.

Liberal reproductive rights were among the envied achievements of Hungarian women. Unfortunately, women tended to use abortion as a method of contraception, and the incidence of abortion skyrocketed. The abortion issue has been widely debated, and a new law was passed by parliament at the end of 1992 that allows abortion for women in a "crisis" situation, defined loosely as one in which the birth of a child "would cause the woman and/or the baby major economic or psychological strife." In essence, abortion remains the choice of the woman concerned. In the course of the debate, however, the discourse surrounding the abortion issue underwent a metamorphosis from liberal humanitarianism to religious dogmatism of the kind that has become familiar in the United States. The language of "reproductive rights" became submerged in talk of "protecting the life of the unborn child."

The parliament is also slated to debate legislation on sex education. The first effort to pass a law mandating sex education in the schools was initiated by the liberal opposition party, SzDSz, in the spring of 1992.[26] At that point the parliament refused to discuss it, but the ruling party has taken up the case and is planning to propose similar legislation of its own.

Marital rape is not covered by Hungarian law. When SzDSz undertook to introduce and define the concept of domestic violence and marital rape, it met with astonished incomprehension. One male representative reportedly asked why anyone would marry if marriage did not bring a man's full power over his wife's sexuality.

Who Are Women's Representatives?

Women in the National and Local Governments

At both the national and the local levels very few women are in powerful decision-making posts in Hungary. In 1992, for example, two of the thirty-three deputy ministerial positions were filled by women. No woman was head of a ministry. Similarly to the communist era, job segregation is observable even at this level: women are likely to work in fields of welfare, health, or education. The first postcommunist local elections were held in Hungary in the fall of 1990.

In 1985 the proportion of women among the members of local councils was 27 percent; after the election of 1990 that figure dropped to 16 percent. Contrary to expectations, smaller communities were more likely to elect women to local government posts than the supposedly less traditional cities. Women head local governments in about 10 percent of smaller communities, about 3.5 percent of cities (the comparable figure was only slightly higher in 1985—15 and 8 percent, respectively).[27] The percentage of women elected was the same as the percentage of women who ran, so in the local elections women did not suffer the disadvantage that reduced their representation in parliament.

Women in the Parties

In 1990 six parties won seats in parliament. Three of them—the Hungarian Democratic Forum, the Christian Democratic Party, and the Smallholders' Party, all conservative, Christian, and nationalist— formed a coalition and established the first government since the communist regime dissolved. The opposition consists of two liberal

Table 8.2

Distribution of Participation and Party Choice by Gender in 1990 and 1994, Hungary

	1990			1994		
	Men	Women	Total	Men	Women	Total
Voted	78.6	77.1	77.8	78.0	77.4	77.7
N	411	475	886	595	694	1,289
Democratic Forum	40.2	34.9	37.3	10.0	11.5	10.8
Free Democrats	24.1	26.9	25.6	25.6	25.8	25.7
Smallholders	15.8	6.4	10.6	11.4	5.9	8.5
Socialist	7.5	9.5	8.6	43.5	42.5	43.0
Young Democrats	7.1	12.2	9.9	5.7	4.6	5.1
Christian Democrats	5.3	10.1	7.9	3.7	9.8	7.0
N	266	327	593	402	461	863

Source: International Social Survey Project 1990, 1994.

parties—the Alliance of Free Democrats and the Alliance of Young Democrats—and the Hungarian Socialist Party, which was formed on the ruins of the reform wing of the old Communist Party.

Four years later, politics moved unexpectedly to the left: the Hungarian Socialist Party won the majority of the seats in parliament and formed a governing coalition with the Alliance of Free Democrats. What was women's role in electing these parties into power?

According to election data from the survey "Social Stratification in Eastern Europe after 1989" (conducted by Ivan Szelenyi and Donald J. Treiman in 1993), there was practically no gender difference in election participation in either years (see Table 8.2). Women and men appear to have cast their ballots in similar numbers. But there are some differences in party choice: in both years, women favored the Christian Democratic Party, while men were more likely to vote for the Smallholders'. While none of the parties addressed women's issues in any depth, the Christian Democrats' program emphasized the welfare safety net as well as the role of families, which may have appealed particularly to women in times of general instability. The party program and campaign strategy of the Smallholders' Party targeted men in rural areas especially, thus their success in this demographic group is not surprising.

An issue of great concern to many female politicians was the significant drop in the representation of women in parliament under the multiparty system. After the first election, where only 9 percent of all candidates were women, only twenty-eight women won seats, a mere 7.3 percent of representatives. This rate climbed up to 13 percent by the second election with the victory of the Hungarian Socialist Party, but it is still far from women's representation in earlier, perhaps less powerful, legislatures. Most of the women MPs gained seats through national and regional party lists, rather than through direct election. It seems that the electorate did not trust women to represent their interests. In fact, a survey asking people qualities they were looking for in candidates in 1990 showed that "male" was third on the list, preceding "college educated" and "locally born."[28]

In 1992 I conducted extensive interviews with eight of the twenty-six women representatives in parliament as well as with the leaders of all large women's organizations and collected data from party offices reviewing women's participation (Table 8.3). On the basis of this information I distinguish three viewpoints on women's role in society, which emerged after the collapse of the postcommunist regime: the Christian nationalist stand, taken principally by the three parties that formed the coalition government in 1990, the liberal views of the Alliance of Young Democrats (FIDESz) and the Alliance of Free Democrats (SzDSz), and the moderate (by no means radical) socialist ideas of the Hungarian Socialist Party (MSzP). The information below represents the situation soon after the collapse of the communist regime, thus it depicts a gender regime in the process of change.

At first glance it is striking that almost half of all members of the Christian Democratic Party are women. It is even more striking that there are no women among its delegates in parliament (there was one, but she defected to another party). The Christian Democrats do have one token woman in the admittedly powerful position of party vice-president. A strong-minded, tactful politician, she is also the leader and founder of the women's section of the party. The women's section claims to have an impressive membership of 8,000, mainly in the countryside.

The Hungarian Democratic Forum, the party with the most seats in parliament and thus the leader of the coalition, has a smaller percentage of women members than any other party and a correspondingly small percentage in its leadership. Its women's section, perhaps the most conservative and rightist of all women's organizations in Hung-

Table 8.3

Number and Percentage of Women in the Six Parliamentary Parties, in Their Top Executive Bodies, and in Their Women's Sections, Summer 1992

Party	Members		Members of Parliament			Members of executive body			Women's section	
	Total	Women(%)	Total	N	%	Total	N	%	Number of members	Date founded
Alliance of Young Democrats (FIDESz)	13,218	40.4	23	2	8.7	13	1	7.7	0	—
Alliance of Free Democrats (SzDSz)	33–34,000	25.5[a]	88	9	10.2	11	2[b]	18.2	0[c]	—
Hungarian Socialist Party (MSzP)	40,000	34.4[d]	33	3	9.1	13	2	15.4	1,000	February 1992
Hungarian Democratic Forum (MDF)	27,438	24.9	166	5	3.0	21	1	4.8	"Few hundred"	Summer 1988
Christian Democratic Party (KDNP)	19,310	4.7	21	0	0.0	7	1	14.3	8,000	February 1991
Smallholders' Party (FKGP)[e]	60–70,000	±33.0	45	4	8.9	12	0	0.0	1,500–2,000	June 1990

Source: Data collected by the author from the parties and their women's organizations. Since these figures were supplied by the organizations, they may be biased.

Notes: Of 18 independent MPs, 3 were women.

[a] Estimate based on a sample of 33% of the membership.

[b] Only one of the two women leaders has been taking part in the monthly organizational meetings in the previous three months. Among the 91 members of the SzDSz's National Council, the executive body below the top leadership, there were four women (4.4 percent).

[c] A few SzDSz women have formed the Foundation of the Women of Hungary (MONA) in an effort to influence policy; it is not intended to be a mass organization.

[d] Estimate based on a sample of 85 percent of the membership.

[e] The FKGP has split into factions, each claiming to be the only legitimate party. The figures pertain to one faction only, and should be viewed with caution in any case.

ary, was in the process of being organized in the summer of 1992 and claimed a "few hundred" members.

The third party in the coalition, the Smallholders' Party, was in turmoil in mid-1992. In any event, its largely rural members hold traditional views. In the years just after World War II, however, it had a strong women's organization, and the party now hopes to revitalize it.

These parties represent a conservative, primarily Christian, but not necessarily dogmatic view of women's role in society. They, like almost everyone else concerned with women's issues, emphasize the need for women to be able to choose whether to work outside the home or as homemakers. At the same time, there is no doubt about which choice they think women should take. They consider it a woman's responsibility to provide her family with physical and emotional nourishment. They see the family (defined in its most conservative sense) as the most important cell of society, the place where moral reintegration after the decadent and ruinous decades of communism can and must begin. Women are seen as bearing the final responsibility for this noble task and should be given financial and moral support in this role. They propose the institution of the family wage and the extension of child-care leave to the child's sixth birthday, together with other policies aimed at allowing women to stay out of the labor force. As nationalists, they are concerned about the falling birthrate; as traditional Catholics, they deplore the large number of abortions performed. Although only a small minority demand an absolute ban on abortion in all circumstances, in general they see abortion as murder, and demand the legal protection of the embryo from the moment of conception. The more liberal wing argues that abortion should be available as a last resort in a grave crisis. Even these people, however, view the "last resort" not as a matter of women's reproductive rights but as a remnant of the lax ethics of the communist era that will disappear when the moral consciousness of the nation is finally awakened.

They also agree that women who are no longer bearing and raising children can be active in the public sphere "in their own feminine ways," engaging principally in charitable activities but some serving as politicians or holding challenging full-time jobs. In fact, the Christian Democrats and the Smallholders intend to make an active search for talented women and train them to run for parliament in the next elections. This is not a high priority, however; meanwhile they are not concerned about women's worsening situation in the job market and in the workplace. They want the state to interfere on behalf of women only to promote women's role as bearers and educators of children, the future of the nation.

All three parties in the coalition now have women's sections, and in fact these are the most successful of all women's organizations at mobilizing grassroots support. Their members, mostly rural women, engage in charitable activities, create information networks, hold classes on such subjects as efficient household management, and organize family entertainment. Ironically, the most widely supported women's organizations emphasize that these gatherings are not exclusively for women but for families.

The women's sections of these three parties have joined with a few nonpartisan organizations of similar political orientations to form the Hungarian Women's Union. They have forged links with the European Women's Union, a similarly conservative offshoot of Christian democratic centrist parties in Western Europe, and hope to gain membership in it. Meanwhile, the Union provides political education programs and attempts to arouse concern about issues neglected during the state-socialist years. It also serves to validate the existence of the parties' women's sections, which the male members tend to see as of no particular importance or even as unnecessary.

On the other side of the fence are the two liberal parties. The Alliance of Young Democrats (FIDESz) has a relatively large number of young women among its members but few among its leaders. In fact, this party openly refuses to make any special arrangements for women—no organization, no affirmative action program, no training program, nothing. True to its classical liberal ideology, it claims that affirmative action for women or any kind of targeted support would reintroduce the paternalism practiced so inefficiently by the socialist state before 1989. Their two women leaders, both independent, strong women, seem to believe that women should be let alone to fight their own battles, and the fit will eventually survive.

At the same time, freedom of speech is one of the Alliance's liberal tenets, so members are willing to provide a forum for feminist ideas, even though they do not endorse them. So far they do not see the vague association with feminism (as one of many "alternative ideologies") as damaging the party image.

The other liberal party, the Alliance of Free Democrats, has the only woman representative in parliament who is willing to devote her energies to women's issues, and her efforts meet with mild support but not much interest within her party. The issues the Free Democrats have tackled in this area are scattered and largely peripheral, but new to the political discourse: they introduced the subject of sex education, sexual harassment, and domestic violence. They are reluctant to integrate a feminist point of view in their general politics, however, and they do not seem to view the important social issues of the day as structured by gender inequalities. This is not quite surprising: though they have a larger proportion of women on their top executive committee than any other party, if we examine the national-level leadership, which consists of ninety-one people, we find only four women (a mere 4.4 percent) among them. Naturally, this should be viewed merely as an indicator rather than a cause of the failure of women's point of view to be represented very effectively in their policy decisions or in the party's long- or short-term strategy.

Signs of a slow change may be visible, though. In 1992 a handful of women in the SzDSz organized themselves as the Foundation of the Women of Hungary (MONA), with the aim of examining the position of women in all areas of life and of evaluating and participating in the formation of policy decisions concerning women directly or indirectly.[29]

Thus the liberals, though they are sympathetic to feminist views on relatively peripheral issues, are not genuinely interested in women's economic and social situation, since they do not consider it necessarily different from that of men. In this spirit, they support legal abortion, and they phrase their views in terms of women's reproductive rights; but they refrain from direct intervention on women's behalf in the labor market because such action evokes memories of state-socialist propaganda and practice, which they want to avoid. More important, affirmative action for women workers would run counter to their free-market policies, if not their sympathies.

The Free Democrats have no grassroots organization for women, nor are they making a serious effort to create one. In their mostly urban, intellectual circles they see women as individuals with perhaps slightly different roles and characteristics but with the same chances for a high-quality life as men.

The Socialists represent a third view of women. They too recognize women's roles in both the workplace and the family, but they place greater emphasis on the need to guarantee women's equality in the workplace. Therefore, they demand the state financing of institutions that would allow women to perform both roles if they wish or must. Interestingly, these institutions that would help relieve women of their family burdens are once again seen as the sole responsibility of the state or of the employer; in no way is the husband's passive role in the household threatened. The mostly male leadership would hardly be willing to endorse the demand that husbands should consider taking child-care leave or getting dinner on the table, nor does it occur to the female representatives to suggest that they should—for the reasons we have seen. Though the Socialists are careful to dissociate themselves from their communist predecessor, the Hungarian Socialist Workers' Party, they are the only party that acknowledges that the "emancipation" of women in the communist era produced some advantages. Its women's section and the party itself have some highly qualified women leaders, who gained political experience and a great deal of information on women's issues and on organizational tactics in the past era. Like the women in the liberal parties, they are urban, college-educated women, but they are less likely to be intellectuals (professors, teachers, artists) and more likely to have had actual hands-on experience in factories or agricultural cooperatives as professionals, engineers, or applied economists. They understand the importance of appealing to female voters and therefore try to reach out of the circle of intellectuals to women working in factories and in low-level white-collar jobs. The women's section they organized deals with issues of health, the environment, motherhood, sex education, and abortion rights from a nonradical liberal perspective, but its primary concern is equal rights in the workplace. It is designed to encourage women of all ages and qualifications with socialist sympathies to participate in meetings and lobby local and national leaders—their preferred means of political influence. They support the liberal abortion policies of the pretransition period and urge the renegotiation of the postponement of the retirement age. They also wish to call upon women's trade union organizations to negotiate the lifting of the restrictions on child-care leave imposed by the new employment laws. Their chances of succeeding improve as the economic situation worsens and as time obscures the associations with their communist predecessors.

Women's Organizations Outside the Party Structure

There are two major independent women's groups in Hungary. The largest, the left-oriented Association of Hungarian Women, has ties to the Socialist Party but attempts to remain politically neutral. As the earliest women's organization to be formed—it arose in June 1989 from the ruins of the Communist Party's women's organization, and took over the international relations of the old organization as well as part of its premises and finances—it offered help to all women who were candidates for office. All but one declined, because the organization was quite unjustly associated with the misuse of women's politics by the old National Council of Hungarian Women. At the moment this is by far the best-organized group and has the most resources and an open and well-trained staff. It gathers information on women's issues, organizes meetings for women, shares its premises with other women's groups that need a place to meet, and lobbies representatives on issues the members feel need attention. Their primary aim is to create a party-neutral council that advises the parliament on issues they deem to be of specific concern to women, in the manner of similar groups in such Western European democracies as France. In the summer of 1991 they attempted to join forces with other women's organizations and form a women's committee in the Council of Social Affairs (Szociális Tanács), which already had committees representing the interests of the young, the retired, and other social groups. In response to their overtures, the minister of social welfare denied the need for a special committee on women, thus effectively cutting them off from the resources and the political voice the Council afforded the other committees. Like other civil associations, however, the Association of Hungarian Women does get some funding from the state.

Though the organization is badly understaffed and has very few active members, they manage to keep an eye on and respond to most issues concerning women. They also inherited and were able to retain the wide circle of international contacts of the communist era's women's organization. They are the representatives of Hungary in the UN Commission on the Status of Women (a right questioned by other organizations) and were the first of all East European women's movements to be admitted to the International Council of Women. Through visits and correspondence they exchange information with women of other countries. One of these visits sparked the idea of collecting and cataloguing all the documents the Association inherited from the old organization, as well as materials assembled from elsewhere. This effort demonstrates that even though the Association can claim about 10,000 members in forty-two member organizations, it is not really equipped or trained to do grassroots organizing; its principal area of expertise and its primary interest lie in the collection and dissemination of information.

The Feminist Network is the only women's organization that openly admits to being feminist—though it has as many ways of understanding the word as it has members. This is a small group of about thirty women of all ages and levels of education, and no two seem to agree on what constitutes a feminist discourse. They have disproportionate press coverage, since they are a real curiosity in the Hungarian stronghold of patriarchy. Unfortunately, in the summer of 1992 they were not yet quite prepared to formulate arguments that could hold the ground against experienced politicians. Although they may carry the seeds of real change, of issues and ideas to be discussed in the future, they find it hard to adapt the solutions offered by Western European and American feminists to the specific situation of Hungary, even with the financial and educational help of various feminist groups and individuals in the United States and the United Kingdom. Foreign feminist groups give a limited amount of financial aid to buy photocopying machines and computers, and they provide opportunities for formal and informal exchanges of information and for participation at conferences and East-West meetings.

Strictly church-related women's groups are of little significance in Hungary, but the trade unions have women's groups, pretty much on the old communist patterns. The role of these trade union organizations could be extremely important inasmuch as they are directly in touch with women workers and could communicate problems on the shop floor to the higher political circles. The trade unions, however, are disorganized and therefore out of touch with their membership, and at a time of steeply rising unemployment they are in a very poor position to bargain with the government. Thus even though the leaders of the women's section of the Association of Hungarian Trade Unions (MSzOSz), for example, have expert understanding of women's situation, the union itself has no credibility among the workers because of its association with the communist trade unions, its misuse of union funds, and its lack of success (and of experience) at negotiating with the factory leadership.[30]

Conclusions

Ilona, the factory woman we met at the beginning of this chapter, knows nothing about any of these organizations. She watches segments of the evening news as she serves dinner or washes the dishes, but these organizations do not appear in the national media. Of course she has her own political opinions: she realizes that her situation is less secure than it used to be and sees that it is a lot harder to make ends meet at the end of the month. None of the women's organizations, however, have the reach to be able to offer her help or even inform her, make her aware of the problems she may be facing.

Lack of grassroots organization and mass support is the greatest problem facing women's organizations at the moment. Civil associations were banned for a long time, and women's organizations suffer the particular disadvantage of association with the hypocrisy of the official women's movement of the past. It seems that the organizations most successful at recruiting members are the religion-based, nationalist, rural ones. What accounts for their appeal?

I believe that part of the explanation lies in the fact that the Christian-nationalist organizations are capable of offering a discourse on women's place in society that differs in all respects from that of the previous era. This discourse places women back in their primary communities, in the family and the village or small town. It views women primarily as members of families, as belonging to some identifiable group that provides security in times of crisis—something highly valued by women. It also emphasizes the national community of Hungarians, a concept of nation based on race and a shared language and culture—a community that is broader than the immediate ones, but still a source of moral strength and support. Neither the communist nor the liberal discourse can do as much. The communists of the past and the socialists of the present view women primarily as wage earners, as workers, and their discourse consciously deemphasizes the family in order to avoid discussion of the power relations within it. Unions and workers' councils cannot conjure up an image of an immediate community. The liberals tend to view women as individuals, not necessarily tied to anyone, independent, surviving on their own. Neither the liberals nor the socialists emphasize the concept of the nation; instead, their discourse focuses on foreign relations, cosmopolitan ideas, internationalism. I believe that the return to the discourse of immediate communities is of primary importance in the recruitment of women, partly because of the social chaos women need to cope with and also because of the values they have been traditionally taught, values that have not changed much in the forty years of communist rule.

All women leaders[31] shuddered at the thought of and bluntly refused any association with "radical feminism" in the Western sense of the term. But I hope I have made it clear that because of women's specific historical situation, the specific meanings they attach to such key words as "work," "liberation," and even "women's movement," their reactions to the challenges presented by the social changes they face may lead in political directions very different from the ones currently in vogue in the West. What exactly this development may mean for women in Eastern Europe is to be decided in the future, but it certainly may provide an opportunity for Western feminists to rethink the meanings of "conservative" and "reactionary" when they examine them in a very different social context.

Notes

I thank all the women who granted me interviews, their time, and the ideas they shared with me. I especially thank Ibolya Ujvari of the Association of Hungarian Women for her dedication to the interests of Hungarian women, the vast amount of information she provided me, and the great amount of time and energy she spent helping me with my work.

1. I conducted a brief participant observation study in a Hungarian factory among female semiskilled workers in the summer of 1992. Ilona is one of those women; only her name is changed.

2. *Statisztikai Évkönyv* [Statistical yearbook] (Budapest: KSH, 1990).

3. Mária Frey, "A nők helyzete és a munkanélküliség" [The situation of women and unemployment]. Manuscript, 1992.

4. *Nők a mai magyar társadalomban.* [Women in Hungarian society] (Budapest: KSH, 1980).

5. Census data collected by the Association of Hungarian Women, 1991.

6. Ildiko Hrubos, "Women's Chances in Intellectual Occupations." Manuscript, 1992.

7. *A nők helyzetének alakulása a KSH adatainak tükrében 1970–1981 között* [The changing situation of women according to Central Statistical Office data 1970–1981], (Budapest: Szakszervezetek Elméleti Kutató Intézete, 1982).

8. *Nők a mai magyar társadalomban.*

9. *A nők helyzete a munkahelyen és a családban* [The situation of women in the workplace and in the family] (Budapest: KSH, 1988).

10. István Koncz, *Nők a vezetésben* [Women in leadership positions] (Budapest: MNOT, 1984).

11. *Nők a mai magyar társadalomban.*

12. Rudolf Andorka, Béla Falussy, and István Harcsa, "Időfelhasználás és életmód" [Time budget and lifestyle], in *Társadalmi riport* [Report on the society], ed. Andorka et al. (Budapest: TARKI, 1990). Note that this does not mean

that men have three times more leisure time than women; men spend more time on second jobs and other additional wage-earning activities.

13. Katalin Koncz, "Nők a politika szinpadán" [Women in politics], *Aula*, no. 4 (1990); and *Statisztikai adatok a nők helyzetéröl* [Statistical data on the position of women] (Budapest: KSH, 1975).

14. Interviews with women in top-level leadership positions during the previous regime, conducted in the summer of 1992.

15. "Nők a választásokon" [Women in elections], in *Pártpanoptikum, 1848–1990* [An overview of parties, 1848–1990], ed. Károly Jónás (Budapest: Interakt, 1990).

16. Interviews with two former women secretaries of the National Council of Trade Unions, autumn 1992.

17. The magazines *Nőmunkás, A Nő,* and *A nő és a társadalom* were all published between 1905 and 1914 in Budapest.

18. Interviews with top executives of the MNDSz and its successor, the National Council of Hungarian Women.

19. Ibid.

20. Ibid. and interviews with female politicians in top party positions at the time.

21. Interviews with current leaders of the Association of Hungarian Women and a review of Council documents, such as those the Council prepared in 1988 in response to the initiative of the Economic Committee titled "On the Reduction of Women's Labor Force Participation."

22. Interviews with top trade union leaders.

23. *Nőpolitikai dokumentumok, 1970–1980* [Documents describing policies concerning women, 1970–1980] (Budapest: Kossuth, 1980).

24. Mária Frey, *Nők és a munkanélküliség* [Women and unemployment] (Budapest: Kossuth, 1992).

25. "A Survey on Sexual Harassment," prepared by Median for SzDSz. Manuscript, 1992.

26. Interview with party representatives, summer 1992.

27. *Két választás Magyarországon 1990–ben* [The two elections in Hungary in 1990] (Budapest: KSH, 1991).

28. Ágnes Bokor, 1990. "A közvélemény a rendszerváltozás folyamatában" [Public opinion in the transition period], in Andorka et al., *Társadalmi riport.*

29. This is not the only effort to create an organization of this sort in Hungary at the moment, but MONA seems to have the best infrastructural and informational resources, since it is backed by a major party. In 1997, an eight-member government commission was established to guarantee equal opportunities for women. According to Katalin Medvedev, efforts to fight poverty among women, improve their health care and social welfare benefits, and to address issues of violence against women were supported by only $160,000 in the 1997 national budget. (*Transition*, vol. 9, no. 1, Feb. 1998, p. 26).

30. Interviews with leaders of the women's sections of three major trade union associations (MSzOSz, LIGA, and the Vasas), autumn 1992.

31. With the exception of the Feminist Network, of course.

Romania

9

From Tradition and Ideology to Elections and Competition

The Changing Status of Women in Romanian Politics

Mary Ellen Fischer

Romanian politics and society have undergone profound change since the collapse of the Ceauşescu regime in December 1989. The communist institutions and ideology that dominated the country for four decades have lost their power and legitimacy, and different structures and beliefs have begun to emerge. Nostalgia for precommunist traditions and values immediately surfaced and mingled with the assumptions and principles of communist rule that had been imposed during four decades. The new institutions and policies now emerging in Romania thus derive in part from the country's precommunist past, in part from the socialization processes of the communist era, and in part from expectations about democracy and market economies prevalent in Romania and in Western democracies at the end of the twentieth century. In this complex new world Romanian women and men have begun to reshape some basic assumptions about work, family, and their own personal roles and priorities. Nowhere are the contrasts and continuities in traditional, communist, and postcommunist beliefs more apparent than on issues relating to gender roles and the status of women.

Romanian Traditions

Romanian society before World War II was characterized by deep social divisions between urban and rural populations, among ethnic groups, and between those with education or property and those without.[1] The overwhelming majority of Romanians were Orthodox peasants, and the implications of such a society for women included a patriarchal extended family structure, a clear division of labor in which all members of the household contributed to economic survival, and there were strictly defined gender roles and suppression of women's sexuality. This patriarchal and hierarchical order subordinated a woman to her mother-in-law as well as to her husband. Rituals reinforced the hierarchy; Gail Kligman describes the wedding, for example, as "a subtle act of incorporation into a subordinate position."[2] Men's domination and women's submissiveness were seen as human and social norms rooted in a natural and religious order beyond human judgment.

The clear division of responsibilities according to gender required distinctive patterns of behavior. Men had to be tough, rational, and intellectually superior, whereas women could be emotional, sensitive, and compassionate. Men's sexuality was glorified, but women's sexuality was a sign of evil, danger, and moral decay. Although the man was the head of the family, the woman was responsible for the smooth functioning of the home and thus had an important source of power and a claim to participate in decisions. She also developed informal strategies to balance the formal male authority. Peasants brought these strict gender roles and the patriarchal system of values and norms with them when they moved from the countryside to the factory towns to form the nucleus of the working class.

These traditions, however, were not uniform throughout society. Aristocratic and upper-class women were part of a small but sophisticated and Westernized elite that rejected significant aspects of peasant culture. In this very different environment a woman's intellectual skills as hostess and conversationalist, her artistic abilities, and her physical attractiveness were important attributes to herself and her family; thus her sexuality was purged of its negative connotations. Such upper-class women were responsible for the home but were freed from daily toil by domestic servants. A number of women at the highest levels of society made use of their talents by engaging in politics, usually indirectly, behind the scenes, as hostesses, wives, or mistresses; some women played prominent roles directly as professionals—often as teachers, nurses, or office staff, sometimes as writers, poets, and artists, and even as graduates of medical, law, or engineering schools.[3] In addition, small numbers of women organized on their own behalf before World War I, maintaining contacts with groups in Western Europe, and the many contributions of women to the war effort led in

1918 to the creation of the Association for the Civic and Political Emancipation of Romanian Women, a group that would remain active throughout the interwar years.[4]

In summary, although Romanian society before World War II was largely peasant and patriarchal, there was a sophisticated veneer of urban cosmopolitanism within which a variety of roles were open to women, and their sexuality was encouraged. Despite the differences between these two worlds, certain attitudes toward women were pervasive throughout society: (1) a recognition of the value (or economic necessity) of women's contributions toward the household; (2) a belief that women held primary responsibility for the well-being of the family and children; (3) the assumption that women were fundamentally different from men in their abilities and attitudes; and (4) acceptance of men's dominance in the public sphere.

The Communist Period

The ideology and practices of the Romanian Communist Party (RCP) would come to influence but not eradicate these four assumptions. First, always suspicious of the nuclear family, the communists denigrated women's contributions to the household and instead stressed the value of paid labor to the personal development of each human being and to the society. This meant that women were expected to work full-time outside the home. Second, the RCP promised that the state would accept responsibility for home and children by providing high-quality child care, canteens, and other public facilities. Such promises were never fulfilled, however, and women continued to shoulder the burdens of home and children. Third, differences between men and women were not officially recognized—indeed women were expected to contribute to the public sphere as much as men and in the same ways. Their sexuality was suppressed, along with gender distinctions, as a means of achieving equality. Fourth, although women were ostensibly welcomed into the public sphere as equals, in reality men continued to dominate political and economic life. As we later see, these policies came to influence the postcommunist transition in a variety of ways. In order to understand the reactions of women and men after 1989, however, we must first examine more closely the patterns of the communist years and especially the era dominated by Nicolae Ceaușescu.[5]

The Romanian Communist Party was ideologically committed to the demise of the patriarchal society and the achievement of complete equality between men and women. Equality, however, did not imply that the household roles women had fulfilled were henceforth to be considered as important as the traditional male roles. On the contrary, it meant that women of all classes had to reject their customary roles as "bourgeois," thus denigrating any work not rewarded by monetary payment. Women responded in various ways to the demands of the new environment. The destruction of the former political, social, economic, and artistic elites produced a new type of "white-collar" working woman: educated and sophisticated, wearing clothes that had once been elegant, and now working for a salary in order to survive. Whenever possible she sold her knowledge of arts, music, and languages to keep herself (and her family) alive as she joined the paid labor force and continued to be responsible for the household tasks.[6] The "blue-collar" working woman continued, as before, to work full-time for wages and simultaneously to meet the always unpaid and now officially unappreciated demands placed upon her in the home.

Meanwhile, the peasant woman was asked to change completely in order to become part of the brave new world. All the old and known values that had defined her place in the family, the village, and the world were now outdated, subversive, and unwanted. The images spread by the new regime's propaganda showed happy young peasant women freeing themselves from the tyranny of family and tradition by working for wages at a nearby factory, state farm, or in the local agricultural cooperative. Indeed the only way to be a human being was to do paid labor for the state. Eventually, as peasants were deprived of land and other property, a good job and the peripheral opportunities it provided acquired the same value in the search for a marriage partner as that formerly associated with landownership. A job became an important attribute of a potential bride or groom.

Extended families did not disappear but changed their tactics in the face of continuing economic scarcity. The proliferation of factories created many commuters (usually male) caught between the double pressure of industrial work and traditional rural homes. Someone in the family had to remain a member of a collective farm because it brought a private plot and the opportunity to grow food; someone else would hold a factory job to provide wages and access to urban goods; children remained in the village with the mother or, if both parents worked in the city, grandparents or other relatives moved into the tiny urban apartments temporarily to help out. Men faced their own multiple burdens: an official job and a second job, usually in the underground economy, often while commuting.[7]

These pressures, although intense, were not unique to Romania. Nor did most patterns of women's participation in politics and the economy during the communist period differ radically from those in other communist countries and in noncommunist ones as well.[8] First, although women were by law equal to men, in politics the proportion of women in any organization varied inversely with its real power. More women could be found in trade union councils than in the more powerful government councils, for example, and very few women were elected to high positions in the omnipotent party; during the 1950s and 1960s, the proportion of women in the Grand National Assembly rose as high as 17 percent but in the RCP Central Committee declined from 7 to 4 percent.[9] Second, women tended to cluster at the bottom of any hierarchy; more were elected to local than to higher government bodies, for example, and their share in total party membership during those decades ranged from 17 to 23 percent,[10] substantially higher than in the Central Committee.

In accordance with communist ideology, women were mobilized into the paid labor force in large numbers and given access to education. Yet in Romania, as elsewhere in Eastern Europe, the sectoral segregation typical of noncommunist societies continued under Communist Party rule. Despite the official rejection of gender differences, women tended to work in sectors where they were deemed to have special competence, such as health, education, light industry, retail trade, and service and consumer specialities. These sectors received less investment and remuneration than more "masculine" areas, yet men still tended to hold the positions of power as managers or directors. Thus women were concentrated in sectors and jobs with low prestige and pay.

Ceauşescu's Variant

The situation of women in Romania began to diverge from East European patterns after Nicolae Ceauşescu was chosen leader of the Romanian party on the death of Gheorghe Gheorghiu-Dej in 1965. Ceauşescu emphasized rapid economic growth to strengthen the Romanian nation, and he required sacrifices by all citizens to achieve his goals. His demands resulted in two distinct and apparently contradictory sets of policies toward women that made Romania an anomaly in the communist world. Not only did he initiate a series of extremely coercive pronatalist campaigns that outlawed abortion and contraception, but he also set rigid quotas requiring the rapid promotion of women into higher political and economic positions.[11] Both sets of policies were widely resented by both women and men.

The first of the pronatalist decrees to increase population growth and the future labor force was issued in October 1966, and the next year the birthrate tripled. By the early 1970s, however, women had found ways to circumvent the restrictions, and births returned almost to 1966 levels. Additional measures and punishments were introduced over the next two decades, including higher taxes for the childless or unmarried and, eventually, frequent and compulsory gynecological examinations for all women of childbearing age to detect early pregnancies and ensure that they went to term.

If an abortion was discovered, the woman (not her partner) was subject to a minimum of two years' imprisonment or a very high fine. If the woman needed emergency treatment related to an abortion, she could be denied hospital care until she named the person who had induced the abortion. Both were, after all, stealing from the community. President Ceaușescu had declared that the fetus was the socialist property of the whole nation, and women who refused to have children were deserters, shirking their responsibility to the community. Society did not provide adequate care for these children, however, just as it had not relieved women of household tasks. Pronatalist demographic policies endangered the lives of millions of women driven to illegal abortions, destroyed many marriages by exacerbating conflicts over sexual relations, and produced thousands of unwanted children, many of whom ended up in the notorious orphanages revealed after the 1989 revolution. By 1989 Romanians had the highest infant mortality rate and lowest life expectancy in Europe.[12]

Despite the desire for population growth, the authorities tried to suppress any sexual activity outside of marriage. Unmarried couples were forbidden to share a room in a hotel or a berth on a train. Police frequently entered hotel rooms at odd hours to discover and punish anyone engaged in extramarital sex. If an unmarried couple were found together, however, the woman was charged with prostitution and acquired a criminal record, whereas the man went unpunished. Scarce housing forced many young men and women to live with their parents until they married and often after marriage, and the resulting tension was aggravated if an unwanted pregnancy occurred. Ironically, this new society re-created some of the difficult conditions of traditional peasant life, including generational hierarchy and lack of privacy. Gender-specific responses reappeared as well: men could indulge in quietly tolerated drunkenness, violence, and occasional adultery; women responded by fearing men, suppressing their own sexuality, and regarding sex as a necessary evil. Many women came to see their job outside the home as an escape—not just an economic necessity that brought them wages and access to the second economy, but also a chance to meet other women, exchange gossip, and leave behind the intolerable drudgery and boredom of the house.[13]

In public and private life, the regime enforced its socialist version of feminism. Outward manifestations of feminine elegance in style, manner, and dress gradually disappeared. Government movie censors excluded kisses and hints of sensuality. Televised modesty required high-necked dresses and long skirts and sleeves. In Romania the ideal woman had to combine the muscles of a communist worker with the modesty of a young peasant, and any women was officially rated according to that incongruous stereotype. Unofficially, however, most women measured their liberation by the extent to which they distanced themselves from the approved model. Nevertheless, strict observance of the stereotype was a prerequisite for political promotion and, at high levels, professional success.

Promotion of women to higher positions throughout the country was the stated goal of Ceaușescu's other extremely coercive campaign involving women. In reality, however, this campaign also aimed at increasing the number of workers. The RCP had been somewhat less successful than most East European regimes in drawing urban women into the paid labor force, and in the early 1970s Ceaușescu began to insist that more women be enticed to seek jobs.[14] Not satisfied with the potential increase in the labor force provided by children, he insisted on immediate growth by adding women.

At first it seemed that the major purpose of the new campaign to promote women was to glorify Elena Ceaușescu, wife of the president, and she joined the top party leadership and the Council of Ministers in 1973 along with a few friends. Six years later, at the RCP congress in

1979, the campaign suddenly broadened; 25 percent of the party's new Central Committee and 20 percent of its new Political Executive Committee were women (a jump from 2 to 11 women and from 34 to 100 women respectively). The next year the proportion of women in the Grand National Assembly rose from 14.3 percent to 32.5 percent. In the decade that followed, high quotas for the promotion of women were set in other political bodies and also in the labor force.[15]

Unfortunately, the quotas (like most of Ceauşescu's economic targets) were unrealistic, and many women were promoted before they were experienced enough to do well in their new posts. Others were coerced into taking posts they did not want and that demanded more time than they had, given their burdens at home. The result was high turnover rates among women. Another disadvantage of these quotas was their close association with Elena and Nicolae Ceauşescu. Not only was this couple deeply hated throughout Romania (as the events of December 1989 would show) but also any promotion associated with them was assumed to be based on political subservience or nepotism.

Indeed, any woman who wanted to be promoted or to retain a job to which she had been promoted could jeopardize her career if she did not play the role desired by the party. She had to be politically quiescent and socially acceptable: married, with children, and without sexuality. She could not dress elegantly or apply makeup to enhance her physical appearance. Women willing and able to play this role drew more antipathy from their compatriots than their male colleagues in positions of power. In part this may be explained by the powerful images of traditional Romanian culture: women were expected to be different from men, wiser and more sensitive, especially now that they had acquired some power for the first time in Romanian history. When communist women such as Elena Ceauşescu proved to be as cold-hearted, ambitious, and ruthless as the men, these dashed expectations produced intense resentment.

Often the women promoted under Ceauşescu had less influence than their male colleagues, whatever their formal titles. Some women served as figureheads, while men wielded the real power. Others, such as those in the Central Committee and the Grand National Assembly, held less prestigious jobs than their male colleagues and were less likely to be chosen for important committees or to be reelected. Women (like the ethnic minorities) tended to hold their positions as representatives of a "disadvantaged" group. In other words, they were there to fill a gender quota. Some electoral districts, for example, were allowed to nominate more than one candidate so that voters actually had a choice on election day. In such cases, however, to preserve the desired balance among demographic categories, women usually ran against women, just as Hungarians ran against Hungarians. They were there not as individual candidates but to fill the quota; any woman would do. (Needless to say, proportionally fewer Romanian men faced opponents, and none of the top party officials was opposed.)[16]

Those members of a "disadvantaged" group who were elected or promoted then faced a dilemma. If they wished to be reelected or to retain their higher status, they had to fit into their new environment by supporting the wishes of their colleagues and superiors. Thus they could not represent the interests of their demographic or social group. Indeed they had to demonstrate clearly that they subordinated their particular interests to the needs of society as a whole—that is, the party. Just as the official trade unions did not represent or serve the workers, so the National Organization of Women neither represented nor served women. Instead it functioned according to directives from above, cheerfully supporting policies detrimental to women and creating deep mistrust in Romania for any group that purported to defend the interests of women. Thus the Ceauşescu campaign to promote women left them disorganized as a social group and tarnished the image of any politically engaged woman.

In summary, communist ideology—especially the Ceauşescu variant—reinforced for women the value of work outside the home, denigrated their unpaid household labor, and denied them the promised public facilities, convenience goods, and appliances to help with family tasks. They were forced to shoulder the onerous double burden of full-time work in the public sphere, often with responsibility rather than real power or sufficient remuneration, and caring for home and family under conditions of extreme economic scarcity. Meanwhile, their health was endangered by the demographic policies, and their right to be different from men or to express their sexuality was destroyed in the name of equality. Small wonder that the end of the Ceauşescu era left many women uncertain as to their personal and professional goals and ready to seek choices different from those available to them before December 1989.

The Postcommunist Period

After Ceauşescu's downfall, the need to break with the immediate past produced a "confusion of values"[17] and led men and women to turn once again to traditional institutions such as church, ethnic group, and family in a search for personal and group identity. Women tended to embrace precommunist assumptions about their own status in society, most notably the value of their role in the family and the deep differences between men and women. At the same time, their resentment over past policies mobilized them to demand certain rights: to hold a paid job outside the home if they chose, as a means of independence or self-expression; to stay home if they wished, remaining outside the public sphere and focusing most of their energies on home and family; but above all to choose whether and when to have children. Not surprisingly, the 1966 decree outlawing abortion and the sections on abortion in the criminal code were among the very first of Ceauşescu's laws to be revoked by the new government.[18]

On most major legislation the new Romanian government acted with less haste. In fact, the entire political and economic transition has tended to move more slowly in Romania than in most other East European states for a variety of reasons. Before 1989, in contrast to Poles and Czechs, Romanians had little experience with spontaneous political activity or dissent.[19] The Ceauşescu regime had allowed no political autonomy and had used harsh and effective measures against dissenters. Indigenous social groups such as the Romanian Orthodox church or the trade unions had not challenged the communist regime as had the Roman Catholic church and Solidarity in Poland. No economic reforms or private economic activity had been permitted as in Hungary. Intellectuals had been coopted more effectively than in other states, especially because of the regime's manipulation of Romanian nationalism to support its policies, and the notorious Securitate had permeated society and compromised almost anyone with political, economic, or administrative experience.[20] In short, Romania lacked that network of autonomous relationships and organizational structures existing in the realm between individual and state often termed "civil society."[21] As a result, it would prove very difficult to create an effective new government.[22]

The overthrow of Ceauşescu was quick and violent. On December 15, 1989, street demonstrations broke out in Timişoara and spread to Bucharest. Ceauşescu and his wife were forced to flee but were soon captured and executed on Christmas Day after a perfunctory and secret trial. A provisional government formed, calling itself the National Salvation Front (NSF), composed mainly of reformist communist opponents of Ceauşescu and a few anticommunist dissidents. Protests continued in the streets by various groups hostile to the government—workers, ethnic minorities, students—and the NSF responded with violence of its own. Disagreements within the ruling coalition led to a series of resignations, and by March the government was clearly dominated by former RCP members and officials. Indeed, anyone in Romania with political or administrative experience had to have been a Communist Party member.

The NSF won a comfortable parliamentary majority in the elections of May 1990, and its presidential candidate, Ion Iliescu, gained an overwhelming mandate with 85 percent of the popular vote. He was a former Communist Party official, who had been demoted by Ceauşescu as early as 1971 but had never broken with him openly. In his electoral campaign Iliescu denounced Ceauşescu, promised democracy and market reforms, and also reassured the population that he would preserve stability, enact economic change gradually, continue state policies of social protection, and (by implication) not prosecute those who had worked for Ceauşescu's regime.

The parliament elected in May 1990 managed to retain a majority in support of the president and his younger and economically more radical prime minister, Petre Roman, long enough to write a constitution, which was approved in December 1991 by popular referendum. Elections were held for president and parliament under the new constitution in fall 1992, thus ending the transition period and initiating constitutional rule. By then, however, Iliescu and Roman had quarreled over the speed of the economic transition. Roman was forced from office in September 1991, and the NSF split into Roman and Iliescu factions the following spring. Meanwhile, a number of opposition parties united into an electoral coalition, the Democratic Convention of Romania (DCR). Sufficient opposition to Iliescu from the DCR and other parties did force the president into a second-round runoff in the fall 1992 presidential elections, but he won easily against the DCR candidate, Emil Constantinescu.

Although Iliescu himself was elected to a four-year term in 1992, his party—renamed the Party of Social Democracy in Romania (PDSR)—fell just short of a majority in parliament. As a result, from 1992 to 1996 a minority government led by Iliescu's chosen prime minister, Nicolae Văcăroiu, governed the country with the tacit support of the small nationalist parties (and for several months in a formal coalition with them). During the 1992–96 parliamentary term legislation was passed leading toward privatization and a market economy, but economic reforms moved very slowly.[23]

By the fall of 1996 the population was ready for more radical change: Iliescu was again forced into a runoff election and this time lost to Constantinescu. Moreover the Democratic Convention, in which the major party was now the National Peasant Party-Christian and Democrat (NPP-CD), won a plurality of parliamentary seats and was able to form a governing coalition with Petre Roman's Social Democratic Union (SDU) and the Hungarian Democratic Union (see Table 9.1). The new government under NPP-CD Prime Minister Victor Ciorbea promised more rapid economic and political change and was convincing enough to gain support from most European states in June 1997 for Romania's entrance into NATO in the first round. U.S. opposition prevented admission, but Romania was named as a prime candidate for the next round. By mid-1997 Romania's long-term prospects for democracy and economic recovery appeared brighter than ever before, although it was clear that considerable economic pain lay ahead in implementing economic restructuring.

As in other postcommunist states, Romanian women and men have been faced by the difficulties of economic transition: runaway inflation, rising unemployment, declining production, erosion of the social safety network (pensions, health care, other benefits), and the need to change the assumptions and coping mechanisms of workers and consumers from those appropriate for Communist Party rule to those required for survival in a market economy. Women face special difficulties in this new environment.

There is no longer a Romanian Communist Party, for example, to demand that most women work outside the home. Nevertheless, most continue to do so because the new market economy requires a second salary to offset inflation and the threat of unemployment. Moreover, the simultaneous collapse of trade barriers and domestic production has led to the import of expensive foreign goods; women can now save

Table 9.1

Results of the November 1996 Romanian Elections

President	November 3 (%)	November 17 (%)
Emil Constantinescu (DCR)	28.2	54.4
Ion Iliescu (PDSR)	32.2	45.6
Petre Roman (DP & SDU)	20.5	
Others	19.1	

Parliament	Deputies (women)	Senators (women)
Democratic Convention (DCR)		
National Peasant Party-Christian		
Democrat (NPP-CD)	83 (6)	27
National Liberal Party (NLP)	25 (1)	17
Others	14 ·	9
Party of Social Democracy in		
Romania (PDSR)	91 (8)	41 (2)
Social Democratic Union (SDU)		
Democratic Party (DP)	43 (3)	22
Romanian Social Democratic Party		
(RSDP)	10 (1)	1
Hungarian Democratic Union	25 (1)	11
Greater Romania Party (GRP)	19 (3)	8
Party of Romanian National Unity		
(PRNU)	18	7
Minority Organizations	15 (2)	
Total (women)	343 (25)	143 (2)

Sources: OMRI, November 6, 8, and 11, 1996, and information supplied omanian parliament.

time by purchasing prepared foods and household appliances, but only if they have the money. Time has become money in the new market system with serious implications for all aspects of men's and women's daily life. Erosion of the social safety network has hit women especially hard; they are the primary caregivers because they accept—and many embrace willingly—the precommunist assumptions about women's responsibility for the private sphere and the social (but not economic) value of such contributions.

Economic and social data on men and women in postcommunist

Table 9.2

Female/Male Comparisons in Postcommunist Romania

	Females as percentage of males
Life expectancy at birth, 1992–94	111
Mean years of schooling, 1995	88
Secondary enrollment, 1994–95	102
Postsecondary enrollment, 1994–95	93
Employment, 1994	87
Unemployment, 1995	123

Source: Romanian Human Development Report 1996 (Bucharest: Romanian Government and U.N. Development Program, 1996), p. 101.

Note: Since 1966 the percentage of women in the overall population of Romania has ranged from 50.7 to 51.0 percent, *Anuarul statistic al României 1996* (Bucharest: Comisia naţionalăpentru statistică, 1996), p. 82.

Table 9.3

Unemployment in Postcommunist Romania

	Total	Women (*N*)	Women (%)
1991	337,440	208,457	61.8
1992	929,019	563,065	60.6
1993	1,164,705	685,496	58.9
1994	1,223,925	693,342	56.6
1995	998,432	551,492	55.2

Source: Anuarul statistic al României 1996 (Bucharest: Comisia naţionalăpentru statistică, 1996), p. 157.

Romania reveal other disadvantages for women (see Table 9.2). They tend to live longer, for example, and therefore depend more heavily on pensions. As a group they have less education than men and are underrepresented in higher educational enrollments. Even more disturbing, at the end of 1995 women made up 43.6 percent of the work force but 55.2 percent of the unemployed.[24] (For more details on unemployment, see Table 9.3.) In addition, considerable sectoral segregation of women workers remains from the communist era, as women are concentrated in certain types of manufacturing (especially food and beverages, textiles and textile products, leather goods), as well as commerce, hotels and food service, education, and health care.[25]

Women in Postcommunist Politics

Most striking—and most important for our purposes—has been the absence of women in politics. In contrast to the Ceauşescu years, very few women played a prominent political role after 1989. In explaining this widespread reaction against women's participation in politics in the early postcommunist years, Romanian women themselves during discussions in 1992 pointed to several factors. First, they argued that the low involvement of women was a natural response to the previous coerced and manipulated involvement. Most women, forced to play an active role in politics before 1989, were no longer interested in making policy, but were seeking peace and quiet and the right to stay home. Second, they invariably mentioned the revulsion against Elena Ceauşescu, the other highly placed communist women, and the corrupt and hypocritical communist organization for women. Third, they insisted that because women were different, they preferred to work behind the scenes in supportive positions as assistants or to advise or criticize as journalists; women did not want their paid positions to absorb all their energies as jobs were supposed to do under Ceauşescu. Finally, the women argued in 1992, after 1989 most women wished to make different choices and to focus any extra energy on their families or on the new economic opportunities and difficulties that appeared during the economic transition.

Whatever the causes, there has been a marked scarcity of women in government and parliament. Several women were major figures in the National Salvation Front during and immediately after the events of December 1989—most notably anti-Ceauşescu dissidents Doina Cornea and Ana Blandiana—but both soon resigned to join the opposition. The 1990–92 government contained only one woman, appointed in fall 1990 as secretary of state for the handicapped. Indeed, since 1989 only one woman has been a full minister, and she was placed in charge of health for just two months before the 1996 elections. Less than a dozen women have been secretaries of state ("junior" ministers), although a number have held positions just below that level. Thus in the 1990s there have been many fewer women in top government positions than in the 1980s, when women headed such ministries as Light Industry, Internal Trade, and Education, as well as the National Council for Science and Technology.

Parliament

Likewise, in parliament, only a tiny number of women have served. For the elections of May 1990 only a few were placed in high positions on the parties' lists of candidates and, as a result, women were elected to only 1 out of 117 Senate seats and 13 out of 383 places in the Chamber of Deputies, a much smaller proportion than the usual one-third of the communist Grand National Assembly. By mid-1992 resignations by men from both houses of this first parliament (to accept another office or for personal reasons) had brought a second woman into the Senate and raised the total number of women in the Chamber to twenty-two, a high of just over 4 percent.[26] The percentage dropped to 2.7 percent in the second parliament, but after the 1996 elections rebounded to 5.5 percent (see Table 9.1). That is still only a tiny group of twenty-seven in the both houses, but interviews in 1992 and 1997 of individual women deputies from the first and third parliaments do reveal significant improvements in the women's professionalism and in the legislative environment, reflecting the greater political maturity of the entire parliament as well as among the women members.

In June 1992 five women deputies were interviewed for this project, each from a different party or faction. They had very little experience in legislative politics (like all Romanians in 1992), but they were bright, articulate, well educated, and attractive, and they ranged in age from about 30 to over 60.[27] Most were fashionably dressed and all took pride in their appearance. The image of the successful woman politician had changed radically between 1989 and 1992; they had regained the right to look and act differently from men.

The women were not happy in parliament, however, and only one of the five said she would be willing to run for another term in the fall 1992 elections. The weekly parliamentary schedule of four days in Bucharest and three days in the electoral constituency was difficult for a woman with a family or district outside the capital, but the principal reason they were unwilling to serve four more years was not just the schedule but their belief that they were not accomplishing enough in parliament to make the sacrifice of personal time and effort worthwhile.

They resented their treatment by their male colleagues and complained that they were not taken seriously, that the men paid no attention when they spoke, and that the reactions they received ranged from resentment and intimidation to scorn and amusement. Several said that they had spoken on the floor in the early days but eventually found that they influenced the votes of their male colleagues more effectively by talking with them in the corridors and using quiet persuasion, flattery, and cajolery. They criticized the leaders of their own parties for not selecting them for important delegations (especially to the West), not putting them into leadership positions on commissions, and not allowing them their own commission on women's issues. Instead the Chamber of Deputies had established a Commission for Labor, Health, Social Protection, and the Status of Women in Society; nine of the women deputies chose to serve on that commission,[28] but it was chaired by a male physician. The women were particularly angry at the Party of Romanian National Unity (PRNU)[29] for its opposition to legislation in support of women's interests and for blocking the women delegates' efforts to use parliamentary facilities to meet regularly among themselves.

Despite their complaints and disappointments, the women in 1992 could point with satisfaction to some favorable legislation passed after 1989. The new constitution, for example, guaranteed legal equality, equal pay for equal work, and paid maternity leave. Under Ceauşescu women had been allowed 112 days of maternity leave with full pay; by 1992 they had the option of remaining at home with the child for one year at 65 percent pay. Two major laws on the handicapped enacted in the spring of 1992 were also particularly important to women as the primary caregivers.[30] A major disappointment for the women deputies in 1992, however, was their failure to persuade their male colleagues to pass a law providing a one-year window during which any woman could choose to be pensioned at age 50 instead of 55 if she had done manual labor for twenty years. Such a law would have eased the situation of many older women, who were becoming unemployed in the new economy, but the legislation was postponed—in effect blocked—by "the men" in parliament.[31]

There was, therefore, among the few women a sense that certain issues had a special impact on women and deserved the attention of women legislators, but they had little confidence in their own ability to succeed within the legislative process. The 1992 women were beginners in politics, and they decided not to stay around for more seasoning. Only one woman deputy from 1990–92 served in the next parliament.[32]

Indeed, the role of women within the legislative process was even weaker in the 1992–96 parliament. The eleven women deputies and two senators were almost evenly divided between Iliescu's governing party, the PDSR, and various opposition parties.[33] They were not in positions of leadership, however, and were too few to have a significant impact on most legislation, although five chose to serve on commissions related to family issues: three on Labor and Social Protection (one as secretary), and two on Health and Family. Nevertheless, these women would prove significant in that they would begin to develop as professional legislators, and six (five deputies and one senator) would be reelected in 1996 to the third parliament—a slightly higher retention rate than the 40 percent overall figure.[34] By then they were becoming effective and influential as legislators.

In 1997 twelve of the twenty-five women in the Chamber of Deputies agreed to be interviewed. They represented a broad spectrum of political parties, and as in 1992 they were bright, articulate, well educated, and fashionably dressed to emphasize their femininity—their right to be different from men. They came from all over Romania and juggled their personal lives accordingly, since they spent two or three days a week in their electoral constituencies. Most were married, most had children, and all were well educated and had extensive political experience. Of those interviewed, two were serving a second term in parliament, three had served in government as secretaries of state, three had held major posts in local politics, and all had done significant work for their party organizations. Indeed, given the party-list electoral system in Romania, aspiring politicians had to make themselves valuable to their parties in order to be placed sufficiently high on the lists to be elected—and the women in the 1997 parliament had developed their own areas of expertise and had earned high posts within their parties.[35]

Most insisted that they were different from men: equal in competence but with contrasting priorities and interests. Three, therefore, had chosen the Commission on Labor and Social Protection; two of them had served on that body in the 1992–96 parliament and now had been elected its vice-president and secretary. A seniority system was emerging. Other commissions with women members included Health and Family (two women), Culture, Art and Mass Media (two), Human Rights, Minorities, and Religion (two), Local Administration, Industry and Services, and Economic Reform and Privatization. Deputies were allowed to serve on one regular commission and on one joint commission of both houses, and three of the women (one as president) served on the European Integration Commission, the body charged with ensuring that all Romanian legislation be compatible with European Union and Council of Europe requirements.

It was not a coincidence that women were serving on and presiding over this particular commission. European governmental and nongovernmental organizations (NGOs) have tried hard to improve the status of women in Romania as part of a general emphasis on human rights.[36] A one-year program with the support of several European groups, for example, led to the formation of a Romanian NGO to prepare women for politics: to teach them how to communicate in a political speech, how to comport themselves in a political arena, and how to convince men to vote for them. Women in several of the parties (especially the DP) took advantage of this opportunity to create a nucleus of women candidates in 1996, and the results were visible in the attitudes of the women members.

The attitudes of these women deputies toward their male colleagues were quite different from the views expressed in 1992. No longer did any complain that they were not taken seriously or given responsible positions. Instead they talked about the need to make themselves necessary to their parties to gain influence and then to formulate strategies to pass legislation. Politics, most had discovered, was a kind of war in which strategy and even deceit were needed to gain electoral and legislative victories. Women in Romania, one pointed out, had been used to having doors opened and chairs held; they waited for an invitation to act, posing, as Westerners might put it, "on a pedestal." Instead, several deputies argued (as did many Romanian women in 1997), women must act without waiting for an invitation; they must insist on what they want and need, and take the initiative in order to succeed. Such echoes of assertiveness training sounded in the words of more than half the deputies, and the results were visible in their demeanor despite their overt femininity in dress and body language.

The women deputies were not a homogeneous group, however, as they divided along generational and party lines. The younger women, as well as USD and Liberals (NLP), tended to be the most assertive, demanding the right to be both equal and different. The PDSR women either rejected gender differences (reflecting communist socialization) or paid lip service to equality and worked from their pedestals. Those in the NPP-CD were torn between their rejection of communist ideas and their unwillingness to let precommunist traditions push them out of the public sphere. By 1997, therefore, Romanian women were developing a spectrum of attitudes toward themselves as women, a positive sign in the development of pluralism, but divisive for women politicians.[37]

This third parliament was just beginning to enact legislation in June 1997, and so it was too soon to assess the impact of these women on policy. One new law had emerged from the Commission on Labor and Social Protection, lengthening maternity leaves to two years without loss of job seniority. However, the women members had not been able to persuade their colleagues to allow parents to choose whether mother or father would remain at home.[38] Several women were interested in a pending law on political parties because one proposed amendment would give extra funding to those parties with an "appropriate" proportion of women in parliament (based either on party membership or votes). Otherwise the women deputies were focusing their attention on the contradictory priorities of shrinking the budget deficit while preserving the social safety network, a difficult dilemma in Romania, where the widespread commitment to deficit reduction in order to join European organizations conflicted with the needs of impoverished families, and especially acute for those women most active in defense of families (SDU) because their parties were in the ruling coalition and most determined to bring Romania into Europe.

Thus party loyalties and the special interests of women were potentially in conflict, and party loyalty was winning. Dependent on party leaders for support in all aspects of political life, the women felt very strongly the division between government and opposition. Those with experience in the 1992–96 parliament stressed repeatedly how much more difficult it was to be responsible for passing and implementing legislation than merely to criticize the government. At the same time, those who had served in government felt considerable resentment at their parties' electoral loss. Neither group was ready to cooperate with the other. Indeed, despite their growing confidence in themselves as legislators, they saw no need to organize themselves within parliament as women. There were too many differences among them, they argued, in personal life, interests, and ideologies.

Postcommunist Society

The difficulties and opportunities in postcommunist society are reshaping the environment and therefore the attitudes of women in Romania.

Although marketization and privatization have already brought significant hardships, restructuring the economy has barely begun. In agriculture, privatization has divided the land into small plots, and the absence of machinery or the capital to purchase it has temporarily reproduced the hardships of the traditional peasant family with its strict gender roles and division of labor; 54 percent of the agricultural labor force by 1995 was "unpaid family members, that is, women."[39] Yet those who can grow food and sell to urban markets are already gaining wealth and seeking to acquire more land and hasten full commercialization and mechanization. This should in the long run bring new forms of transport and communication, a gradual decline in the rural population, and more variety and choice in the roles of men and women as they stay in the villages or move to cities or suburbs. Many variables, however, including the outcome of legislative debates in Bucharest and the development of domestic and foreign markets for agricultural products, make the future evolution of gender roles in the Romanian countryside— where 45 percent of the population lives—difficult to predict.

In other sectors privatization has emerged most rapidly in the form of small family businesses such as restaurants or shops where again all members of the family must work together to survive, but where the gender roles are less stereotyped than in traditional society. Depending on the restaurant or store, men or women may cook, take orders, wait on tables, work behind the counter, or do the bookkeeping. As in agriculture, among the most immediate consequences of privatization has been a strengthening of the family unit, although in less traditional ways.

Much of the economy remains in the hands of large enterprises, and here the news for many women remains bleak. Traditional misogynism and the excuse of Elena Ceauşescu and the communist period continue to mitigate against their promotions. In addition, their concentration at lower levels means that in many cases they are the first to be fired; hence their higher rates of unemployment. Those who lose their jobs (or in rural areas their land or family support) may be driven to prostitution in the new environment of open sexuality. They may even choose their own postcommunist variant of migrant labor: going abroad for several years to sell their bodies and returning with a dowry sufficient to start a business.

There are more positive possibilities. Many women who have lost their jobs have been forced into new sectors of the private economy (advertising, marketing, retail services) where there is the greatest potential for growth. Also, within manufacturing, women have tradition-ally worked in those sectors that must now be developed to make the Romanian economy viable: textiles, furniture, household goods, and the food and wine industries, as well as such currently depressed areas as health and education, where there is considerable potential for growth. In such areas they will face greater competition from men, who will seek jobs as their own sectors shrink, but women will have the immediate advantage of expertise, and there will be less prejudice against them than in the traditional male preserves.

Finally, and perhaps most important, any successful business will have to produce what is needed in Romanian society. In the long run, consumer sovereignty should give women (and men) more power over economic decisions than the omnipotence of a Communist Party domi-nated by the priorities of heavy industry.

In 1992 Romanian women rejected feminism as an ideology or as a form of political discourse for many of the same reasons that Alena Heitlinger found it was absent in the Czech Republic: mistrust of "emancipatory" ideological promises; association of women's equality or emancipation with a discredited communist regime; rejection of "collective" action; regard for themselves as strong women, rather than victims; placing a high value on motherhood and family; and a percep-tion that feminism was anti-male.[40] The horrors of Ceauşescu's cam-paigns, however, gave a different twist to the experience of Romanian women. Not only had women's private needs and public organizations been distorted, manipulated, and discredited by the Communist Party in its efforts to destroy the traditional society, but also, ironically, the family had been weakened by pronatalist policies, and women's capa-bilities had been disparaged by the campaigns to promote them. Im-mediately after 1989 both precommunist traditions and the reaction against communist rule combined to persuade most Romanian women that the family must be the major focus of their attention, at least in the near future.

By 1997 the situation was changing. Women had discovered eco-nomic and professional reasons to remain in or rejoin the paid labor force, and their frustrations were leading at least a few of them to political action. In the mid-1990s over a hundred NGOs relating to women were established involving specific issues in politics, econom-ics, education, social services, and many other fields, and a number were avowedly feminist in their orientation. Such groups received considerable encouragement from a project on Women in Development, established in 1994 by the UN Development Program, together with the Romanian Ministry of Labor and Social Protection, to sensitize the public and decision makers on gender issues, to promote equal opportunities for women and men, and to initiate programs to generate employment for women. The clout (and funds) of the UN have been well used in pressuring government officials and empowering women to act for themselves.

One of the many NGOs, for example, ANA, the Romanian Society for Feminist Analyses, was founded with support from PHARE (European Union), the UN Development Program, and other sources. ANA operates a library, puts out a bulletin, keeps in contact with women throughout the world on e-mail, and publishes materials focusing on gender and education in an effort to reduce sexism in the schools from the primary years through the university. The subtitle of ANA's most recent book is revealing: *Gender and Education: Equality through Difference, a Program for Non-sexist Education*.[41] Romanian feminism in the 1990s insists that women have the right to be different from men.

Conclusions

The status of women in Romanian politics as of mid-1997 can be summarized as marginal but considerably more promising than in 1992. Widespread adversity faces most Romanians in their new environment, and Romanian women have responded in a variety of ways. Many have chosen to become active on their own behalf. Most are working directly in the economy, and some have formed or joined NGOs to meet their needs. Others—still only a small number—have chosen politics as an appropriate way to help themselves and their constituents.

Those who have gone into politics at the national level have become much more professional than in 1992. Whether this will translate into effective legislation to help other women remains to be seen. Most of the women in government and parliament certainly see themselves as specialists on women's issues and express their desire to help other women on social and economic problems. They also have obligations to their parties, however, and at times there is a direct conflict between the policy needs specific to women and those of the parties—on deficit reduction, for example, a priority not only for Romanian party leaders but also for the European states and organizations most supportive of women's rights.

Before World War II, Romanian society was largely peasant and patriarchal. The rural population is now down to 45 percent, but patriarchy still dominates much of Romanian rural and urban life. The sophisticated veneer of urban cosmopolitanism that was present in the 1930s now reaches much further down into urban society, and within it a variety of roles are now open to women. Nevertheless, assumptions about women that were pervasive in Romania before World War II remain widespread today: (1) the importance of women's paid and unpaid contributions toward the household; (2) women's primary responsibility for family and children; (3) the existence of fundamental differences between women and men; and (4) men's dominance in the public sphere. The communist regime tried to change some of these attitudes by denigrating women's unpaid labor in the home and eradicating differences between men and women. After 1989, therefore, as they sought a new life, women demanded the right to focus on their homes and to be different from men, and they continue to assert these rights. Most cannot afford to leave the paid labor force, but they can assert their right to be different, and they are doing so.

Only the last of the precommunist assumptions is being widely questioned, but certainly not rejected, by Romanians in the late 1990s. The communists had paid lip service to women's equality in the public arena, but they had not ended men's dominance. They did, however, raise women's expectations, and now that women are adversely affected in the new social and economic environment, they are beginning to recognize that the political process is important for them and for their families and to demand the promised power in the public sphere. This process is just beginning, but Romanian women (and men) have come a long way since 1989.

The state has been reshaping the economy and society as it legislates privatization and rebuilds a network of social services, and in this political transition women are still playing much too small a role. The various parties and political groups—and women themselves—are starting to see politics as an arena in which women can and should make extensive contributions. They can no longer rely on tradition or ideology to give them a secure place in society. Instead they must develop their own options in the new Romania and in doing so master the process of political competition. As time passes and the memories of the Ceauşescu era fade, the revival of the family and women's new economic roles are creating needs that push women into the political process. They do not agree among themselves as to their goals, but they are beginning to join the struggle to implement them. In 1992 women were watching from the sidelines; by 1997 they were moving onto the field.

Notes

The final text of this chapter for both editions of this volume was prepared by Mary Ellen Fischer. In the first edition a paper written by Doina Pasca Harsanyi was very useful for the analysis, and she therefore was listed as co-author. This chapter has been considerably revised since then, however, and unless otherwise noted the ideas and text are mine alone. I should like to thank Virginia Gheorghiu, who provided data and arranged a number of interviews in June 1992, and Lucian Mihai, Maria Sandor, and Stelian Tanase, all of whom made important contributions to my 1997 interviews. I should also like to thank the many Romanian citizens who took time from their busy schedules to speak with me, especially the women in parliament.

1. Sources on the Romanian social background include Keith Hitchins, *Rumania, 1866–1947* (New York: Oxford University Press, 1994); Michael Shafir, *Romania: Politics, Economics and Society* (Boulder, CO: Lynne Rienner, 1985); Kenneth Jowitt, ed., *Social Change in Romania, 1860–1940* (Berkeley: Institute of International Studies, University of California, 1978); Daniel Chirot, *Social Change in a Peripheral Society* (New York: Academic Press, 1976); and Mary Ellen Fischer, "Politics, Nationalism, and Development in Romania," in *Diverse Paths to Modernity in Southeastern Europe,* ed. Gerasimos Augustinos (Westport, CT: Greenwood Press, 1991), pp. 135–68.

2. Gail Kligman, "The Rites of Women," in *Women, State, and Party in Eastern Europe,* ed. Sharon L. Wolchik and Alfred G. Meyer (Durham: Duke University Press, 1985), p. 328. For a detailed description of such rituals and the daily life of women in a Romanian village, see Kligman, *The Wedding of the Dead* (Berkeley: University of California Press, 1988).

3. The most famous woman was Queen Marie, who influenced the outcome of the treaty negotiations following World War I. See Hannah Pakula, *The Last Romantic* (New York: Simon and Schuster, 1984). Another example was Elena Văcărescu, poet and member of the Romanian Academy, who was involved extensively in international diplomacy in the 1920s and 1930s; for a collection of her writings, see Constantin I. Turcu, ed., *Hélène Vacaresco: Une grande européenne* (Bucharest: Editura fundaţiei române, 1996). See also Adam J. Sorkin and Kurt W. Treptow, *An Anthology of Romanian Women Poets,* 2nd ed. (Iaşi: Center for Romanian Studies, 1995), with poems and biographical sketches of fifteen nineteenth- and twentieth-century poets.

4. For a survey of women's activities before 1939, see Aurora Liiceanu, "Rivalitate şi solidaritate: începuturile feminismului în România," in Mădălena Nicolaescu, *Cine suntem noi? Despre identitatea femeilor din România moderna*

(Bucharest: Ed. Anima, 1996), pp. 20–39; and Walter M. Bacon Jr. and Louis G. Pol, "The Economic Status of Women in Romania," in *Women in the Age of Economic Transformation,* ed. Nahid Aslanbeigui, Steven Pressman, and Gale Summerfield (New York: Routledge, 1994), pp. 44–47. On World War I see Maria Bucur, "Între mituri, icoane și tăceri: femeile române în primul război mondial," in ibid., pp. 40–50. A number of women politicians interviewed by Fischer in 1992 and 1997 stressed the professional accomplishments of women before 1939 and cited them as role models.

5. For an earlier and more detailed study of these issues during the communist period, see Mary Ellen Fischer, "Women in Romanian Politics: Elena Ceaușescu, Pronatalism, and the Promotion of Women," in Wolchik and Meyer, *Women, State and Party in Eastern Europe,* pp. 121–37, 388–93.

6. For this description and that of the peasant women below, see Doina Pasca Harsanyi, "Women in Romania," in *Gender Politics and Post-Communism,* ed. Nanette Funk and Magda Mueller (New York: Routledge, 1993), p. 42.

7. On these issues, see, for example, William Moskoff, "Sex Discrimination, Commuting, and the Role of Women in Rumanian Development," *Slavic Review* 37 (September 1978): 440–56.

8. On the Soviet experience, see Gail Warshofsky Lapidus, *Women in Soviet Society: Equality, Development, and Social Change* (Berkeley: University of California Press, 1978).

9. See Fischer, "Women in Romanian Politics," Tables 7.1 and 7.3, pp. 128 and 131.

10. The cited figures were given by Gheorghe Gheorghiu-Dej at the 1960 party congress and in *Scînteia,* March 20, 1970. Figures reported on other dates fell within this range.

11. For more details on both of these policies, see Fischer, "Women in Romanian Politics." On the pronatalist policies, see Gail Kligman, "The Politics of Reproduction in Ceaușescu's Romania," *East European Politics and Societies* 6 (Fall 1992): 364–418. For the broader political context, see Fischer, *Nicolae Ceaușescu: A Study in Political Leadership* (Boulder, CO: Lynne Rienner, 1989), chs. 7–9.

12. *Cotidianul,* June 12, 1992.

13. A semiclandestine survey of women textile workers in 1988 revealed that although their jobs made their lives very difficult and gave them no leisure time at all, the women preferred work over being "home alone"; Harsanyi, "Women in Romania," pp. 45–48.

14. For more details, see Fischer, "Women in Romanian Politics, pp. 125–27, and the sources cited there.

15. Ibid., pp. 128–32.

16. Ibid., pp. 132–35.

17. This was Virginia Gheorghiu's phrase at the Prague conference in 1992.

18. See *Adevărul,* December 27, 1989, p. 1. Timișoara, a week ahead of Bucharest in its revolution, declared itself a free town on December 20, and gynecologists immediately began to perform abortions without charge. Over a million legal abortions per year were performed in Romania in 1990 and 1991, saving the lives of an estimated 500 women. By mid-1992, however, a backlash had appeared: concern about a "demographic crisis" and the need for 125,000

more children each year; see, for example, *Cotidianul,* June 12, 1992, and *Adevărul,* June 12, 1992. This backlash would be reflected in the low number of women elected to parliament that year.

19. For an overview of the Ceauşescu era, see Fischer, *Nicolae Ceauşescu,* or Trond Gilberg, *Nationalism and Communism in Romania* (Boulder, CO: Westview Press, 1990).

20. On intellectuals, see Katherine Verdery, *National Ideology Under Socialism: Identity and Cultural Politics in Ceauşescu's Romania* (Berkeley: University of California Press, 1991). The best source on the Securitate is Dennis Deletant, *Ceauşescu and the Securitate: Coercion and Dissent in Romania, 1965–1989* (Armonk, NY: M.E. Sharpe, 1995).

21. On the absence of civil society in 1990 Romania, see Gail Kligman, "Reclaiming the Public: A Reflection on Creating Civil Society in Romania," *East European Politics and Societies* 4 (Fall 1990): 393–438.

22. For a thoughtful survey of Romanian events in 1989–90, see Nestor Ratesh, *Romania: The Entangled Revolution,* Center for Strategic and International Studies, The Washington Papers/152 (New York: Praeger, 1991). See also my "The New Leaders and the Opposition," in *Romania After Tyranny,* ed. Daniel N. Nelson (Boulder, CO: Westview Press, 1992), pp. 45–65.

23. On the Romanian economy, see Lavinia Stan, "Romanian Privatization: Assessment of the First Five Years," *Communist and Post-Communist Studies* 28 (1995): 427–35; and Yves G. Van Frausum, Ulrich Gehmann, and Jürgen Gross, "Market Economy and Economic Reform in Romania: Macroeconomic and Microeconomic Perspectives," *Europe-Asia Studies* 46 (1994): 735–56.

24. *Anuarul statistic al României 1996* (Bucharest: Comisia Naţională pentru statistică, 1996), pp. 152–57. See also Bacon and Pol, "The Economic Status of Women in Romania," pp. 53–57.

25. Ibid.

26. Members who resigned were replaced by the next name on their party's list of candidates. This system makes it difficult to keep an exact count of women deputies throughout the life of a parliament. Note that the Chamber of Deputies was called the Assembly of Deputies from 1990 to 1992, but the present term has been used in the text throughout to avoid confusion.

27. The interviews were conducted by Fischer in June 1992; about a dozen other women involved directly in politics at various levels and from different parties also submitted to extensive interviews.

28. Members of parliament were allowed to join whichever commissions they chose.

29. The Romanian nationalist party of the extreme right based in Transylvania. A second such party with roots in Bucovina and Moldova is the Greater Romania Party (GRP).

30. As described in 1992 by their sponsor, Rodica Munteanu, secretary of state for the handicapped, the new laws were designed to mainstream the handicapped through programs financed by a 1 percent tax on all wages.

31. Women of different parties had evidently united in support of this proposal, and they blamed "the men" for blocking it.

32. Floarea Calotă, a popular singer from Teleorman.

33. Party affilations of women in the 1992–96 Chamber of Deputies were as

follows: PDSR—5; Greater Romania Party (GRP)—2 (including one moved from the NPP-CD to the GRP); Petre Roman's Democratic Party (DP)—1; the Social Democrats (RSDP)—1; a Liberal faction (PL-93)—1; Turkish minority—1; see *Tot ce voiaţi să ştiţi şi nu v-aţi gîndit să întrebaţi despre Parlamentul României* (Bucharest: Asociaţ ia PRO DEMOCRAŢIA, n.d.).

34. The party affiliations of women deputies reelected in 1996 would include 2 PDSR, 2 Social-Democratic Union (DP and RSDP), and 1 GRP. The senator was PDSR. On the overall retention rate, see *Telegrama*, no. 678 (November 12, 1996): pt. 2, item 6.

35. The interviews were conducted by Fischer in June 1997. The party distribution of the 12 women was: PDSR—2, NPP-CD—2, DP—2, RSDP—1, National Liberals (NLP)—1, GRP—1, Hungarian Democratic Union—1, ethnic minorities—2. All those interviewed had completed higher education and were professionals. Seven were married, 1 was widowed, 2 were divorced, and 2 had never married. Five had 2 children, 2 had 1 child, and 5 had no children. Several were grandmothers. The 2 reelected included 1 DP and 1 RSDP; the former secretaries of state had administered culture (PDSR and GRP) and economic reform (PDSR).

36. European and global organizations such as the Council of Europe, the European Union, the United Nations, the World Bank, and a variety of NGOs have tried with considerable success to influence the behavior of the new democracies in Eastern Europe on a variety of issues involving women, religious and ethnic minorities, and any disadvantaged or persecuted groups. In Romania the rights of Hungarians, gypsies, and homosexuals have been cause for particular concern.

37. For similar conclusions regarding the party differences, see Mihaela Miroiu, "Hrana conservatorismului: antifeminismul," *Sfera Politicii* 5, no. 47 (1997): 7, note 7.

38. The failure, one woman deputy explained, was due to her colleagues' conservative "mentality" as well as to weak "technology": the inability to prevent both parents from illegally taking leave. Once a system of crosschecking could be instituted, they would try again for "parental" rather than "maternity" leave.

39. Miroiu, "Hrana conservatorismului," p. 5.

40. Alena Heitlinger, "Framing Feminism in Post-Communist Czech Republic," *Communist and Post-Communist Studies* 29 (1996): 90.

41. Laura Grünberg and Mihaela Miroiu, eds., *Egalitate prin Diferenţa: program de educaţie non sexistă* (Bucharest: Societatea de Analize Feministe ANA şi Uniunea Europeană, 1997). Another important volume, Nicolaescu, *Cine suntem noi?* (see note 4) was published as part of the project "For a Community of Women's NGOs," sponsored by the Center of Feminine Identity Studies GENDER (Centrul de Studii ale Identităţ ii Feminine GENDER), with the support of the European Community's PHARE. In addition, two of the most important political journals carried special issues on gender in 1997; see *Sfera Politicii* 5, no. 47 (1997); and *Dilema* 5, nos. 220 and 226 (1997).

The Former Yugoslavia

10

In Pursuit of a Framework

Delayed Modernization and the Emancipation of Women in the Balkans

Silva Mežnarić and Mirjana Ule

East European researchers on gender relations and politics have often wondered how to explain two seemingly incongruous processes in East European societies: the ever-higher social visibility of women in education and employment and their declining rates of participation in politics and decision making. In Marxist societies these two processes were expected to be positively correlated to converge toward "emancipatory social settings" so that the equality of the sexes in at least the major sectors of modern life could be postulated. The major sectors encompassed industry, employment, a mobile work force, a secularized life, a diversified public sphere, and "civilized" households and other institutions of civil societies. Contrary to expectations, it has been found time and again that in East European societies the "emancipation of women" took the form of constant growth in the rate of female employment in manufacturing and agriculture, in combination with restricted and controlled mobility, strict control of spiritual and creative work, a nondiversified public sphere, and a double burden of labor in the workplace and in the household. Moreover, the household—the stronghold of privacy—became either entirely dependent on the social environment or, in some East European societies, isolated in its self-sufficiency.

It is safe to argue that women's emancipation in these East European societies has kept pace with their modernization; both are delayed or incomplete because of the absence of both a diversified public sphere and a civil society. Their absence is due to the elimination of private ownership and of any kind of market; that is, sovereign individual and autonomous economic agents. In such a setting, the true relationship between gender and power has been hidden behind the walls that shelter the *nomenklatura;* the apparent relationship has been displayed in the sectors of social activities, far from the seats of power: manufacturing, health services, education. Thus for almost three-quarters of this century the "emancipated and equal" woman of Eastern Europe gingerly sailed through muddy waters toward almost complete physical and mental exhaustion, supporting the reproduction of patriarchy within well-defined channels of power.[1]

No wonder, then, that support for emancipatory models of women in politics failed both as strategies for various emancipatory movements and as explanatory tools in the social sciences. Moreover, such failure fitted very well with an almost total absence of negotiation between the state and society. This lack reinforced the reproduction of known patterns of power, and by the same token has been conducive to traditional patterns of gender relations.

With new democracies coming to power in Eastern Europe, one would expect a diversified public sphere to emerge in the twilight zone between state and society and a civil society to emerge as the traditional patterns of power and gender relations are dismantled and the cornerstone of democracy is laid. But the new East European (mostly nationalistic) governments are closing themselves off from the rank and file in order to control the diversification of the public sphere and for the most part are repeating the old gender/power relations. These relations are inimical to civil societies and to women's participation in the political sphere.

Hence we argue that the modernization of the public sphere and the construction of a market economy form an appropriate framework within which to seek the place of women in the politics of Eastern Europe, past or present. In particular, the twilight zone between the household and the state is the area to watch to detect the first signs of the emergence of the new woman and of new gender relations in Eastern Europe.

Delayed Modernization in Eastern Europe

Modernization comprises the processes by which Western countries became organized as industrial, secular, and pluralistic societies. For the most part these processes were synergistic and congruous. They worked through the migration of populations, through the infusion of capital into markets, through the establishment of parties, newspapers, and parliaments, and through the confinement of religious institutions within their respective niches. The major ingredients of the modernization process are mobile workers, motivated capitalists and bankers, the work ethic, private ownership, and differentiated public spheres; their major outcomes are, for better or for worse, organized capital and labor, urban conglomerations, free elections and democratic institutions, and a tolerant clergy separated from the state.

A modernized society is easily recognizable. It is based on private property, which is protected by law. Religious discourse does not direct public affairs; various kinds of knowledge are generated and maintained within their own realms, which are not ruled exclusively by either church or state. A modernized society invests, has entrepreneurs and rentiers, people who are actively working or seeking work. It has parties, assemblies—parliaments, elections, campaigns, supporters and followers; it has mass media and their controllers; it has judges and lawmakers. When we say, as we customarily do, that modernized society is complex, we mean that this intricately interwoven fabric has some big loopholes: unprotected labor and unconcerned employers, decayed cities and environments, corrupt politicians and cronyism, unconcerned or cynical citizens, rotten institutions and compromised judges, controlled media. Yet despite these shortcomings, the very tension between state and civil society manages to reproduce procedures to keep these societies going, without major disruptions.

A modernized society is one in which people are mobile, or at least do not have to surmount institutional obstacles to mobility; in a modernized society not only people but also goods, information, ideas circulate with a degree of ease and flexibility. Therefore migration and mobility, inseparable from markets, are the hallmarks of incipient modernization. In a modernized society, books, newspapers, teachers, students, artists, and their products circulate. Obstacles to their circulation are embedded in modern societies, but so are procedures for overcoming those obstacles.

And at the level of everyday life? What does "modernized society" mean for women in contemporary Western society? They would probably define a "modern" society as one that provided opportunities, jobs, safety; but uppermost in their minds would probably be the state's role as pro-

vider of services for the community, for the society. The state is responsible for these services and pays for them. The citizen has her duties and
obligations toward the family and expects the state to listen to her and to
the groups that make up the society. This separation of private (household, family) and public (market) is the strength of modernized Western
society; it enables, it feeds both the state and the civil society; it gives
stateness to society and civility to the state. The mutual feeding of
private and public deprives the state of its exclusivity and society of its
"natural innocence."[2] Modernization of the private and public spheres
would then mean that the boundary between state and society was being
redefined and maintained through independent processes and at the
same time that state institutions were being restructured, civil liberties
expanded or shrunk, various pitfalls (anarchy, bureaucratization) of
modernization avoided or regulated. Such processes are vital forces of
modernizing societies and states; they create and re-create the living
tissue of society, the plurality of its public and private spheres. The vital
tension between society and its state is thus created and maintained by
private units, households, voluntary organizations, community-based
services, legally guaranteed self-organization. Modernized society limits the "state of nature" by its own self-organization; it thus prevents the
state from abusing its powers, even if the state is what Tocqueville
termed a "popularly elected despotism."[3]

A modernized society, then, is an industrialized, secularized, and pluralistic society that is capable, within limits, of handling the major conflicts that arise in the contemporary Western world—conflicts of
ethnicity, race, class, gender—within the institutional framework of its
polity. In other words, a Westernized polity is a necessary but not a
sufficient condition for the ability to handle conflicts (including those of
gender) without major disruptions. The threshold of possible disruption of
the polity is probably historically, culturally, and environmentally determined. Disruptive conflicts are possible in any modernized polity, let
alone a nonmodernized one. Yet arrangements for dealing with conflicts
within modernized societies make the threshold of disruption rather high.

The formerly socialist societies of Eastern Europe and the Balkans
lacked such arrangements; they had no ongoing means to maintain the
boundaries between public and private, none of the protections afforded by the institutions of democratic procedure. Therefore, with
very few exceptions, these societies simply lacked the institutional and
procedural means to contain any kind of conflict.

Modernization of the Borderlands and the Socialist State

In the nineteenth century the whole Balkan region lacked the set of social arrangements needed for economic growth and modernization, while the countries' politics were directed by forces beyond their own boundaries. John Lampe, a prominent Western historian of Balkan economic development, sees the region's development as "delayed," its modernization as "arrested," and the region itself as an "imperial borderland" of the "capitalist periphery."[4] The Balkans were untouched by the forces that began to modernize the rest of Europe in the sixteenth century because they had no contact with the West. When at last contact was established in parts of the western Balkans, such as Croatia, modernization began with the commercialization of agriculture and some protoindustrialization. These contacts brought a certain uniformity in the development of administration, education, and fiscal and banking systems; as peripheral administrative units before 1918, Slovenia and Croatia were governed by uniform larger state systems. But the great, overwhelming impact of the West on Eastern Europe was political. Western commerce may have been economically constructive or destructive, but Western political intervention always posed a deadly threat to local elites.

The former Yugoslavia exemplifies rapid modernization in sectors typically associated with modernization: expansion of the female work force, mobility within the work force and out of it, mobility of whole households, and a shrinking rate of women's participation in politics. After the end of the "war economy" in 1950, when Yugoslavia's economy was expected to take off, it persisted in lagging behind other countries in Southern and Eastern Europe. In 1950 the Yugoslav gross domestic product (GDP) per capita ranked twenty-second in Europe. Only Romania, Bulgaria, and Turkey ranked lower; Greece was not much higher. From 1950 to 1970 Yugoslavia raised its GDP to around two-fifths of the figure attained by developed Western European countries, so it was improving. In the same period, however, three comparable Southeastern European countries—Greece, Bulgaria, and Romania— shot ahead of Yugoslavia. From 1980 on, it was obvious that the Yugoslav economy was on a downward slope; in GDP per capita Yugoslavia dropped behind the European market economies; it advanced only in comparison with Hungary and Poland. Thus the gap in economic development between Yugoslavia and other Southern and

Eastern European countries has become wider.[5] More recent data show that at the end of 1990, Yugoslavia was at the bottom of European economic development, below the place it held in 1950.

Dismantling the Party Center and the Emergence of New Democracies

The social setting partly explains the nature of the transition to postcommunist politics in which Yugoslavia found itself after the center fell apart. The dismantling of the parties and of the member states in the 1990s varied in style and timing among the former republics. Slovenia experienced no major stress; there the communists have smoothly orchestrated the transition to a rather diversified and balanced democracy. In Croatia, "democratization" meant the installation of an ineffective parliamentary system and an authoritative presidential system, new oligarchies, and war with Serbian and Yugoslav armies. Serbia has not yet made a transition to postcommunist politics; there a new communist center has been substituted for the old. In Croatia and Serbia the major Balkan problem in political modernization has been brought into sharp focus: the systematic incompatibility of weak political institutionalization and growing political mobilization of the people.

We shall now proceed to an examination of the Slovenian case.

Notes

1. The heavy workload of women in Eastern Europe is manifested in chronic exhaustion and increasing apathy, ignorance, and lack of information. For the impact of the removal of women from public life on their political opinions, see Anuška Ferligoj, Mirjana Ule, and Tanja Renner, "Sex Differences in 'Don't Know' Rate: The Case of Slovenia," *Wisdom* 4 (1991): 3.

2. John Keane, *Democracy and Civil Society* (London: Verso, 1988), p. 14.

3. Alexis de Tocqueville, *De la Démocratie en Amérique* (Paris: Centre National de la Recherche Scientifique, 1981), p. 158.

4. John Lampe, "Imperial Borderlands or Capitalist Periphery? Redefining Balkan Backwardness, 1520–1914," in *The Origins of Backwardness in Eastern Europe,* ed. Daniel Chirot (Berkeley: University of California Press, 1989), p. 177.

5. Aleksandar Vačić, *Jugoslavija i Evropa* (Belgrade: Ekonomika, 1989), pp. 211–17.

11

The Case of Slovenia

Silva Mežnarić And Mirjana Ule

Women in Politics

Slovenian politics is undeniably still the domain of men. In the first free elections in 1990, only 15.7 percent of all candidates for the Assembly of the Republic of Slovenia and 10 percent of those elected were women.[1] The picture is much the same at the local level: 15.7 percent of delegates to local assemblies are women, with slightly higher representation in the Social Democratic Party.[2] Although the United Party claims to support gender equality, it has no more women delegates than any other party.

These figures are significantly below those for the communist era; women filled 26 percent of elective posts in 1982, 22 percent in 1986.[3] They are certainly lower than the comparable figures in some European countries (women occupy 30 to 40 percent of all parliamentary seats in the Scandinavian countries, close to 50 percent in Norway). The higher percentage of women delegates in the communist era was mainly a consequence of the quota system, which has been jettisoned along with the other trappings of the communist system. Even if a third or half of all candidates on a list are women, they are not elected because they are concentrated at the bottom of the list. In 1991, after the first free elections, the top echelons of the Assembly were exclusively male: all legislative committees were chaired by men. Women chaired five of the Assembly's forty administrative committees; only two of twenty-four ministers were women. In 1992 the Liberal Democratic Party won 23.3 percent of the vote, followed by the Slovenian Christian Democrats (14.5 percent), the United Party (13.6 percent), the Social Democratic Party (3.3 percent), and the Socialist Party (2.8 percent). All of the twenty-seven registered political parties are headed by men; women's representation on their executive boards ranges from 33 to 0.6 percent. The only party to preserve a quota for women's participation is the Liberal Democratic Party. Since almost all other forms of organizational activity have disappeared, very few opportunities are left for women to break through. As a result of financial difficulties and the media's loss of interest in independent women's movements since the mid-1980s, women's initiatives in almost all fields lack support and have difficulty attracting public recognition.[4]

Women Citizens and Politicians: Attitudes, Views, Problems

In the spring of 1990, on the eve of Slovenia's independence, a few surveys and interviews of women voters and politicians were conducted.[5] Seventy-six interviews of professional politicians (89 percent with university degrees, 65 percent between 36 and 55 years old) yielded findings that provide insight into the political situation during the transition period. Judging from the reactions of respondents on almost all questions about their expectations for the future multiparty system, one could argue that women politicians showed split loyalties. On the one hand, they are still loyal to the old party's positions; on the other, they are considering the possibility of shifting to new associations or parties, mostly with ecological (22 percent) or generational constituencies. Only 6 percent contemplated joining the newly established Association of Women of Slovenia; none expressed a wish to join any feminist group.

A comparison of the attitudes of these women politicians concerning the status of women in politics with those of a sample of 338 female citizens polled in the autumn of 1989[6] reveals interesting differences between the two groups (see Table 11.1). These groups differ significantly on the three items that are contingent on actual experience in politics and on one item that is embedded in almost every Slovenian woman's experience: abortion. Women politicians are overwhelmingly against legally prescribed quotas for women in politics, are evenly divided on women leaders if they have a choice, and would be likely to accept a political job if they were offered one; and the vast majority want to keep abortion legal.

It seems that both populations, "initiated" (politicians) and "uninitiated" (women with no experience in politics), agreed on most of the commonly cited reasons for women's lack of visibility in politics:

Table 11.1

Percentages of Female Citizens and Female Politicians Who Agreed with Nine Statements Concerning Women's Status

	Citizens (N = 338)	Politicians (N = 76)
Women are underrepresented in politics	63.5	82.4
If yes, the reason is family and home responsibilities	53.8	61.8
Women's representation in politics should be enforced by law	34.9	8.8
Women should have their own political party	8.2	7.4
Women have problems in the public sphere that men do not share	76.8	80.0
I favor the multiparty system[a]	64.8	75.0
I favor women leaders	23.3	50.0
I personally would accept a leadership position if it were offered to me	25.2	57.3
Abortion should remain legal	38.7	89.7

Source: Tanja Renner, "Ženske in politika v Sloveniji," in *Ženske in politika,* ed. Mirjana Ule, pp. 21–43 (Ljubljana: Varianta, 1990); Milica Antić, "Razvoj politike v podjetje," in ibid., pp. 47–65.
[a]December 1989.

tradition, socialization, family, and the women themselves. The first three reasons are all too familiar; the last one, women themselves, has not been subjected to rigorous research and therefore is worth investigating in more detail. Women believe that women are not politically active because:

- Women lack self-reliance.
- Women are too sensitive.
- Women's professional performance is too emotional.
- Women are demanding; they question their own performance all the time.
- Women assume full responsibility for family and child care.
- Politics is not a creative endeavor; women are more creative than men.
- Women do not like to be too visible.

What can be done?

The women interviewed offered many suggestions, from the radical (special-interest groups, a women's party) to the pragmatic (changing job shifts). Most of them seemed to feel that women are on their way to power.

Women politicians sought minimal policy measures:

- Programs to raise the educational level of both women and men.
- Programs for joint political endeavors by men and women.
- An affirmative action program for women managers.
- European working hours (from nine to five).
- More flexible forms of employment.

Women in the Labor Market

The position of women in the labor market in Slovenia is similar to that in many Eastern European countries; the difference between the employment rates of women and men is even smaller than in the majority of other European states, and it is steadily decreasing (Table 11.2).

Most women have been employed in the state sector; only 4.2 percent of all women in the work force are self-employed (compared to 5.1 percent of all employed men).[7] They represent more than one-third of all people employed in agriculture and manufacturing, and more than two-thirds of all those employed in services and banking. The distribution of employed women in the various sectors of activity, however, shows a different picture: 1.7 percent of women work in agriculture, 38.7 percent in manufacturing, 20.6 percent in services, 34.7 percent in banking and administration. It would be safe to say that the Slovenian labor market is divided by gender; there are "male" and "female" sectors of employment, and those in which women predominate—education, health, social welfare, and the textile and shoe industries—are graded lower on the social scale.

Within the work hierarchies, women are concentrated in lower-paid jobs, with lower prestige and less autonomy than men; research findings show, for example, that in 1991 8.4 percent of employed women had no autonomy on their jobs (compared to 5.4 percent of men); 41.5 percent of employed women but 34.1 percent of men felt physically exhausted by their full-time jobs. Women rank lower in work hierarchies even in "feminized" employment sectors, and even if they are better educated than men. Slovenian women's mobility in the work-

Table 11.2

Women in Work Force, Slovenia, 1987–92 (in thousands)

	1987	1988	1989	1990	1991	1992[a]	1993	1994	1995
Total employed	867.8	861.7	851.3	817.8	746.0	700.9	845	851	884
Women employed	395.7	395.8	392.9	379.9	349.8	330.7	395	397	409
Percent	45.6	45.9	46.2	46.5	46.9	47.2	46.7	46.6	46.4

Source: Statistical Bureau of Republic of Slovenia, Ljubljana, 1992; *Republic of Slovenia 1996 Statistical Yearbook,* XXXV (Ljubljana, 1996), p. 193. Information for years 1993, 1994, and 1995 was provided by Jill A. Irvine, University of Oklahoma.
[a]March.

Table 11.3

Percentage of Women in High-Skilled Jobs and Management in Selected Employment Sectors, 1986

Sector	High-skilled jobs	Management
Manufacturing (textiles)	74.0	33.5
Trade	54.0	16.0
Catering, tourism	61.0	25.4
Education	73.0	39.4
Judiciary	56.6	29.0
Health insurance	84.0	68.0
Child services	97.7	83.0

Source: Republic of Slovenia, *Report of the Government on the Position of Women in Slovenia* (Ljubjana, April 1992), p. 8.

Table 11.4

Women and Men Employed in Slovenia in 1986, by Years of Education
(in percent)

	Women	Men
Lower education (up to 8 years of education)	32.7	22.8
9 to 11 years of education	24.8	44.9
12 to 14 years of education	36.8	23.7
University graduates (up to 16 years of education)	5.7	8.6

Source: Republic of Slovenia, *Report of the Government on Position of Women in Slovenia* (Ljubljana, April 1992), p. 8.

place is severely limited. The number of women in a firm's managerial jobs is not proportionate to the pool of highly educated and competent women the firm employs (Table 11.3).

In general, women receive slightly less education than men in Slovenia; in 1986 men averaged 10.8 years of schooling, women 9.9 years. More employed women (36.8 percent) than men (23.7 percent) were high school graduates in 1986, but only 5.7 percent of women had university degrees, in comparison with 8.6 percent of men (Table 11.4).[8]

Women accounted for a smaller share of the unemployed than men (43.7 percent)[9] in March 1992, though those who are unemployed have to wait longer for jobs (an average of 14.4 months in 1992, compared to 12.5 months for men). This is a new development; in the four preceding years, the waiting period was no longer for women than for men, and sometimes shorter. A government report offers two possible explanations for this phenomenon: (1) the initial tide of bankruptcies swept up firms in which the majority of workers were men; (2) women are more averse to risk than men; they are not job-hoppers and are not attracted to jobs that offer no security. At the same time, women are more willing than men to change their occupations; 84 percent of unemployed women (compared to 77 percent of men) would like to be included in a training program if one were available. This finding may be related to the fact that unemployment is rising among young women; in the cohort of Slovenians aged 18 to 30 years, more women than men are without jobs.[10]

Women in Management and Entrepreneurship

The twilight zone between the household and the state is the area to watch for the first signs of the emergence of the new woman in the modernizing process. Slovenia may be a good place to look for such signs; it has a fairly high standard of living, well-equipped households with appliances, a large percentage of employed and educated women, and well-endowed supports for women who work outside their homes. Yet, as we have seen, women are less well represented now than they were in the predemocratic era. Where, then, are the signs of the new woman? We find them in small private firms.

Liberalization and privatization of the postsocialist economies left enough space for new, unconventional economic activities. Since the procedure for registering a new firm was not difficult and the initial capital required was not great, many entrepreneurs entered the market. At the beginning of 1992 almost 30 percent of the new entrepreneurs were women. Most of them fill niches in modernizing activities—finance management, data management, information and administrative consulting, travel agencies—sectors that were men's domains in the socialist economy. Women entrepreneurs are young (between 30 and 45) and well educated. They have significant previous experience in relatively well-paid jobs, and as a result of various social incentives they had been promoted to senior positions. Their work days are significantly longer than men's (male entrepreneurs tend to work shorter days than they did in their previous jobs). They are fully absorbed in their work for their firms, whereas about a third of men also do outside work for other firms.[11]

Women managers and entrepreneurs are a highly selected segment of the population; they are distributed along quite an unconventional spectrum of economic roles. As entrepreneurs and managers, they demand a great deal of themselves and of their co-workers. They are sensitive to social problems around them, are strongly self-reliant, and are oriented toward risk-taking.[12]

Convinced that the abolition of women's quotas would diminish women's opportunities to participate in political and corporate life, these women have devised their own strategies for advancement in the pluralistic society in the making. According to the women we interviewed, there are three clusters of viable promotional strategies, for both the short and the long term:

1. Strategies to be developed and implemented during primary and secondary socialization, within in-groups, among significant others, and in institutions: sharing and teaching how to share male and female roles in everyday life. On this issue women are very specific and inventive; their ideas are based on experiences accumulated during their own socialization and in hard work in corporate (socialist) and domestic life while they developed their careers.

2. "Consciousness raising": increasing both men's and women's awareness of the necessity and rationality of letting go of the patriarchal mentality. In their view, modernization of life through a market economy will introduce new criteria of success, quite contrary to the socialist standards. These criteria—education coupled with job performance, the ability to communicate, command of foreign languages, tact and good manners, the capacity for continuous learning—would hardly fit with the patriarchal mentality common among Slovenian women as well as men. "It's hard work, but worthwhile as a beginning," says one of the respondents.

3. Organized, farsighted, and well-orchestrated action designed to get more women into the legislature. "There will be no spontaneous selection according to the quality of the candidates in the new elections," one woman politician said. "We [women] have to realize that in the future, the most important decisions will be based on laws, and the most important laws will be those concerning education, social policy, reproduction of society, and the

position of the individual in relation to the state and society. In addition to the economy, all legislative areas are especially gender-sensitized, which means, in our circumstances, that their outcome could easily be gender-biased. To avoid that, men and women have to work together on restructuring power relations in society; since men are not likely to do it, women should get organized and enter all three levels of government [local, regional, and national] in considerable numbers as representatives."[13]

"Abortionstrife": Conflict over a New Distribution of Ideological and Political Power

As elsewhere in (mostly Catholic) Eastern Europe, family planning and pro-life/pro-choice issues took center stage as soon as the new political parties began to identify target issues. Conservative or right-of-center parties almost without debate stood for limiting the right to abortion. "Abortionstrife" was on everyone's mind in 1990 when the proposed new constitution was being circulated for public discussion. Article 52 concerned the right of women to decide upon abortion. The Catholic church was opposed to the freedom of choice that the majority of women and other groups demanded. The issue split both governing parties and the opposition. Pro-choice politicians argued that to deny women and couples the freedom to choose would be to erase the boundary between the state and the private sphere, and consequently to eliminate the bedrock condition of civil society from the coming democracy. Pro-life politicians, including some liberals, argued for the "sanctity of life" and demanded that Article 52 be removed from the new constitution. Women became organized: various pressure groups in and out of the Assembly, publications, and public opinion polls helped persuade parliamentary groups to commit themselves to vote in favor of freedom of choice.

A comparison of a public opinion poll on abortion conducted in 1969 with the same poll conducted in 1990 (identical wording) reveals intriguing similarities and differences, both over time and between male and female respondents. Within the span of two decades, the percentage of Slovenians who opposed the right to abortion was almost halved; the somewhat cautious pro-choice approach (in favor of abortion when medical and social circumstances are taken into consideration) gained adherents; and the proportion of respondents "strongly in favor" of free choice more than tripled (Table 11.5). Such a liberalization of public opinion was certainly strongly supportive of women when Article 52 was contested. The responses also suggest that in two decades women became more liberal than men.

In 1969 almost 45 percent of women (41.2 percent of men) opposed abortion; in 1990, 25.2 percent of women (29.5 percent of men) opposed abortion unconditionally or only under "certain conditions." Two decades also brought changes within generations: in 1969 the majority of respondents who opposed abortion, both men and women, were at least 61 years old; in 1990 the opponents of abortion were almost evenly distributed among men and women under 30 years and over 60. Such findings suggest that the younger generation is becoming more conservative, at least where abortion is concerned. There are indications, researchers suggest, that the lower socioeconomic groups are developing more conservative tendencies, while the middle and upper socioeconomic groups are becoming more tolerant of the right to abortion.[14]

Conclusion: Delayed Modernization Means Delayed Women's Politics

Earlier we defined our framework of "delayed modernization" as one in which women are absent from the public sphere, a civil society is lacking, the labor market is divided by gender, and "emancipatory" models serve to reproduce the nomenklatura's patterns of power. We have also argued that the first sign of real democratization in the new democracies of Eastern Europe would be the breakthrough of a civil society through incorporation of gender issues in the new society's institutions. Can we see in Slovenia any signs of modernization with the introduction of private property, the rule of law, a secular state, and a diversified public sphere, all conducive to the promotion of the interests of vulnerable social groups, women in particular? Are there signs that women are organizing for autonomous action in their own belief?[15]

We have seen that the new institutions of power have reverted to the ways of the old boys' network and have systematically excluded women. Nevertheless, we have seen signs that women are finding their own niches in the new polity. These niches are not within the economic sectors characterized by "delayed modernization"; most of them

Table 11.5

Responses to Questions about Abortion, 1969 and 1990

"Arguments for and against abortion have become heated again; What is your opinion about abortion?"

	1969			1990		
	Men	Women	All respondents	Men	Women	All respondents
Strongly opposed	12.7%	17.5%	15.2%	8.7%	5.3%	6.9%
Opposed with some exceptions	28.5	27.1	27.8	20.8	19.9	20.3
In favor when socially/ medically indicated	45.3	43.7	44.5	45.6	52.7	49.3
Strongly in favor	5.3	4.3	4.8	17.3	15.1	16.2
Undecided	5.3	5.2	5.2	6.6	5.6	6.1
No answer	2.9	2.2	2.5	1.0	1.4	1.2

Source: Slovensko javno mnenje, *SJM '69* and *SJM '90* (Ljubljana: Center for Public Opinion Research, Faculty for Social Sciences, University of Ljubljana, 1969, 1990).

are in the expanding service sector, in small-scale manufacturing, and in education. There are also encouraging indications that women will realize their goals in institutionalized politics; only organized action through the legislative bodies at all levels can increase women's influence in the new state's politics. Research indicates a new awareness of the sort of framework needed to advance women's interests.

Slovenia may become one of the success stories of women's politics in the Eastern Europe of tomorrow. Women's breakthrough could be seen as a sign of the emergence of civil society in the state and the stateness of civil society. Yet as the delay of modernization and democracy is prolonged, optimism may be premature. One woman we interviewed commented: "It seems to me that women could easily start to go backward. Nobody would notice."

Notes

1. Out of 1,477 candidates and deputies elected to the National Assembly of the Republic of Slovenia in 1992, 219 were women. Information provided by Jill A. Irvine, University of Oklahoma.

2. Of the 2,779 members of municipal councils in 1994, 299 were women. *Republic of Slovenia 1995 Statistical Yearbook,* vol. 35 (Ljubljana, 1996), p. 119. Information provided by Jill A. Irvine, University of Oklahoma.

3. In 1974, 26 percent of all representatives in the Slovenian Assembly were women; see Tomšić, *Ženska, delo, družina, družba,* p. 66.

4. Komisija Skupščine Republike Slovenije za žensko politiko, *Poročilo o položaju žensk,* p. 12.

5. Tanja Renner, "Ženske in politika v Sloveniji," in *Ženske in politika,* ed. Mirjana Ule, pp. 21–43 (Ljubljana: Varianta, 1990); Milica Antić, "Razvoj politike v podjetje," in ibid., pp. 47–65.

6. Ule, *Ženske in politika,* p. 2.

7. After World War II, the rate of female employment in the state sector grew more quickly than that of men; between 1958 and 1968, the number of men employed rose by 28 percent, while that of women increased by 62 percent. See Vida Tomšić, *Ženska, delo, družina, družba* (Ljubljana: Komunist, 1976), pp. 180–85.

8. Republic of Slovenia, *Report of the Government on the Position of Women in Slovenia* (Ljubljana, April 1992), p. 8.

9. In 1995, of the 70,000 unemployed in Slovenia, 39,000 were men, while 31,000 were women. *Republic of Slovenia 1996 Statistical Yearbook,* vol. 35 (Ljubljana, 1996), p. 193. Information provided by Jill A. Irvine, University of Oklahoma.

10. Komisija Skupščine Republike Slovenije za žensko politiko, *Poročilo o položaju žensk v Republiki Sloveniji* (Ljubljana: Skupščina Republiki Slovenije, July 1992), p. 9.

11. "Research: Women in Politics; Opinion Makers. Subpopulation," in ibid., p. 60.

12. For quite different research findings concerning women managers in Croatia, see Vesna Pusić, *Vladaoci i upravljaci* (Zagreb: Novi Liber, 1992), p. 82. According to Pusić's typology, women tend to be "traditional" rather than "modern" managers.

13. Ule, *Ženske in politika,* p. 141. This interview was conducted on the eve of the first free elections, in the fall of 1989; in the second national elections, in December 1992, women accounted for only four of the twenty-one persons elected to the State Council and nine of the ninety elected to the legislative body, the National Assembly.

14. We suggest some caution in interpreting pro-choice/pro-life opinions as indicators of either conservatism or open-mindedness. It may well be that these opinions are influenced by extraneous variables, such as the quality of health services and access to contraceptives. Twice as many couples in Slovenia compared with Western Europe use no contraceptives at all; more than half of the women who had abortions in 1991 had practiced no form of contraception. There are strong indications that well-organized gynecological centers, by distributing contraceptives freely, succeeded in eliminating the need for almost two-thirds of the anticipated abortions. See Komisija SRS za žensko politiko, *Poročilo o položaju žensk,* p. 19; Mirjana Ule, "Javno mnenje o splavu," in Ženske za politiko, *Abortus: Pravica do izbire* (Ljubljana, 1991), p. 9.

15. Various autonomous women's groups have sprung up in the last few years: a hotline for battered women and children (1989); Women for Politics (1989); Women with Ideas, the women's section of the Management Club (1990); Initiative for Equal Opportunities (1990); Initiative of the Women of Capodistria (1990); Women's Section of the Party of Democratic Reforms (1990); Women against Violence (1991); Committee for Women's Politics in the Slovene Parliament (1990); and Action of Women Farmers (1972).

12

Public Opinion and the Political Position of Women in Croatia

Jill Irvine

The rapid social, political, and economic change characteristic of postsocialist systems has had a significant impact on the political role of women. Perhaps most striking has been the decrease in women's political participation, both at the elite and mass levels, and the resulting marginalization of women in political life. Croatia has been no exception. Whereas women typically filled 20 to 25 percent of elected positions in Yugoslavia during the state socialist period, they now fill significantly fewer of these posts. For example, in 1986, 54 of the 341 representatives in the Croatian parliament (Sabor) were women; in 1990, of the 80 representatives elected to the House of Representatives in the Sabor, only 3 were women. In 1992 this number rose slightly to 8 out of 138, and in 1995 to 10 out of 127. In the upper house, the House of Counties, 3 women out of 63 representatives were elected in the 1993 elections. Thus at the most visible level of decision making, women's political participation and representation dropped dramatically in 1990 and has risen only slightly in the ensuing several years.[1] While women's political participation under state socialism was often formalistic and did not necessarily translate into real political power, this drop nevertheless indicates a real shift in the political position of women in postsocialist Croatia.

Scholars have provided various explanations for this change in women's political status in Eastern Europe during the past several years. Some have attributed it to a male grab for power in the popular movements instrumental in effecting the collapse of state socialism, movements in which women participated heavily.[2] Others have pointed to women's rational desire to withdraw from public life after years under state socialism of bearing the triple burden of job, family, and political obligations.[3] Whatever the immediate cause, however, changing patterns of women's political participation reflect a deeper societal debate about the proper social and political role of women in these newly transformed polities. Central to this debate is the prevailing concept of public and private spheres and women's relation to them. A long tradition in Western social and political thought has associated men with the former and women with the latter.[4] That is, while men's identity has been seen to rest on their actions in the political realm, the *polis,* women have been confined to the private domain of discourse and activity. Although this concept began to change as women entered the work force in large numbers in both command and market economies, remnants of the public-private dichotomy in defining gender roles remain. In Croatia, traditional social actors, such as the Catholic church, which have become more influential in recent years, have promoted this view by emphasizing the importance of women in the private sphere—of their bearing and raising children in the proper moral environment. This view has also been advocated by nationalist and extreme-right ideologies, which believe a patriarchal family structure is best for fostering the "moral cleanliness and willingness to sacrifice" necessary to the survival and growth of the nation.[5]

This brief chapter analyzes public opinion toward women's political position in Croatia using survey data on a variety of questions relating to women's social and political roles.[6] Should women's activity be related primarily to familial obligations in the private sphere? What is the proper mode of women's participation in political life? Which social actors should have the most influence in determining gender roles? Should women have the right to choose an abortion? Which system—socialist or postsocialist—has most effectively ensured the proper political position of women? Has the social, political, and economic position of women improved since the introduction of multiparty elections? The chapter then considers how these opinions relate to ideological orientation and electoral choice. That is, to what extent are voters' views on the political position of women reflected in their electoral choices? Is there a gender gap in the voting behavior of the Croatian electorate? The chapter concludes by discussing the implications of these data for the future political position of women in Croatia. Although a complete explanation for trends in women's political participation is beyond the scope of this chapter, an examination of available survey data can provide preliminary hypotheses and raise further questions about the impact of popular opinion on women's political role.

Public Man, Private Woman in the Croatian Context

What does the population in Croatia think about the activity of women in the public sphere? Should women participate in public life on equal terms with men, or is their primary place in the private domain? Two components of popular attitudes toward this issue are explored in the survey data. The first involves the proper sphere of labor for women. Is women's work to be defined in domestic terms, that is, as caring for the home and family? Or should women work outside the home in all sectors of the economy? The answers to these questions have implications not only for employment practices but, more importantly, for the way in which women's social being is defined. The second component of popular attitudes toward women's public role involves women's aptitude for politics, both as voters and as officeholders. Is the public role of political life somehow "unnatural" to women as traditionally conservative or extreme-right ideologies often suggest?

A look at public opinion data reveals that while one-half to two-thirds of the population strongly supports women's participation in social and political life on equal terms with men, a significant group of the population opposes this view (see Figure 12.1). According to a 1997 survey conducted throughout Croatia, roughly half the sample (56 percent) completely disagreed with the statement that a women's place is in the home, where she should occupy herself with raising children and domestic matters. Nevertheless, about 20 percent, or roughly one-fifth of the sample, agreed or strongly agreed with this idea.[7] The remainder of the sample was distributed between these two viewpoints. Thus, while at least half the population rejects a primarily domestic definition of women's social role, a significant portion of the population supports this view, suggesting a core of support for the reassertion of private woman as a public virtue.

To what extent do these views reflect the reality of employment trends in Croatia? Has there been a significant decrease in women's participation in the labor force since the collapse of state socialism? Women entered the labor force in high numbers during the state-socialist period as a result of the League of Communists of Yugoslavia's

Figure 12.1 **Attitudes toward the social and political position of women**

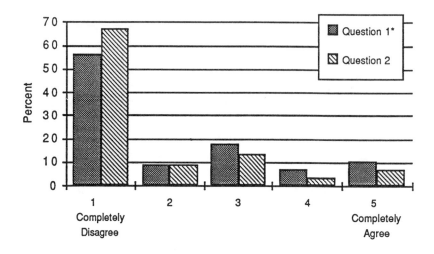

*Question 1: A woman's place is in the home where she should occupy herself with
        raising children and with domestic matters.

Question 2: Women should stay out of politics because they were not born for it.

(LCY) ideological commitment to the equality of women and the exigencies of rapid industrialization.[8] Nevertheless, as in other industrialized democracies, women's participation remained concentrated in those sectors of the economy related to their traditional role of nurturing and caring for others.[9] Similarly, while women were now working outside the home in large numbers, they were still expected to carry the primary burden of raising children and caring for the home.[10] Thus traditional norms about the social role of women coexisted alongside this greatly expanded, more public role for women in the economy.

A similar situation persists today concerning women's economic and social roles. While women's employment outside the home has continued to rise in the four years after 1990,[11] and much of the population supports this activity, social norms concerning women's primary responsibility for home and family undoubtedly remain.[12] Moreover, those advocating women's withdrawal from the labor force have been able to articulate this view in a way that was not permissible during the state-socialist period. The impact of their voice on redefining women's social role remains to be seen, but, coupled with the dislocations caused by economic restructuring, it could be significant indeed.

Support for women's political equality is higher among the populace than for social equality. When asked whether women should stay
out of politics because they "are not born for it," three quarters (76
percent) of the population disagreed or completely disagreed. Similarly, the percentage of respondents who agreed or completely agreed
with this question was lower (10 percent) than that which placed
women's social role in the home. Thus, many respondents who view a
woman's primary place as in the home are not prepared to exclude
women from political life. These data are consistent with data on political participation in Western liberal democracies where a significant
portion of the population supports equal opportunity for political participation at the same time that it advocates differential gender roles.[13]
The portion of the population that believes a woman's primary place is
in the home but rejects the idea that women should stay out of politics
may prefer more limited political participation by women than by
men—for example, voting but not running for office.

To what extent are these views about the public role of women
consistent with ideological orientation? Have the rise of right-wing,
religious, and conservative ideologies prompted a greater support for
the privatization of women's public role? Survey respondents were
asked to rank their beliefs on a left-right scale in order to determine
their general ideological orientation. A preliminary look at the data
suggests a strong relationship between ideological orientation and beliefs about women's political participation, with those on the left more
supportive of women's political participation than those on the right.
While about 65 percent of those on the left disagree with the idea that
women belong in the home, approximately 45 percent of those on the
right disagree (see Figure 12.2). Nevertheless, respondents on the ex-
tremes of both left and right show a similar rate (17 percent) of positive response to this question. Thus there is a hard-core group on the
extreme left that holds an equally conservative approach to women's
social role. This small group of hard-core leftists (12 percent) also
completely agrees, along with its extreme-right counterpart (13 percent), that women should stay out of politics.

This association between ideological orientation and views on
women is reflected in the electoral choices of voters. Voters who take
the most conservative position on women's participation in public life
generally vote for parties on the right, while those who are most supportive of women's public role tend to vote on the left. The political

220

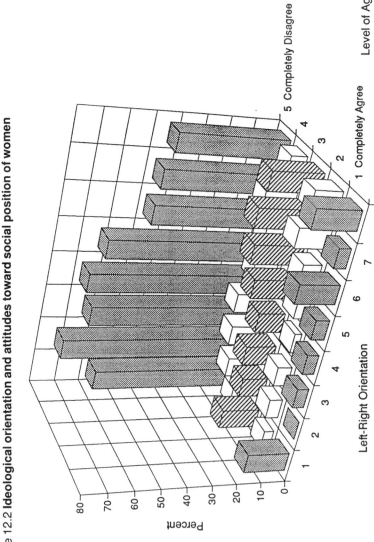

Figure 12.2 Ideological orientation and attitudes toward social position of women

*A woman's place is in the home where she should occupy herself with raising children and domestic matters.

party with the highest level of support for women's public role, however, is the centrist liberal party, the Croatian Social Liberal Party (CSLP). While the CSLP has sometimes adopted nationalist rhetoric, it has consistently positioned itself as the main party of liberal opposition to the ruling Croatian Democratic Union (CDU), and it has occasionally championed women's issues, such as abortion rights. While the leftist Social Democratic Party (SDP), the reconstituted League of Communists, also displays a high level of support for women's participation in public life, some extreme leftists, many of whom vote for this party, are opposed to this view.

The political parties that display the highest level of support for restricting women's public role are the ruling CDU, the extreme right Croatian Party of Rights (CPR), and the Croatian Peasant Party (CPP). The CDU has consistently taken a conservative position on women's political issues, emphasizing the central importance of family and women's special role in raising children and caring for the home.[14] Although the CPP has attempted to forge a political alliance with parties of the liberal opposition, its primarily rural constituency has retained its conservative attitude toward women's social role. Indeed, CPP voters show the most conservative attitude of any portion of the electorate in their belief that women's proper place is in the home, and they are inclined to punish their leadership for straying too far from their core values by voting for the CDU. Thus, attempts by CPP leaders to adopt a more liberal profile on these and other issues have not been successful. Interestingly, voters for the CPR display a less conservative attitude on the question of women's social role (i.e., that her place is in the home) than do CPP and CDU voters, but they indicate the highest level of support (20 percent) for the idea that women should not participate in political life. This may reflect the more entrepreneurial attitude displayed by CPR voters, which coupled with their more hard-line nationalist views may result in their belief that women should take advantage of new business opportunities but that they do not possess the militaristic traits needed by politicians "in these times."

In order to evaluate the significance of these different views on the position of women expressed by political parties and their electorates, it is necessary to describe briefly the current political context in Croatia. The present system in Croatia can best be described as semi-democratic. While Croatia has established the requisite institutions of democracy—competitive elections among political parties—it has failed to meet the criteria of a fully consolidated democracy. There has been no turnover of government nor have the results of the elections been respected in all cases. Moreover, the ruling CDU has used non-democratic methods to harass and weaken the opposition. The authoritarian tendencies of the ruling party and its preeminent political role have allowed it to translate its conservative positions on women into legislative rulings and to propagate its views in the largely government-controlled press.

The Role of the Church

As the social and political roles of women have been debated during the past several years, so too has the question of which social actors and institutions should define these roles. Before 1990, the LCY determined public attitudes, or at least public behavior toward women. Since then, other institutions, such as the Catholic church, have become instrumental in shaping public and private norms. In a country where two-thirds of the population are practicing Catholics, the Catholic church has tremendous social influence.[15] Public opinion polls consistently rank the church higher in terms of popular approval than political institutions such as the parliament.[16] To what extent does the populace believe, then, that the church should have the most powerful voice in shaping the debate about the public role of women?

Despite the high level of approval of the church as an institution, there is little support for increasing the church's influence concerning women's role in society (see Figure 12.3). Fully 69 percent of the population completely disagrees with this idea, while a mere 5 percent completely agrees with it. The most significant opposition to the church's influence comes from individuals who are ideologically on the left and are SDP voters. Thus, even those extreme leftists who wish to restrict women's role in political life do not believe the church should have a say in this matter. Greatest support for the church's role in defining the position of women in society comes from individuals who vote for the CDU, 12 percent of whom completely endorse this view. The high correlation between religious beliefs and CDU voting goes a long way toward explaining this greater level of support within the CDU for expanding the church's social influence.[17] The CDU's position on this question, and attempts by CDU leaders to foster a closer relationship with the church, have resulted in a more significant

223

Figure 12.3 **Party choice and attitudes toward the church's role in defining the position of women**

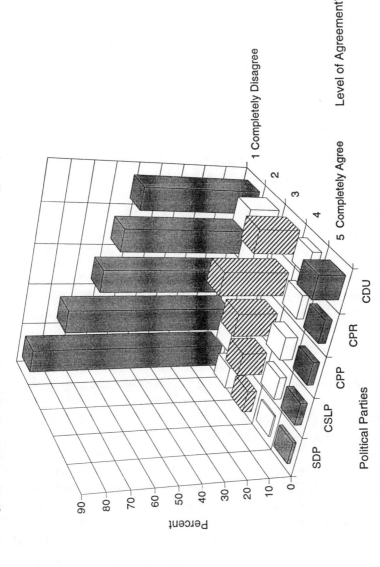

*The church should have the main influence on the position of women.

voice for the church in defining gender roles in the largely government-controlled press.

The Struggle over Abortion Rights

As elsewhere in Eastern Europe, the struggle over abortion rights has
become symbolic of the changing social and political roles of women
in Croatia. The right to a legal abortion, which existed under state
socialism, was publicly contested in the 1990 elections by various
members of the CDU and other political parties and groups.[18] Although this issue did not provoke the public outcry and demonstrations
that occurred in Slovenia, which resulted in a constitutional article
ensuring the right to choose, it has remained a point of political contention during the ensuing several years. Unlike the debate over abortion
in the United States and Europe, which has been framed primarily in
terms of individual rights, in Croatia this debate has centered on nationalist precepts and has been closely linked with attempts by the
ruling party to increase the Croat population. President Tudjman cited
this goal in his speech to the parliament in 1990 when he outlined the
ten major tasks of his regime.[19] Subsequently, the government enacted
legislation designed to encourage women to have more children. The
incorporation of demographic renewal into the CDU's political program has also led to a strong move to ban abortion in order to ensure a
higher rate of population growth.

These attempts to restrict abortion have met with little support from
the populace. Nevertheless, evidence suggests that popular support for
the right to choose, while still high, may be falling as a result of
opposition to abortion in the popular press. In 1990, 79 percent of the
population supported a woman's right to have an abortion, but this
support dropped to 74 percent in 1995 and still further to 70 percent in
1997. Support for a restriction of abortion rights is highest, as we
might expect, among those whose ideological orientation is on the
right (See Figure 12.4). The extreme-right CPR has adopted opposition
to abortion as an official part of its political program, and 19 percent of
CPR voters oppose abortion in all circumstances. Ultranationalists
have emphasized that legalized abortion is "both national genocide as
well as national suicide."[20] The CDU, which has a much more diverse
electorate, has backed away from its initial efforts to ban abortion.
While 13 percent of its voters support such a ban, 60 percent of them

Figure 12.4 **Ideological orientation and attitudes toward abortion**

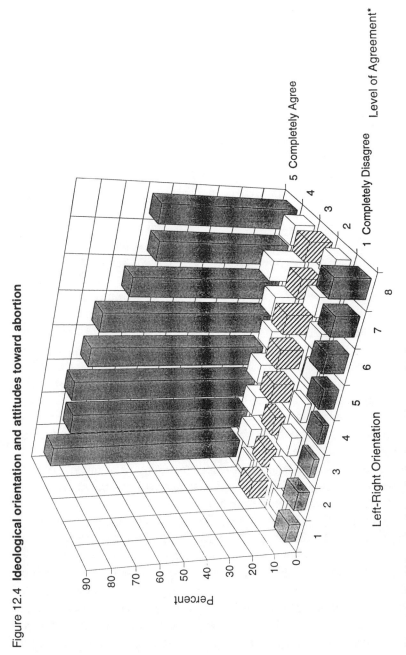

* A woman should have the right to freely choose to have an abortion.

completely oppose it. Thus, although many party officials continue publicly to call for a partial or total ban on abortion, the CDU has gone no farther than passing legislation requiring women to undergo compulsory counseling before having an abortion.

Is the Political Position of Women Improving?

The ambiguous legacy of state socialism for the political position of women is still being debated today by scholars, activists, and the popular press. The Communist Party's official commitment to social and political equality and party-imposed quotas on female participation in governmental bodies meant that women were represented to a greater extent than today. This participation, however, often did not increase women's real decision-making authority. By eradicating the power of the party to impose its dictates on women, and by expanding the real competency of representative institutions, the postsocialist political environment ultimately appears to offer a better chance for political equality. This environment also has involved a rapid expansion of the private sphere, however, and pressure on women to return to it.

To what extent does the populace in Croatia think that the position of women has improved under the present system? Recent survey data indicate that most citizens believe women to be no better off today than they were under state socialism (see Figure 12.5). Forty-six percent of survey respondents reject or completely reject the idea that women's position has improved since 1990; another 33 percent are not certain if it has. Thus, while a majority of citizens rates the current political system positively in comparison with its predecessor, this feeling of optimism does not apply to the position of women. Whatever the shortcomings of the state socialist approach to achieving women's political equality, most Croats appear to believe that it afforded better protection to women's rights than the current political system.

Viewed from a different perspective, those respondents who completely agree that women's position has changed for the better in recent years tend to be ideologically on the right and to be CPR voters (37 percent of whom feel this way) or CDU voters (26 percent of whom feel this way). Since these parties and many of their supporters advocate a more restricted public role for women, it may be that they are satisfied with the steps that have been taken in that direction. Nevertheless, even large numbers of CDU and CPR voters doubt whether the

Figure 12.5 **Evaluation of impact of state socialist and post-socialist systems on the position of women**

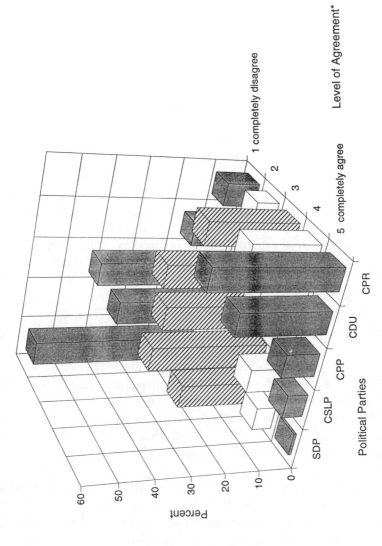

*The position of women today is better than it was under communism.

position of women has improved under the postsocialist system. Most of them, like the rest of the population, express ambivalence or uncertainty about the impact of recent political developments on women's political equality. Thus, while this group of the population is most enthusiastic about social, political, and economic developments since 1990, they are less willing to see the benefits of these developments as extending to women as well.

A Gender Gap in Croatian Politics?

Research on political participation and voting behavior in the advanced industrial societies has documented significant differences in the ways in which men and women approach politics, from their views on the issues and candidates to their modes of participation.[21] Evidence of such a gender gap in Eastern Europe might help to explain changes in women's political participation in at least two important ways. First, it can tell us something about why women are participating in lower rates than previously. Are women choosing to withdraw from public life, and if so, why? Or does a more restricted political role for women primarily reflect the views of men? Second, what might be the impact of declining rates of female political participation ? If women's views are considerably different from men's, a decrease in their rates of participation might have a significant effect on the process of representation.

Answers to survey questions about the proper social and political roles for women, the church's influence on defining gender roles, and the position of women under the current political system reveal consistent differences in the views of men and women, though overall the agreement between them is high (see Table 12.1). Fewer women accept the view that women's place is in the home, and more believe that women should play an equal role with men in politics. For example, while 65 percent of women completely disagree that a woman's place is in the home, 50 percent of men completely disagree with this statement. A roughly equal difference exists in the views of men and women concerning political equality. While 75 percent of women completely disagree that women should stay out of politics, 61 percent of men completely disagree. Thus, although there are clearly discernible differences in the beliefs of men and women about these questions, women's beliefs tend to mirror those for the population as a whole in their greater commitment to political over social equality.

Table 12.1

Answers to Survey Questions by Gender (in percent)

Answers by women (W) and men (M)	Completely disagree 1		2		3		4		Completely agree 5	
	W	M	W	M	W	M	W	M	W	M
Question 1: A woman's place is in the home where she should occupy herself with domestic matters	65.3	48.9	7.3	11.5	14	20.1	4.2	9.0	9.3	10.5
Question 2: Women should stay out of politics because they were not born for it	74.5	60.6	5.4	10.3	11.2	16.9	2.8	4.9	6.2	7.4
Question 3: The church should have the main influence on the position of women	71.6	68.1	8.1	10.7	12.5	15.6	2.6	3.1	5.2	4.5
Question 4: Women should have the right to have an abortion	6.2	10.7	2.8	4.3	7.5	13.0	6.2	9.5	77.4	62.5
Question 5: The position of women is better today than it was under communism	71.6	68.1	8.1	10.7	12.5	15.6	2.6	3.1	5.2	4.5

Source: Calculated from data in the 1997 election survey conducted by the Department of Political Science at the University of Zagreb.

Women and men also show different levels of support for a woman's right to choose an abortion with 77 percent of women completely agreeing with this right compared to 63 percent of men. But they are closer in their answers about the role of the church in defining this and other issues. Seventy-two percent of women disagree that the church should be the main influence on women's position; 66 percent of men hold this view. Levels of support for the church's role in this matter are the same between men and women, at about 5 percent. How the current system affects the position of women is subject to some differences of opinion between women and men. While 40 percent of women completely disagree that things are better now than they were under communism, 28 percent of men feel this way. Only 10 percent of women completely agree that things are better now than before; slightly more men (16 percent) feel this way.

To what extent do these differences in views translate into differences in voting behavior? Has a gender gap appeared in Croatian politics? A preliminary look at the data suggests that women's higher level of support for social and political equality has not been expressed at the polls. In other words, women have not punished those parties that have adopted the most conservative positions on women's public role. For example, roughly equal numbers of women and men voted for both the extreme-right CPR and the ruling CDU in the 1995 elections.[22] Indeed, an analysis of the CDU's social basis of support indicates that housewives, who vote in overwhelming numbers for the ruling party, constitute a significant element of its popular support. Ironically, these conservative women have found a powerful political platform, despite their support for a more restricted public role for women, by virtue of the CDU's stranglehold on Croatian political life.

In sum, levels of support vary among men and women concerning women's political position. So do their evaluations of the impact of the current political system on the position of women. Women's less positive evaluation of the postsocialist political environment can be explained in part by their greater support for social and political equality and their perception that not enough has been done by the current regime to achieve this goal. The differences between men and women concerning gender equality suggest that lower rates of political participation by women are likely to have a negative impact on their future political role. They also suggest that lower rates of women's political participation could reflect resistance by a segment of the male population. But it is also probable that many women have simply chosen to stay out of politics for the past several years. This choice may reflect a variety of factors, including the belief held by 14 percent of the female population that a woman's place is in the home.[23] Finally, despite these differences in men's and women's views, it is important to keep in mind the substantial agreement between them about women's social and political position during the current political transformation. At the present, a gender gap does not characterize the voting behavior of the Croatian electorate, nor has it affected significantly the political positions or campaign strategies of the major political parties.

Conclusion

Despite fears of a backlash against women's political equality in postsocialist systems, survey data in Croatia reveal a high level of support for an equal public role for women. The majority of Croatian citizens believe that women have the capacity and that they therefore should have the right to participate equally with men in political life. Though a significant portion of the population supports a conservative definition of gender roles, which emphasizes women's domestic obligations, there is little popular support for giving more voice to the Catholic church in defining these roles. Popular opinion in Croatia is overwhelmingly opposed to the church's stance on abortion and its right to determine other aspects of women's lives. Despite popular consensus on defining women's lives in public as well as private terms, however, most citizens believe the current system is less capable of achieving these aims than was its state-socialist predecessor.

The only group of the population more satisfied with women's political opportunities under the present system is composed of CDU, CPR, and CPP voters who are ideologically oriented toward the right. This group supports a more restricted public role for women and their withdrawal to the private sphere. Some of these voters oppose women's political equality on nationalist grounds; they conceive of women's political role primarily as bearing and raising "good Croats" and support such policies as demographic renewal and banning abortion. Others are ultraconservative in their emphasis on family, subordination to traditional sources of authority, and a greater role for the church in defining gender roles. In any case, the large number of these voters within the ruling CDU, and the support among its leadership for a more restricted public role for women, means that a relatively small number of well-placed rightists could thwart the full political equality of women desired by the rest of the population.

Notes

I would like to thank Gary Cohen, Carol Lilly, and Cindy Simon Rosenthal for their comments on an earlier draft of this chapter.

1. Women currently fill significantly fewer of the elective posts in representative bodies at the local level as well. In the 1993 elections, women were elected to a total of 300 out of 8,454 of these positions. See *Statistički Ljetopis 1993* (Zagreb: Državni zavod za statistiku, 1994.)

2. For example, see Barbara Einhorn, *Cinderella Goes to Market. Citizenship, Gender and Women's Movements in East Central Europe* (London and New York, Verso, 1993).

3. For example, see the chapter by Sharon Wolchik in this volume.

4. For a discussion of this concept and its roots in classical and modern political theory, see Jean Bethke Elshtain, *Public Man, Private Woman, Women in Social and Political Thought* (Princeton: Princeton University Press, 1981).

5. Author's interview with prominent nationalist and CDU official Bosiljko Mišetić, July 12, 1994.

6. The public opinion data in this article are taken from surveys conducted by the Department of Political Science at the University of Zagreb during the 1990, 1993, 1995, and 1997 election campaigns. I am very grateful to Dr. Grdešić, the principle investigator of this project, for sharing these data with me. For a treatment of this subject in Croatian see Smiljana Leinert Novesal, *Žene—politička manjina* (Zagreb: Radničke novine, 1990).

7. Respondents were asked to mark their level of agreement on a scale of 1 to 5. Only two of the numbers were further labeled as completely disagree for 1 and completely agree for 5.

8. Despite their massive entry to the labor force, in 1980 the percentage of women employed (33 percent) had not reached the 50 percent mark of most other East European countries.

9. For a discussion of how women's participation in sectors of the economy relating to women's traditional nurturing roles (teaching, counseling, medicine, social work) remains disproportionately high, see Arlie Russell Hochschild, *The Managed Heart: Commercialization of Human Feeling,* (Berkeley: University of California Press, 1983).

10. For an account of how this burden affected women during the state socialist period see Einhorn, *Cinderella Goes to Market.*

11. Women constituted 41.2 percent of the work force in 1986; 42.6 percent of the work force in 1989; 43.1 percent of the work force in 1990, 43.7 percent of the work force in 1991; 44.8 percent of the work force in 1992; and 45.7 percent of the work force in 1993. Calculated from data provided by the Sociajalistička Republika Hrvatska Državni zavod za statistiku and the Republika Hrvatska zavod za statistiku, 1987–94.

12. The survey data considered here do not measure these attitudes in Croatia. However, extensive research in advanced industrial democracies points to the persistence of these social norms even after women have begun to participate in the labor force in high numbers. These attitudes had an impact on women's work patterns in a variety of ways. For example, women's participation in sectors of the economy relating to women's traditional nurturing roles remains disproportionately high. Similarly, despite their participation in full-time work outside the home, women are still perceived of as having primary responsibility for caring for children and the home. See Arlie Russel Hochschild with Anne Machung, *The Second Shift* (New York: Avon Books, 1990).

13. Indeed, this research suggests that it is discussion about gender roles that tends to be divisive, not about political participation. Among the first scholars to point out the disjunction between public support for equal rights and support for changing gender roles is Jane J. Mansbridge, *Why We Lost the ERA* (Chicago: University of Chicago Press, 1986.) Her basic observation was that support for the abstract notion of equality of rights is strongly held by large majorities; however, the ERA failed in large part because the conservative right was able to shift the focus away from abstract rights to more concrete questions (though distorted and manipulated) of changing social roles—women in the military, unisex bathrooms, and gay marriages. Thus, it is not unusual to get very widely conflicting public opinion depending on how questions about women's participation in politics are framed.

14. For example, see Franjo Tudjman, "Papa zaštitnik Hrvatskog naroda i moralni autoritet civiliziranoga čovječanstva," in *S vjerom u samostalnu Hrvatsku* (Zagreb: Narodne Novine, 1995), pp. 367–72.

15. According to 1995 survey data, 33 percent of the sample were strong believers while 50 percent were "customary believers," those who attend church several times a year on holidays or to celebrate marriages and baptisms.

16. For example, in a *Globus* poll from 1994, 31 percent of the respondents named Cardinal Kuharic as the most respected person in Croatia, while 22 percent of the sample chose Franjo Tudjman. *Globus,* September 23, 1994, p. 11, cited in Sabrina P. Ramet, "The Croatian Catholic Church since 1990," unpublished paper.

17. This correlation is particularly high among the one-third of CDU voters who are ideologically on the extreme right, 47 percent of whom are seriously religious, and 50 percent of whom are "customary believers."

18. For example, at his inauguration ceremony, President Franjo Tudjman (who was also head of the CDU) tucked a feather in an empty cradle to honor unborn Croatian babies. See Jill Benderley, "Feminist Movements in Yugoslavia, 1978–1992," in *State-Society Relations in Yugoslavia 1945–1992,* ed. Melissa K. Bokovoy, Jill A. Irvine, Carol S. Lilly, (New York: St. Martin's Press, 1997).

19. Franjo Tudjman, "Očuvanje punog suvereniteta Hrvatskog naroda i gradjanskih prava svih državljana Republike Hrvatske," in *S vjerom u samostalnu Hrvatsku* (Zagreb: Narodne Novine, 1995), pp. 79–90.

20. *Nedjeljna Dalmacija* (September 2, 1994), in FBIS-EEU, September 15, 1994, pp. 51–53.

21. For a concise discussion of research on the gender gap in public opinion

and voting behavior, see M. Margaret Conway, Gertrude A. Steuernagel, David W.Ahern, *Women and Political Participation, Cultural Change in the Political Arena* (Washington, DC: CQ Press, 1997).

22. Calculated from 1995 survey data.

23. Nine point three percent of female respondents completely agreed that a woman's place is in the home. Another 4.2 percent chose catagory 4, which can best be understood as expressing agreement, though not the strongest agreement.

13

Reflections on Nationalism and Its Impact on Women in Serbia

Branka Andjelkovic

If the woman question is a test of democracy, then the new postcommunist Yugoslavia is certainly far from a democratic society. Communist Yugoslavia represented a happy past in the eyes of many women, regardless of the fact that official ideology underlined the importance of gender equality only at the surface and that the high level of women's employment was considered an indicator that the women's question had been successfully resolved. The impressive corpus of legislation on women and the family in the former Yugoslavia has been seen as a proof that women in communist times were treated with respect.

Women Under Communism

The law of the former Yugoslavia was a copy of the Bolshevik declaration of policy on women made at the First International Conference of Working Women in Moscow in 1920. The essential goals of the statement were to bring women out of the home into the working world, to end the traditional household organization that kept women in subservience, to provide equal educational opportunities for women, to mobilize them into political work, and to provide adequate working conditions to satisfy the particular needs of women.[1]

The evidence suggests that women had considerable problems in reaching equal status with men as far as their social and political positions were concerned. In Yugoslavia, women held equal rights to the vote, to political office, to education, and to employment, but in practice they did not achieve equality. They were still overwhelmingly responsible for domestic duties, their earnings were less than those of men, they clustered in low-paid professions. They were under-represented at the upper level of career hierarchies, and they only rarely reached the highest levels of economic and political decision making.[2] Equal choice was an illusion whose weaknesses were apparent: most working women remained trapped within traditional patriarchal discourse. The favorite slogan of socialist Yugoslavia was "Woman as a housewife, a lover, and a worker." The message was clear: the profession was important, but only if a woman successfully fulfilled her first two tasks.

Nevertheless, all these problems were overseen by the ideologists of communism. The fact that the rate of employed women was high was taken by the Yugoslav authorities as a parameter of development. This was generally seen as a proof of completed emancipation. The result was that all other women's issues were considered to be of an individual character or "the result of the negative historic and patriarchal legacy." What is more, for this reason women's issues never came to the focus of serious academic study.

Hidden discrimination against women was a trademark of socialist Yugoslavia. Instead of getting better jobs, which would bring them higher status, women faced discrimination and segregation. Increased numbers of educated women led to the "feminization" of such professions as health and social services. Segregation along gender lines led to a decrease in salaries, a weakening of the unions in these sectors, and so on.[3] What is more, the surplus of educated women resulted in their massive unemployment or their employment in professions for which they were overqualified. In this sense, the socialist version of freedom of choice was, in fact, a forced choice.[4]

Over the years, gender segregation became more ingrained in the society, and work was divided into male and female sectors.[5] In accordance with this division, salaries were also divided, regardless of the similar qualifications of females and males. In typical male professions, a man would always have a higher salary than a woman with the same qualifications. Interestingly, women were mainly employed in occupations with the highest productivity and the highest export rate to the Western market, such as the textile industry.[6]

In the late 1980s, as Yugoslavia's political and economic system eroded, the distance between the genders deepened. Research conducted by Belgrade's Department of Sociology in 1990 under the title "New Technologies and Gender Relations" led to the conclusion that a concentration of men was evident at the top of the pyramid, while women were concentrated at the bottom. Women were also paid less: 85 percent of women were classified as low-income earners, whereas 75 percent of the men fell into the high-income category.

With the economic crisis of the 1980s, women's positions were for the first time apparently seriously jeopardized. According to official estimations, 13 percent of the working population was unemployed. Women were first to bear the impact of unemployment, especially women with better qualifications. Two-thirds of the unemployed were women who were about to enter the labor market for the first time.[7] A similar situation influenced the women's revolt in the West, which resulted in women's greater penetration into the economic, political, and professional spheres of society. This was not the case in the former Yugoslavia.[8] For the first time, a critical mass of dissatisfied women was needed to effect change, but women did not raise their voices.

Why did women fail to manifest their dissatisfaction with such inequality, since, at least officially, they had the support of the communist ideologists? Why did the feminist movement fail to turn into a serious and important force? Analysts suggest that

> the reluctance of Yugoslav women to participate in public life may be considered a reflection of the profound impact of Yugoslavia's transformation from a traditional-agrarian society to a modern-industrial one. Many Yugoslavian women felt confused by the social change, trapped in between tradition and the new modern age. The feminist movement was weak and remained in embryo as it was with all aspects of civil society. Therefore, the advocates of women liberation never managed to gain massive support, and in this sense, the feminist movement, as one of the main revolutions of the 1980s, bypassed Yugoslavia.[9]

In other words, women remained invisible both as social and political actors, and this situation had an important impact on their future role in postcommunist Yugoslavia.

Women in Postcommunist Yugoslavia

In the new multiparty society communists were partly accused of hypocrisy because gender equality was achieved only at the surface. That was the reason why women had great hopes for the new system, which emerged after the fall of communism. Instead of winning more freedom, however, women were returned to "history," from which they were forcefully pulled out not too long a time ago. In this sense, the former one-party system had at least minimal egalitarian ideas, which included women as a matter of principle, though it was far from achieving gender equality.[10]

The worsening of women's position in postcommunist Yugoslavia was determined by three factors: by the collapse of the Yugoslav state, by a new nationalistic understanding of political life, and by the newly introduced market economy. In their desire to annul the achievements of the previous political system, the "slavish treatment" of women in socialism came under the fire of public critiques. New political actors came up with an alternative plan: women should return home, to the family. At the same time, women's positions were affected by the worsening of the social and economic situation. An orientation toward the private sphere and a distancing from social and political life were women's reactions to these new developments. The outcome was disastrous: women in post–Cold War Yugoslavia were completely marginalized. Feminist groups, which were actively participating and shaping political life at the beginning of the 1990s, with the outbreak of war almost entirely vanished from the Serbian political theater. Since then, these groups have been primarily focused on women as victims of war crimes and sexual harassment, and in this sense they have become the victims of nationalist ideology.

The Collapse of the State

The collapse of the state and the beginning of the war in Croatia and Bosnia deeply disrupted society. The security and safety of citizens were severely endangered with the breakdown of institutions and the emergence of a legal void. The obstinacy of the minority who took the power created a deep political and economic crisis.

With the disintegration of the state the family was seen as the only hope and refuge. The family, as an ideal model, never really lost its power in traditional Yugoslav society. When key social and political institutions collapsed, the family had priority over all other forms of social activity. What is more, the family remained the sole financial base for an individual while society was passing through radical and severe political, economic, and social changes.

Women withdrew to the security of the family. More generally, the family as a buffer zone became a basis for collective identification, which was misused by the enforcers of nationalism. The result was the blossoming of values rooted in ideas of collective rights. The rights and freedoms of individuals were pushed aside. The promotion of women could have been achieved only within the family framework because the family was the only cell of society that was still intact. In such casting, what else could women praise other than maternity and family life?[11]

Economic Change

It was not only the disintegration of Yugoslavia that contributed to regressive tendencies with respect to women in postcommunist Yugoslav society. The economic crisis, which was accelerated with the beginning of the war, seriously undermined women's position in Yugoslavia. Liberal policy bears responsibility for such developments, too. Underlining the importance of economic transformation, privatization, and the introduction of market mechanisms, the woman's question was pushed aside as a question of less importance. The rights meant to protect women under state socialism (such as maternity and child-care leave and the right to return to employment) now meant that women were seen as expensive labor by enterprises looking for cheap labor. Furthermore, women were perceived to be unreliable workers because they were compelled to take time off to have children, care for their families, and cope with domestic responsibilities; tasks that increased as the state reduced public welfare provision. As a result, in the newly competitive market economies of the former Yugoslavia, women are more likely to be unemployed than men and are likely to be unemployed for longer periods. As the director of the Serbian Labor Institute says, employers are mostly the victims of their prejudices. They believe that women are less capable than men, less ambitious, and, by and large, a bad choice.[12]

What is more, economic transformation had been accompanied by high inflation and the UN embargo (which was lifted in October 1995). The result was a rapid pauperization of the society. Mainly employed in sectors that were the first to bear the brunt of economic crisis (textile, food, and leather industries) because of their dependence on export, women were affected the most.[13] With increased unemployment, and industry on the edge of existence, women were the first to be left without jobs. The majority of the employed sent to unpaid leave (a compromise between the state and employees for the sake of social peace in which the state keeps workers employed only officially and covers only health insurance) were women. Those who managed to retain their jobs were employed in sectors offering low incomes or in state sectors with a huge financial deficit resulting from the collapse of the state.

Today, 75 percent of the unemployed are women, who typically must wait a few years for the chance to get a job.

Nationalism

At the same time as market reforms and political change were contributing to a narrowing of women's options in the public sphere, the nationalist discourse in the former Yugoslavia was redefining women's roles in line with traditional patriarchal expectations. The policies of socialism were officially committed to the emancipation and equality of women; the new nationalist movement blames these values for their association with socialism, and patriarchal gender relations are claimed as natural, traditional, and national. This has provided an ideological justification for the limitations on women's participation in the labor force and in the public sphere and has acted as a stimulus to the tendency to see women as primarily concerned with reproduction.

Nationalism, which became a prevailing force in Yugoslavia in the first half of the 1980s, has been directed against women from the beginning. Hidden antagonism turned into open hostility with the collapse of the communist regime at the beginning of 1990s. Aggressive nationalist ideologies were used to return women to "where they belong": to family, home, and maternity.[14] The primary role of women is to be the regenerator of the nation. Since the care of the nation has been the essential goal of the state creators, reproduction is meant to be the political fuel for creation of the nation-state. In other words, a main theme of nationalism has been the family.

In the new anticommunist politics of nationalism, men and women are seen to have specific, separate responsibilities, corresponding to their "essential natures." Men should provide financial support for their families, while women should take care of their children and home. Thus, the most important thing in the life of any woman is to be a mother and wife. If she fulfills this task successfully, she can then spare time on her profession, in other words, on her social and economic status. Unfavorable social conditions cannot be an excuse for not giving birth or not trying to form a family. At the beginning of the war with Croatia it was not rare to hear a call to women to make up for war losses by bearing not just babies but warriors. Women who rejected the role of mothers to the nation were at best failures, at worst unnatural or traitors, allies of communism, and enemies of the nation. Therefore, the women who did not act "naturally" and did not follow the "ethical imperatives of national society" were classified as abnormal.

The woman, within a nationalist paradigm, in some twisted manner can reach equality with the man only if she waives all her social roles and responsibilities, except the one that is a direct product of her biological nature.[15]

The irony is that nationalism, underlining only one of woman's capacities—her reproductive role—does not act directly against women. In fact, nationalism successfully creates a picture of the woman as an important and valuable member of national society, but only if she accepts her obligation to reproduce. In this sense, nationalism succeeds in awakening a woman's self-respect, helping her to articulate and manifest her specific female identity.[16] Therefore, it has not been a surprise that many women swallowed the bait, and in the atmosphere of the chaos, of the collapse of the state and the general economic crisis, withdrew to the family nest.

The redefinition of women's roles away from the socialist "working women" toward the newly resurrected "mother of the nation" has taken place on a number of levels, from that of political rhetoric to that of formal legislation. There has been an explicit tendency for these conservative ideologies to be translated into new legislation. Debates about the duties and responsibilities of women to the nation have emerged. Insistent patriarchal propaganda was fostering traditional values, limiting the few women's rights and sending women back to their families. The economic crisis was a perfect cover for the silent return of women to the family nest.

The most exploited issue was that of the birthrate and population policy. The "white plague" (a term widely used to refer to low natality) was attributed to Yugoslav socialism, which allegedly had weakened the family and thus the nation by upsetting the "natural" gender order. The blame for the "white plague" was placed mostly on women who, during the communist era, began to believe they should be equal to men. The response to fears over national survival has been to pursue pronationalist legislation calculated according to national interests and aimed primarily at women as "mothers of the nation." Restricting abortion was one of the ultimate goals, and the unrestricted right to abortion is repeatedly challenged. National interest has been prominent in discussions of the issue; individual interests must be subordinated to the collective interest of the nation. This issue affects women directly: the emphasis on returning women to the home and legislation aimed to encourage motherhood, without reference to women's desires, has a direct effect on women's rights to self-determination.[17]

Other legislature proposals revolved around population policy. Families without children were to be additionally taxed, while families with more than two children were rewarded with numerous social benefits. Paid maternity leave (now nine months with the possibility of a three-month extension, actually requested by most women) for the third child was to be extended to three years. The strategy was clear: while the woman is generously rewarded for the fulfillment of her national duty, she is taken away from work for a considerable time. In this way, women are factually eliminated from the labor market, while men are gaining immense advantages. All these restrictive acts were meant to disrupt women's individual goals.[18]

In postcommunist Yugoslavia women are first subordinated to the collective and only then are they able to address their own needs and desires. Nationalist policy in Yugoslavia intends to reassert "natural" gender roles, reaffirm the traditional patriarchal family, and regenerate the nation by emphasizing patriotic motherhood and subordinating women's autonomy to the demands of the national collective.[19] Women are denied autonomy and full participation because of their gender, just as other minorities are because of their national origins. Limitation of their autonomy to the interests of the nation makes women an internal minority.[20] As a consequence, women who do not fit into officially sanctioned roles are open to criticism as enemies of the nation. Women's liberation and emancipation are concepts that directly contradict nationalist ideals.

Women in Politics

Simultaneous with the deterioration of women's position in postcommunist Yugoslavia, women have been disappearing from formal political institutions; the socialist institution of quotas for women have been abandoned. Women as a targeted group have not been on the agenda of any political party. Political actors have been permanently ignoring women and their needs.

The constitution and development of political parties coincided with the beginning of the war in Yugoslavia. Since nationalism was the prevailing discourse, most political parties followed the nationalist course. Aggressive performance and a *macho* stance by the main political actors were not attractive models for women. That was one reason why women's participation was significantly reduced. Preelection tests, which include gender variables, showed that in the first democratic elections in Serbia in 1990, 26 percent of the women decided not to vote. The reasons included doubts about whether the election would be democratic and the unsatisfactory political options dominating the political scene. Only 13 percent of women were members of political parties at that time, while 70 percent stated that they did not want to be members of any party.[21]

At the beginning of party pluralism, however, women through various feminist groups and political parties tried actively to oppose nationalist policy. Nationalists and other political forces, in order to bring the communist regime to the end, supported women's political activity. At the same time, because of the delay in solving women's problems, women were publicly pleading for understanding. Women soon realized that there was a chance to capture strategic positions in political life from the beginning of the democratic process.

Bearing that idea in mind, a Women's Party was formed. The promotion of the new political party brought to the surface many new and well-known women. Formally, growing opposition forces even supported the formation of this party. But the fact was that major political actors were aware of the marginal position of this political organization, which could never become a serious competitor in the political struggle. What is more, the presence of women's organizations and parties improved the image of the new democracy. The first democratic elections in 1991 had a positive impact on women's activism and speeded their struggle for better treatment in society, although the reformed communist party, the Serbian Socialist Party, gained the majority. Unfortunately, the Women's Party failed to participate in the 1991 elections. The reason was mainly financial, but at the same time the party's political leadership hesitated to enter the race for parliament. Nevertheless, the exposition of this party during the election campaign forced other political actors to pay more attention to women's issues and to try to attract women both as voters and as politicians.

The 1991 elections activated feminist groups such as the Women's Lobby and the Women's Parliament. Their primary task was to alert the Serbian public to such women's problems as population policy and family planning. Many legal amendments, such as the restriction on abortion, were stopped as a result of the activity of these groups. A very important field of feminist activities was in the sphere of high politics. Numerous antiwar actions were organized by the Center for Anti-War Activities and by the Women in Black, both constituted in 1991. Other spontaneous women's activities occurred at this time as well. Mothers' Protests in the summer of 1991 surprised many with their forcefulness. They ultimately required the end of men's recruitment into the Yugoslav People's Army (JNA), the end of JNA activities in conflict areas, and so on. The regime soon brought such activities to an end, using an impudent and offensive media campaign to label these women as traitors and enemies.

As the war machinery in Yugoslavia speeded up, the feminist protests began to lose strength. Media blockades and regime oppression led to women's activities remaining publicly concealed. Simultaneously, the attention of women activists concentrated more on the victims of the war, who were mainly women. Parallel with the internal media blockade, an international one was imposed, too. Since the Serbs in the international media were unofficially proclaimed aggressors, antiwar activities in Serbia were not of any interest.[22]

Simultaneous with the decline of the public feminist resistance to the war, women's activity in the political parties declined as well. The strengthening of nationalism turned women's initial enthusiasm for political activity into disappointment. What is more, women themselves were ambivalent: on the one hand, they were opposed to the idea of participating in political life, and on the other, they rejected the possibility of better self-organization. Insufficient popularization of women's political activity and protest resulted in women's withdrawal from political life. One of the reasons for women's failure to organize politically on a massive scale was the small number of emancipated and self-conscious women. In Yugoslavia every tenth woman is still illiterate, every fifth is without appropriate education, and only one-third of the female population has a high school or university degree.[23]

Although women in today's Serbian political life do participate, their presence is evident only at the lower levels. The most important ministries, such as home affairs, foreign ministry, army, traffic, industry, and economy, are entirely under male domination.[24] What is more, Yugoslavia does not have any female representative working as an ambassador or consul. Only one political party, the Serbian Citizen's Union (SZU), is led by a woman. But, as Vesna Pesić, the leader of this party says, SZU would have ten times as many members if its leader were a man. In other words, in patriarchal society, the sphere of politics is more than ever considered to be "man's business."

Comparison between the number of women in the parliament of the former Yugoslavia and the current one leads to the conclusion that women are completely excluded from Serbian political life. In the former Yugoslavia (from 1974 to 1992) at least 17 percent of MPs were women. In the new Yugoslavia this number has been radically cut down. The current federal parliament has only one female MP, out of 178 representatives. In the Serbian parliament, only 8 MPs (3.5 percent) out of 250 parliamentary members are women, although 904 women (17.5 percent) out of 5,163 candidates stood for parliament.

Women who are delegates in the Serbian parliament are mainly members of leftist parties and liberal democratic ones, while the main nationalist parties generally avoid women in official political life.

Apparently, the electorate, the majority of which consists of women, brought to the end the process initialized by political parties: the door of the Serbian parliament is almost closed for female delegates. Analysts indicate that the Serbian electorate tends to choose an increased number of older male candidates.[25] The result is that Yugoslavia, along with Turkey and Malta, shares one of the last places in Europe where women delegates are concerned.[26] Out of 186 parliaments in the world, the new Yugoslavia is in 142 place.[27] This indicates that politics is still one of the most conservative spheres of social life, in which women usually take part only as decoration. Probably this is the reason why the number of women withdrawing from politics constantly increases in postcommunist Yugoslavia. Recently processed data for the local and federal elections of 1996 indicates that 60 percent of women decided not to vote.[28] Data in the earlier election indicated that when they voted, younger and educated women voted for democratic liberal parties, while older women, housewives, and peasants in general voted for the reformed communist parties, such as the Serbian Socialist Party (SPS).[29]

Conclusion

Unity, which is the main goal of every nationalist movement, was reached through an immense dose of xenophobia toward any other ethnic group regardless of its origins. In order to homogenize the society, nationalists show hostility toward liberal and democratic values and distrust any independent political activity, even in its weakest form. In this sense, nationalism and feminism were meant to clash from the beginning. This is the reason why women's movements and feminism as advocates for women's rights never had a real chance to get rooted and spread their ideas. Women's activities were disabled shortly after "democracy" entered Yugoslavia.

Faced with the nationalists' glorification of war and the subordination of social interests to the interests of the nation, feminists channeled their energies into pacifist and antinationalist activities.[30] Participants in these antiwar actions were labeled traitors, cowards, non-Serbs, and antipatriots by the state media and official propaganda. Condemnations and threats frightened women who were inexperienced and unprepared for this sort of battle. Therefore, this antiwar nucleus remained a minority.

Although never really rooted in socialist Yugoslavia, the new nationalist political elite considered feminism to be a subversive movement. The elite assumed that feminism endangers the consolidation of society on a nationalist basis. Since the feminist movement was already weak, it was not difficult to marginalize it entirely. Yugoslav feminism is on the verge of nonexistence; women are more and more concentrated on their families and home. On the other hand, women are increasingly exposed to violence. Every fifteen minutes a woman is beaten, and every half hour a woman is raped. But, there are only two "women houses" where women can protect their lives, and then only for six nights.[31] The support of the Serbian and federal governments is simply lacking. The conclusion is that women are deliberately expelled from all spheres of social, political, and public life.

Limited interest in the party contest and marginal presentation at the elections resulted in the complete defeat of women in the sphere of political representation. Women remain without any political representation; what is more, they are left without protection at the state level. From the beginning of the war, a woman's role has been mainly that of victim, either as a victim of violence, as a refugee, as a mother opposed to the war, or as a member of antiwar groups and initiatives.[32]

The tendency of state nationalism has been to reduce the role of the woman to her biological, reproductive role, and to marginalize and push aside women's activity on the political scene. Women were meant to act strictly within an assumed patriarchal model. And most women themselves reacted in accordance with their assigned role, that of passive observers and victims of the regime.[33]

Notes

1. Barbara Jancar, "The New Feminism in Yugoslavia," in *Yugoslavia in the 1980s,* ed. Pedro Ramet (Boulder, CO: Westview Press, 1985), p. 201.

2. Wendy Bracewell, "Women, Motherhood, and Contemporary Serbian Nationalism," *Women's Studies International Forum* 19 (January/April 1996): 25–33.

3. Andjelka Milić, "Aspekti društvenog položaja žene," in *Žene, politika, porodica* (Belgrade: Institut za političke studije, 1994), p. 42.

4. Beatrice Dupont, *Unequal Education: A Study of Sex Differences in Secondary School Curriculum* (Paris: Unesco, 1981), p. 41.

5. *Statistički bilten* (Belgrade), no. 1892 (Fall 1991).

6. Andjelka Milić, "Društveno-ekonomski položaj zaposlenih žena u bivsoj Jugoslaviji," in *Žene, politika, porodica* (Belgrade: Institut za političke studije, 1994), pp. 70–73.

7. Ibid., pp. 73–74.

8. Andjelka Milić, "Aspekti društvenog položaja žene," pp. 39–41.

9. Jancar, "The New Feminism in Yugoslavia," p. 204.

10. Rada Iveković, "The New Democracy—With Women or Without Them?" in *Beyond Yugoslavia,* ed. Sabrina Petra Ramet and S. Adamovich (San Francisco-Oxford: Westview Press, 1994), p. 396.

11. Andjelka Milić, "Porodicna transformacija i ženska politika neformalnih mreža," in *Žene, politika, porodica* (Belgrade: Institut za političke studije, 1994), pp. 112–15.

12. *Politika,* October 18, 1995.

13. Andjelka Milić, "Aspekti društvenog položaja žene," pp. 61–64.

14. Andjelka Milić, "Društveni raspad, nacionalizam, seksizam," in *Žene, politika, porodica* (Belgrade: Institut za političke studije, 1994), pp. 123–25.

15. Ibid., p. 153.

16. Ibid., p. 152.

17. Iveković, "The New Democracy—With Women or Without Them?" p. 399.

18. Wendy Bracewell, "Women and Nationalism in the Former Yugoslavia," p. 57.

19. Ibid., p. 61.

20. Ibid., p. 62.

21. Nada Milicević, "Mudre i oprezne" *Nada,* no. 386 (November 24, 1990). Interestingly, the Serbian Socialist Party, clearly nationalist up to the mid-1990s,

as the successor to the Communist Party, also had the largest number of female members and officially advocated gender equality as well as support for the welfare state and opposition to privatization.

22. Iveković, "The New Democracy—With Women or Without Them?" p. 408.

23. Milić, "Društveni raspad, nacionalizam, seksizam," p. 165.

24. *Borba* (Belgrade daily newspaper), March 8, 1997.

25. *Novosti* (Belgrade daily newspaper), March 24, 1996.

26. *Politika* (Belgrade daily newspaper), November 24, 1994.

27. *Novosti,* (Belgrade daily newspaper), March 25, 1996.

28. *NIN* (Belgrade weekly), October 18, 1996; the overall turnout was about 59 percent.

29. Vesna Pesić, "The Impact of Reforms on the Status of Women in Yugoslavia." Paper for the seminar "The Impact of Economic and Political Reforms on the Status of Women in Eastern Europe and the USSR," Vienna, April 1991, p. 19.

30. Iveković, "The New Democracy—With or Without Women?" p. 396.

31. *Borba,* April 24, 1995.

32. Vesna Pesić, "The Impact of Reforms on the Status of Women in Yugoslavia," p. 19.

33. *Borba,* December 27, 1995.

Bulgaria

14

Similar or Different?

Women in Postcommunist Bulgaria

Dobrinka Kostova

The impact of the political, economic, and social changes that engulfed Central and Eastern Europe at the end of the 1980s on the status and activity of women can throw light on women's behavior in societies in transition. The changes have not yet reached a stage that permits us to draw any final conclusions, but even now some assessments can be formulated. One far-reaching change is in attitude: whereas socialist ideology proclaimed that women as a group should be advanced, the special conditions and problems of Bulgarian women are now ignored.

Women's behavior has changed, too. Bulgarian women's political representation declined in the first year of the transition, then rebounded slightly as increasing numbers of women participated in political institutions. The economic activity of women has been declining because of a reduction in predominantly female occupations. Both fear of economic crisis and the transition to market economy seem to have reinforced family solidarity.

The transition period is a time of constant changes in paradigms, attitudes, values, and behavior. After forty-five years of suppression of religious rites, the country's religious traditions are being restructured.

The Communist Tradition

The first women's association in Bulgaria, called Milosurdie, was established in 1857 in the city of Lom. It had two main aims: educational advancement and cultural enrichment of women. Following the example of the women of Lom, women in other cities and towns soon organized

249

similar associations. They established women's educational centers, foundations for the financial support of young women who wished to study abroad, libraries, and theaters. The activities of these groups helped to draw women into the movement to liberate Bulgaria from the Turks.

After the national liberation in 1878, several influential women's groups were organized, such as the Bulgarian Women's Union, the Association of University Women, the Bulgarian Women's Agrarian Union, the Union of Women's Cooperatives, and the Mothers' Union. The aim of these organizations was to achieve equality of men's and women's political, economic, and social rights and to create equal conditions with respect to education, work, and income. As the new Bulgarian state took over responsibility for education, the women's organizations involved themselves predominantly in charity and cultural activities.

With the establishment of socialist rule in 1944, women's issues were given unaccustomed attention in an effort to implement communist ideology. The equality of men and women was legally proclaimed in October 1944 with the passage of a special law.

Women's emancipation was an element in the overall Communist Party program. The program was designed to equalize conditions of work and retirement, political participation, and compensation for children, among many other things.

The model of full female employment—women accounted for 50 percent of the labor force in 1989, up from 24 percent before World War II[1]—did not solve the problems of women's emancipation. Gender conflicts were constantly reproduced. The most significant reason was the difficulty of matching full-time employment with women's family duties. A legal framework was established to institutionalize social policy: women were guaranteed, among other things, two years' paid maternity leave after the birth of a child plus a third year without pay; modern kindergartens; and allowances for children until they reached the age of 16, or 18 if they were still in school.

In general, women's role in the workplace was their primary role during the socialist period; their role in the family took second place. Mothers even received their children's allowances at the workplace. The high level of women's involvement in the labor market during their prime childbearing years led to conflicts between women's work and family roles. The contradictions were resolved most often in favor of their occupational activity. This situation created many demographic problems (see Table 14.1). The proportion of older people in the population increased

Table 14.1

**Births and Abortions per 1,000 Bulgarian Women of Childbearing
Age, 1970–91**

Year	Births	Abortions
1970	63.5	64.5
1975	67.0	65.9
1980	60.4	72.9
1985	56.6	62.5
1988	55.6	62.6
1989	52.8	61.7
1990	11.7	61.8
1991	10.7	62.1

Source: National Statistics: Quality of Life (Sofia: National Statistics Press, 1991), p. 12.

markedly as the population growth rate fell year by year. The growth rate in 1990 was negative (–0.4) for the first time in Bulgarian history.[2]

The political involvement of women in the socialist period was to a great extent designed to solve labor problems. The Bulgarian National Women's Union, founded in July 1945, mobilized women's support for the establishment of cooperatives and state enterprises and for the fulfillment of the country's economic plans. In 1950 the Union was absorbed by the Fatherland Front.

In 1968 a committee of the Bulgarian Women's Movement was elected to coordinate the national and international activities of Bulgarian women. This committee still exists. It is trying to break with its communist past and find its own place on the Bulgarian political scene. As in the majority of political organizations in the transition period, the leadership of the committee initiates all of the organization's activities, from national to local. Its main aim now is to pressure the political parties and institutions to accept it as the representative of the country's women.

On the one hand, the main political forces are resisting the committee's efforts to claim a place in the Bulgarian political scene, seeing it as a legacy of the old communist Women's Union. On the other hand, the few other women's associations have no well-developed local structures and are concerned with short-term, rather than long-range, objectives. The neglect of women's issues could be a negative sign for the emerging democratic order. In that sense the committee has its chance to acquire some political influence and to become an active political force.

Table 14.2

Percentage of Women in Leadership of Fatherland Front, 1975 and 1979

	1975	1979
Local	41.0	47.1
Municipal	—	38.5
Regional	41.0	41.1

Source: R. Gancheva, M. Vidova, and N. Abadjieva, *One Hundred Questions about Bulgarian Women* (Sofia: Sofia Press, 1983), app.

Table 14.3

Percentage of Women in Leadership of Bulgarian Trade Unions, 1974 and 1980

	1974	1980
Local	48.0	52.2
Regional	43.0	45.0
National	38.0	42.4

Source: R. Gancheva, M. Vidova, and N. Abadjieva, *One Hundred Questions about Bulgarian Women* (Sofia: Sofia Press, 1983), app.

Table 14.4

Percentage of Women in Leadership of Communist Youth Organization, 1977 and 1980

	1977	1980
Local	51.3	51.7
Regional	43.7	45.2
National	37.6	38.4

Source: R. Gancheva, M. Vidova, and N. Abadjieva, *One Hundred Questions about Bulgarian Women* (Sofia: Sofia Press, 1983), app.

Statistical data from the socialist period show that women were proportionately very actively involved in the leadership of various political organizations at the local, regional, and national levels (see Tables 14.2, 14.3 and 14.4).

Whether the times are stable or dramatic, Bulgarian men and women are never indifferent to politics. According to survey data, women devote as much time as men to reading political news, watching television news, and engaging in political discussions.[3] Statistics relating socioeconomic status to level of interest in political news indicate that retired women, women students, and women with small children are even more interested in political developments than their male counterparts. Among the employed, the proportion of men interested in political news is not significantly greater than that of women. As a whole, the factors that most greatly affected interest in political life in the socialist period were membership in a political organization and participation in its leadership.[4]

Data from a longitudinal survey carried out between 1968 and 1986 (Tables 14.5 and 14.6) show the dynamics of party membership. The relation between place of residence and membership in political organizations is revealing. Every fifth person in Sofia but only every tenth in the villages was a member of the Bulgarian Communist Party (BCP). The age structure of party members (Table 14.7) reveals that most were middle-aged or elderly. Party membership was associated with the period of "political awareness." According to the prevailing belief in the BCP, "political awareness" developed around the age of 28. That is the main reason why so few young people belonged to the party. This situation contributed directly to the difficulty of arousing political enthusiasm within the communist organizations. With most members over the age of 28, the model of behavior was that of older generations—not necessarily the most appealing model for younger Bulgarians. Every new generation has its own truth, its own feeling, and when its inclusion in the political system is deferred so late and the condition for its inclusion is emulation of the thinking and behavior of the older members, the impact of the older generation on the young may indeed be minimal.

As there was no basis for political conflict between generations within the Communist Party, the organization as a whole lacked dynamism. Until 1989, membership in the Communist Party was linked with one's positions in other social institutions. Membership was a condition for active participation in the society and for personal success, so membership in the Communist Party was not necessarily linked to people's real political goals.

Acceptance of new party members was contingent on adherence to a model of occupational, age, and gender structures that would ensure the power of the party within all social strata. The party's command

Table 14.5

Membership in Bulgarian Political Organizations, 1968 and 1986 (in percent)

	1968	1986
Bulgarian Communist Party	10.35	13.87
Bulgarian Agrarian Union	2.88	2.17
Communist Youth Organization	19.23	20.11
Fatherland Front	56.69	59.94
None	10.85	3.90

Source: Empirical Sociological Survey: Town and Village (Sofia: National Statistics Press, 1988), 3: 230.

Table 14.6

Membership in Bulgarian Political Organizations, 1986, by Urban/Rural Residence (in percent)

	Sofia	Provincial city	Town	Village
Bulgarian Communist Party	19.17	16.40	15.90	9.95
Bulgarian Agrarian Union	0.88	1.32	1.62	3.41
Bulgarian Youth Organization	24.28	23.74	21.64	15.64
Fatherland Front	53.19	55.50	56.85	66.54
None	2.48	3.01	4.80	4.46

Source: Empirical Sociological Survey: Town and Village (Sofia: National Statistics Press, 1988), 3: 231.

Table 14.7

Membership in Bulgarian Communist Party and Bulgarian Agrarian Union, 1986, by Age Group (in percent)

Age Group	Bulgarian Communist Party	Bulgarian Agrarian Union
< 24	1.52	2.68
24–38	5.82	2.23
29–38	27.29	7.59
39–48	27.35	22.32
49–55	12.40	13.84
56–60	8.86	11.61
61–70	11.22	23.66
70 +	5.54	16.07
All ages	100.00	100.00

Source: Empirical Sociological Survey: Town and Village (Sofia: National Statistics Press, 1988), 3: 234.

administration defined its structures. It was definitely not an organization eager to recruit supporters with congenial ideas. These characteristics of the monoparty system generated extensive political problems. The first signs of the changes of 1989 resulted from this type of party policy.

With the start of the political transformation, the old silent generations were quickly removed from the political scene. From the beginning of the transition from socialism to a new social order the younger generations were very active, defining their critical response to the years past and seizing the opportunity to make a place for themselves at the center of the political stage.

Women in Politics

Three quantitative variables can be used to describe the dynamics of women's involvement in politics in Bulgaria in the transition period: membership in political organizations, in women's organizations, and in elected governing bodies.

Official data on the membership of the political parties are still not available. The main reason is probably the weakness of the organizations during the first years of their existence. The political leaders are presenting their organizations' membership as quantitatively significant in order to increase their appeal to the population. If one sums up the membership figures claimed by the leaders, the adult Bulgarian population could reach some 24 million; in reality, it is only about 6.5 million.

A significant degree of women's political representation depends on the structure of the political system and the political culture of the population. As a multiparty political structure is under formation, the election system is becoming a very important mechanism for the formation and influence of various parties. In the four parliamentary elections since 1989, different electoral methods were accepted—the mixed proportional and representational system in 1990 and proportional representation in 1991, 1994, and 1997. In all cases, a party had to win 4 percent of the vote to enter parliament.

The proportional representation system could have promoted the election of women if they had been high enough in the party lists. With the list system, however, any priority given to women candidates could conflict with the need to recognize claims based on ethnicity, age, and other factors. When a simple majority is needed to win, the preferences of voters are the decisive factor.

The numbers of men and women among political leaderships in the transition period differ significantly. The results of surveys[5] and the outcomes of parliamentary elections (Tables 14.8 and 14.9) show a decline in the proportion of women elected. Whereas women accounted for 20.75 percent of delegates in the last communist parliament, their proportion in the Great National Assembly (1900–1991) was just 8.76 percent; later it rose slightly to reach 9 percent in the National Assembly elected in 1997. The explanation for the fact that women's representation in leadership positions is so low even though they are as interested as men in politics should be sought both in structural factors and in women's activities.

Tables 14.8 and 14.9 show that the proportion of women candidates in 1990 was larger than the proportion of the parliamentary seats they received. There are several major reasons for this outcome. The first is the fact that significant numbers of women are members of parties that won no seats in the Assembly. More parties lost their bids for seats than won. The second reason is the position of men and women in the proportional lists of the parties. Few women were near the top of their lists, and so the probability of their election was correspondingly low.

It is difficult to suggest that the women's strategies and programs differ from the ones proposed by the parties they represent. The observations and analyses conducted in half of the voting districts during the election campaigns of 1990 and 1992 reveal that the candidates represented their party programs and did not develop their own.[6]

The mechanisms for selecting party candidates vary among the parties and between the elections. Because the Union of Democratic Forces (UDF), a coalition of sixteen anticommunist groups till 1997 and now a democratic party, was newly formed at the time of the first elections, its candidates were chosen by the organization's coordinating council. In the following elections there was relatively greater participation in the decision-making process of the representatives of the local councils. This method was applied also by the Bulgarian Socialist Party (BSP) and the Movement for Rights and Freedom (MRF). On the eve of the parliamentary elections of 1997 the Union of Democratic Forces made an unsuccessful attempt to define its candidates for parliament on the basis of primary regional elections. Neither did the electorate show an interest in this type of elections nor were the

Table 14.8

Proportion of Male and Female Candidates for Great National Assembly, 1990, by Party (in percent)

	Bulgarian Socialist Party[a]	Peasant Party	Movement for Freedom and Rights	Union of Democratic Forces[b]	Other
Men	89.3	91.4	90.3	92.2	85.8
Women	10.7	8.6	9.7	7.8	14.2
	100.0	100.0	100.0	100.0	100.0

Source: N. Naidenov, P. Stojanova, and D. Kostova, *Political Campaign 1990: A Sociological Survey* (Sofia: ITUSSR, 1990).
[a]Former Communist Party.
[b]Coalition of sixteen anticommunist organizations.

Table 14.9

Male and Female Members of and Candidates for National Legislative Bodies, 1989–91 (in percent)

		Great National Assembly, 1990		
	Members of last Communist Congress, 1989	Candidates	Members	Members of National Assembly, 1991
Men	79.25	88.41	91.24	86.20
Women	20.75	11.59	8.76	13.80
100.00	100.00	100.00	100.00	100.00

Source: N. Naidenov, P. Stojanova, and D. Kostova, *Political Campaign 1990: A Sociological Survey* (Sofia: ITUSSR, 1990).

results of importance for the final selection of the parliamentary candidates.

For the parliamentary elections based on the principle of proportional representation, which in this system required voting for a list rather than for an individual, it was important to have candidates who were well known to the voters. There was also necessarily a degree of continuity between the process of decommunization and restructuring. Faces that had become well known from parliamentary and television discussions were particularly appropriate. Among them, however, were few women.

Table 14.10

Percentage of Women in National Assembly, 1991, by Party

	Bulgarian Socialist Party	Union of Democratic Forces	Movement for Rights and Freedom
Women	18.9	10.0	8.3
Men	81.1	90.0	91.7
	100.0	100.0	100.0

Source: Labor (newspaper), October 1991.

The proportion of women represented in the various parties varied (Table 14.10). Women's participation was greater in the parties of the left than in those of the right. To some extent this difference reflected the ideological commitment to the formal equality on the part of the left-leaning parties and the liberal approach of the other parties.

There were substantial changes in the parliamentary elections of April 1997. The development of the postsocialist political process shows the ideology of male/female equality losing strength. The increase/decrease of the parliamentary seats consequently increase/decrease the portion of women parliamentarians. The rule of the left orientation and the connected higher degree of support for the female parliamentarian candidates cannot be applied to the results of the parliamentary elections of 1997 (Table 14.11). For example, the European-oriented social democratic party (the Euroleft) has the highest portion of women parliamentarians. However, the Bulgarian Socialist Party was losing half the seats it had in the parliament of 1994, while the number of women parliamentarians from this party has decreased.

The voting process has been democratized, yet the decline in women's representation in political institutions cannot be considered an expression of increased discrimination against women. During the forty-five years of socialism gender equality was honored more in the occupational sphere than in the political arena. With the abolition of quotas for women, their representation diminished. To a great extent the explanation for this phenomenon can be found in the strong consolidation of the family in the difficult years of economic and social changes, when women have had to devote more energy to family difficulties than to societal problems. Despite the intense interest that women have demonstrated in the political changes in the country, the

Table 14.11

Percentage of Women in National Assembly, 1997, by Party

	BSP[a]	UDF[b]	UNS[c]	Euroleft[d]	BBB[e]
Women	5.2	11.7	0.0	14.3	0.0
Men	94.8	88.3	100.0	85.7	100.0
	100.0	100.0	100.0	100.0	100.0

Source: Darzhaven Vestnik (State Gazette), April 1997.

[a]Bulgarian Socialist Party.

[b]The United Democratic Forces (including Union of Democratic Forces, Bulgarian Agrarian National Union, the Democratic Party).

[c]Union for National Salvation (including Movement for Freedom and Rights, The Green Party, and other liberal oriented organizations).

[d]European Traditions Oriented Social Democratic Party.

[e]Bulgarian Business Block.

majority of them have no choice but to concentrate on protecting their families from the negative consequences of the transition.

The Women Vote

Let us investigate the political attitudes and voting behavior of women in the presidential elections of 1992. Were there any significant differences between men's and women's preferences? A survey in that year questioned 1,200 Bulgarian voters—607 men, 593 women. The women's group was representative of women in the country as a whole: 15.6 percent of the women surveyed were 30 years old or younger, 22.6 percent were between the ages of 30 and 40, 18.2 percent were between 40 and 50, 17.6 percent were between 50 and 60, and 26 percent were 60 or older. Five percent of these women were peasants, 20 percent workers, 19.8 percent low-level white-collar employees, and 11.8 percent professionals; 2.9 percent were students and 41.3 percent were pensioners. As for education, 13.2 percent of the women had had elementary schooling, 23.1 percent had had at least some education, 43.7 percent had received some education beyond secondary school, and 20 percent had attended a university. A substantial number of women—33.4 percent—lived in villages, 26.6 percent in small towns, 28.3 percent in provincial cities, and 11.7 percent in Sofia, the capital. The majority of the women—66.3 percent—worked in state enterprises; only 2.6 percent worked in private firms. The rest were either students or pensioners. The sample was also representative of the main ethnic groups in the country: roughly 90 percent were Bulgarian Orthodox, 7 percent Turkish, 1 percent Bulgarian Muslims, and 2 percent Gypsies.[7]

Twenty-two pairs of running mates were candidates for the presidency and vice-presidency. Three of those pairs included women. Of the three women, only one was a candidate for the presidency. The election law allows great freedom to those who wish to run for these offices, so the list of candidates included many people who were not well known to Bulgarian voters.

Both the campaign and its results were expected to reveal the dynamics of voters' behavior after the second free parliamentary elections in October 1991. One important issue was whether the national political institutions—parliament, presidency, government—would be dominated by one political party; if so, would that outcome bring greater stability to the development of democratic processes in the country, or would it result in a more authoritarian approach to the country's problems?

The strongest parties at the time of the presidential elections—the Union of Democratic Forces (UDF) and the Movement for Rights and Freedom—agreed that the restructuring of democracy required a united front. They decided to support Zhelyo Zhelev and Blaga Dimitrova—a woman writer—who ultimately were victorious. The Bulgarian Socialist Party did not nominate a candidate of its own but supported the independent candidates Velko Valkanov and Rumen Vodenicharov.

The running mates George Ganchev and Peter Beron were of special interest because they represented developments that appeared in other East European countries as well. Beron assumed the leadership of the UDF after Zhelev was appointed president of the country by the National Assembly in 1990, but he was soon forced to resign when the newspapers exposed his close contacts with the Bulgarian secret police. Ganchev had left Bulgaria during the communist period but returned as soon as the communist government fell. Like many such men in other countries of Eastern Europe, he presented himself as one who had learned and prospered in the West and now was coming back only to give his country the benefit of his valuable experience.

The many changes in the political, economic, and social environments in recent years have led to a low level of political information, knowledge, and experience. The election results confirmed this im-

Table 14.12

Support of Three Front-running Presidential Candidates by Nonpolitical Women Voters and by Female Supporters of Nine Political Organizations, 1992 (in percent)

	Zhelev (UDF/MRF)	Valkanov (Independent)	Ganchev (Independent)
No preference	17.5	13.9	42.4
Union of Democratic Forces	70.0	–	21.1
Bulgarian Socialist Party	1.5	83.9	19.2
Bulgarian Democratic Center	0.7	–	–
Peasant Party "NP" (Nikola Petrov)	–	1.3	3.8
Peasant Party (u)	1.4	–	1.9
Movement for Rights and Freedom	3.0	0.9	3.8
Nationalists	4.9	–	–
Bulgarian Business Bloc	–	–	5.9
Monarchists	1.0	–	1.9
	100.0	100.0	100.0

Source: V. Tomov, Z. Naidenova, Y. Maneva, *Elections 1992: A Sociological Survey* (Sofia: President House Press, 1992).

pression, especially with regard to the group of "hesitant" voters. In that respect the group of women is significant. Most of the hesitant women voted for Ganchev (Table 14.12). Probably they were influenced by his reiterated promise to defend women's rights if he were elected president. It appeared, however, that the majority of voters did have stable attachments to specific political groups (Table 14.13), and that these attachments basically defined women's attitudes toward the presidential candidates.

The differences between men and women were not significant in the case of voters who were members of or supported a political party. Thirty percent of the women studied but only 13 percent of the whole sample voiced no preference for any political party. These women voted overwhelmingly for Ganchev. An analysis of his program and the methods by which he proposed to carry it out lead me to suspect that their votes were motivated by emotion rather than by rational evaluation of his platform. At the same time, the votes for Ganchev two and a half years after the beginning of the democratic changes in the country show some new tendencies in voting behavior and attitudes toward politics in general. The deteriorating quality of life for many

Table 14.13

Support of Three Front-running Presidential Candidates by Nonpolitical Voters and by Supporters of Nine Political Organizations, 1992 (in percent)

	Zhelev (UDF/MRF)	Valkanov (Independent)	Ganchev (Independent)
No preference	12.0	12.0	40.0
Union of Democratic Forces	67.0	3.0	27.0
Bulgarian Socialist Party	3.0	79.0	16.0
Bulgarian Democratic Center	2.5	3.0	3.0
Peasant Party "NP" (Nikola Petrov)	1.5	–	1.0
Peasant Party (u)	4.0	1.5	4.0
Movement for Rights and Freedom	7.0	–	–
Nationalists	1.0	1.5	2.0
Bulgarian Business Bloc	1.0	–	7.0
Monarchists	1.0	–	–
	100.0	100.0	100.0

Source: V. Tomov, Z. Naidenova, and Y. Maneva, *Elections 1992: A Sociological Survey* (Sofia: President House Press, 1992).

people in the first years of the transformation destroyed trust in the main political parties and in their ability to bring about the needed changes. Women seem to have more courage than men to strike out in a new direction.

Zhelev and Dimitrova were the only running mates who received substantial support from women who expressed a party preference. A factor analysis shows that this behavior owed more to the candidates' personal characteristics than to support for the parties and their programs. This circumstance does not contradict my earlier assertion that a party preference had a greater impact on voting behavior than the personal characteristics of the candidates. These women account for only 30 percent of the sample, and Bulgarian women are typically quite flexible in their political preferences; they try to assess for themselves the ability of the candidate to live up to the office he or she is seeking. The large number of university-educated women especially feel free to vote against their own party if they believe that it is in the interest of their country to do so.

Information about the extent of knowledge about the candidates clarifies the picture. Zhelev, who had already been president of the country for a year, was very well known by 84.3 percent of the women respondents; 6 percent of them had only general knowledge about him; 6.5 percent knew who he was but little more; and 3.2 percent knew nothing about him. Nearly 20 percent of the women had heard nothing about Valkanov, an Assembly delegate. Ganchev was an unknown quantity to 15 percent of the interviewed women. These data, together with the electoral behavior of the women, confirm the stable interest in politics of the majority of them. The data also indicate that most of them based their behavior at the polls on conscious political preferences and good knowledge of the principal political actors. At the same time, a third of the women seemed to be casting protest votes. Perhaps this behavior is only to be expected after forty-five years of "elections" in which they were offered only one candidate to vote for. The understandable inability of the transition government to achieve substantial changes in two and a half short years had a disorienting effect on the "hesitant" female electorate. At the same time, such disorientation in a time of transformation, when women have more frequent opportunities to vote for new people, may be useful if it brings some good politicians to the fore. This nontraditional behavior also supports the suggestion that Bulgarian women are independent in their political choices.

Between the presidential elections of 1992 and 1997 Bulgarian society has passed through significant changes. Since the transition, eight governments have been in power. Their policy can be characterized with a shift from liberal democracy to socialist populism and in 1997 with a reversal of the political and economic orientation of the state to democratic preferences.

The economic reality has been characterized with a path to marketization, some degree of privatization of the state sector, an expanding private sector, increased unemployment, a deteriorating style of life for the middle class, and a broadening of the gap between the rich and the poor.

The social response to these changes has been demonstrated in the elections of 1997, as well as in numerous political activities. In 1997, for the first time since the transition began in Bulgaria there was a massive disapproval of the socialist policy and a strong orientation toward democracy. Regardless, many people continue to idealize the socialist full employment, the "unpaid" health care and education, the low prices of goods and services under socialism.

Table 14.14

Support of the Six Front-Running Presidential Candidates in 1997 Elections By Female/Male Voters (in percent)

Candidate	Women	Men
Petar Stoyanov	28.0	28.0
Ivan Marazov	18.0	18.0
George Ganchev	11.0	11.0
Alexander Tomov	5.0	5.0
Reneta Indzhova	3.0	2.0
Vera Ilieva	0.0	1.0
Still not decided	18.0	19.0
No wish to vote	17.0	16.0
	100.0	100.0

Source: Public Opinion Poll, October 1996. Sofia: National Center for the Study of the Public Opinion, vol. 7, no. 5, p. 13.

Petar Stoyanov, candidate of the united democratic forces, uniting UDF, Movement for Freedom and Rights and the BANU (Bulgarian Agrarian National Union).

Ivan Marazov, candidate of the Bulgarian Socialist Party.

Alexander Tomov, candidate of the Euroleft Party.

Reneta Indzhova, independent candidate.

Vera Ilieva, candidate of the Bulgarian Communist Party.

The economic and political changes in the time of transformation significantly influence the life of women. They have lost some of the labor privileges they enjoyed under socialism. That has taken place through the abolishment of these rights in the Labor Code.[8] Women's unemployment is high, and they form the prevailing portion of the unemployed people in the country.[9] Nevertheless, the transition from the totalitarian regime is an ongoing challenge for the women of Bulgaria. For them it is bringing substantial political freedom.

The sociological data from a survey of the National Center for the Study of the Public Opinion published in October 1996 reveal the active political behavior of women (Table 14.14). Of the 1,167 people interviewed, half of them were women. The data represent the development of the following main tendencies:

1. There is a disapproval of the socialist candidate and a strong preference for the candidate of the united democratic forces. The representative of the democratic forces, Petar Stoyanov, is getting such strong support because of his program and the new

political behavior he demonstrates. He is proposing hope, dignity, and strength based on people's abilities and knowledge to overcome the economic and social difficulties.

2. Women give their preferences to strong personalities able to be successful political leaders. In this regard, female candidates are preferred only if they have shown their political abilities as reliable and capable leaders. The disapproval of the communist representative Vera Ilieva and the support for Reneta Indzhove, a former prime minister, are a confirmation of that.

3. The attraction of G. Ganchev is decreasing. Women have stopped trusting populist slogans. Their political experience with four parliamentary and three presidential elections has an important influence on their voting behavior.

4. The comparison between the sociological data on the eve of the last two presidential elections reveal that the portion of women with no preferences and with no wish to take part in the elections remains high. The results of the elections in 1997, however, show that the hesitant women have voted for the candidate of the united democratic forces. The main reason for that has been the inability of the socialist government to make appropriate decisions and to stop the galloping inflation and quickly deteriorating life of all social strata at the end of 1996 and the beginning of 1997. The vote for Petar Stoyanov has not been so much a negative vote for the socialists, however; instead, it has been a positive vote for the new policy of the democratic forces.

Conclusions

The historical, cultural, and social experiences of the various countries of Central and Eastern Europe vary. At the same time, the similarity of their development during the forty-five years of communist rule play a significant role in the emergence of common patterns in the transition from socialism to democracy.

One common characteristic is the neglect of women's problems. No simple explanation for it is possible. Among the important factors are the stages of the countries' development and their current efforts to restructure the very basis of their societies. In this framework women's problems seem not to be the first order of business. The final direction that development will take is not yet clear, but the economic model that is expected to develop—the model that determines all the rest—emphasizes the family rather than its individual members.

The change in women's political representation is influenced less by the abolition of the quotas they once enjoyed than by the past legal framework that gave women much security while encouraging passivity and inertia. In the transition period, some of the rights accorded women are still maintained. Women are not aware strongly enough of the fact that these rights have to be defended now. They show little interest in investing their time and energy in extensive political, social, and legal activity. The women's organizations and associations are concerning themselves with either cultural or economic matters to the neglect of women's representation and defense of their legal interests. Women are very wary of drawing attention to women's problems for fear of increasing tensions and creating a backlash. This approach may be tactically expedient but strategically disastrous. If the women of Bulgaria lose their legal rights now, it could take years to reestablish them. Doubtless the experience would teach them the importance of actively defending their interests, but it is doubtful that the lesson would be worth the price.

Notes

1. *National Statistics: The Bulgarian Economy, 1990* (Sofia: National Statistics Press, 1991), p. 31; *Statistics 1939* (Sofia: National Statistics Press, 1939), p. 48.

2. *National Statistics: Population* (Sofia: National Statistics Press, 1991), p. 5.

3. *National Statistics: Town and Village Survey* (Sofia: National Statistics Press, 1988), 2: 280–85.

4. Ibid., p. 361.

5. D. Kostova, *The Economic Leaders in Bulgaria: Sociological Survey* (Sofia: ITUSSR, 1990); and N. Naidenov, P. Stojanova, and D. Kostova, *Polticial Campaign 1990: A Sociological Survey* (Sofia: ITUSSR, 1990).

6. Naidenov et al., *Political Campaign 1990;* V. Tomov, Z. Naidenova, and Y. Maneva, *Elections 1992: A Sociological Survey* (Sofia: President House Press, 1992).

7. Tomov et al., *Elections 1992.*

8. *Labor Code* (Sofia: Confederation of the Independent Trade Unions Press, 1992), p. 30

9. *Statistics* (Sofia: National Statistics Press, 1996), p. 71

15

Disappearing from Politics
Social Change and Women in Albania

Fatos Tarifa

Despite the similarities created by the failure of the socialist system in all East European countries, their development, and particularly the position of women in the political and social life, cannot be explained simply by the nature of the system itself. At least in Albania, and I believe in other Balkan countries as well, a large part has been played by these countries' historical traditions. In Albania, even today, many traditions of the distant past still have tremendous impact on the status of women.

Historically, the gravest misfortune for Albanian women was the Ottoman invasion, which disrupted the natural process of sociopolitical and cultural development of Albanians. Other peoples of the Balkans, too, fell under Ottoman domination, but the Albanians' experience was more bitter than that of their neighbors; first, because Ottoman rule lasted almost 500 years in Albania, and second, because the invaders managed to convert more than 60 percent of the country's population to Islam. The concepts and standards traditionally applied to women by the *shariat* (Islamic law) and women's place in Islamic society are well known.

In the Catholic northern highlands of the country, which the Ottoman invaders never managed to control, the Albanians preserved de facto autonomy and governed themselves by unwritten norms and laws that were codified and orally transmitted from generation to generation through the centuries. This customary law, known as *Kanuni i Lekë Dukagjinit* (The Code of Lekë Dukagjini), became the only law the Albanian highlanders recognized, and for this reason it was probably the principle factor in the Albanians' ability to preserve their national identity during the Ottoman occupation.

Originating in the Middle Ages, the customary law was very conservative, designed to preserve the archaic patriarchal structures of Albanian society. Its role in the development of a civil society was largely negative. It institutionalized the savage custom of blood feud, for example, and it was extremely damaging to women. The code defines a woman as "a sack, made to endure as long as she lives in her husband's house," and prescribes among her duties the obligation "to submit to her husband's domination." A husband, according to *Kanun,* has the right *"to beat and bind his wife when she scorns his words and orders."*[1]

Imprisoned within the four walls of her home, the Albanian woman had no idea what was going on in the outside world. In many regions, custom prohibited women from appearing before men who visited their families. For a woman the world was the size of her house or her village. The average woman had never been beyond the boundaries of the village where she was born or where she was taken by the husband her parents chose for her. Many women were betrothed by their parents when they were still in the cradle, or even before their birth—another barbaric custom codified in the *Kanun.*

Women's relations were restricted solely to members of their extended families. No woman could take part in a public meeting. In the family women's opinions were almost never solicited, and in public life they felt totally alienated and despised.[2] In short, women were permitted no life of their own.

Only with the last century were Albanian women permitted access to education. In 1887, at a time when some European women were gaining access to higher education,[3] the first elementary school to give instruction in the Albanian language was opened, and in 1891 the first Albanian girls were admitted. Until the end of World War II, 80 percent of Albania's population and more than 90 percent of its female population were illiterate.

Postwar Development

The Code of Lekë Dukagjini is by no means a relic of the past. Many of its precepts and other old traditions still play important roles in the lives of Albanians today, particularly of women. Albania's rural character and its extreme economic backwardness have kept it a very traditional, strongly male-dominated society. After World War II, however, advances in education and the massive employment of women conspired to change the status and role of women.

The eradication of illiteracy became one of the primary goals of the Albanian government after the war. In 1946 elementary education became compulsory, and a year later the Albanian government instituted a literacy program for all men and women up to age 40 who could not read and write. In 1952 compulsory schooling was extended to seven years, and by the end of 1955 illiteracy had been eradicated among all men and women under the age of 40.[4]

The immediate need to reconstruct the country after the devastation caused by the war and to develop the nation's economy created massive employment opportunities for Albanian women in various sectors of the economy. Though the industrialization of Albania brought no profound change to the social structure of the country (even today two-thirds of Albania's population live in the countryside), it had an obvious impact on the social status of women. Not only did it enlist urban women in the work force, raising their economic position close to men's, but it also enabled thousands of rural families to move to the towns. Tens of thousands of rural women settled in a new environment, were integrated into urban life, secured employment, and expanded their social world. The proportion of women employed in various sectors of the economy increased from 35.9 percent in 1960 to 46.7 percent in 1989.[5]

During the 1960s, and especially after the 1970s, Albania's educational system expanded, the proportion of women in secondary schools (grades 9 to 12) increased considerably. In 1991 women accounted for more than 60 percent of the students in general secondary schools. In the 1950s the first Albanian women gained access to higher education. In 1957, when the University of Tirana (until recently the only university in the country), opened its doors for the first time, few of the students were women; but as the years passed, especially in the 1970s and 1980s, the number of women who went on to higher education increased steadily, as Figure 15.1 indicates. Consequently, the number of educated women in the work force rose from 11.9 percent in 1965 to 37.9 percent in 1989, a tremendous increase in three decades. Today slightly more women than men earn university degrees. Figure 15.2 shows the proportion of employed women with higher education and with vocational secondary education.[6]

After World War II Albanian women appeared for the first time as

Figure 15.1 **Proportion of female university students, Albania, 1960–89**

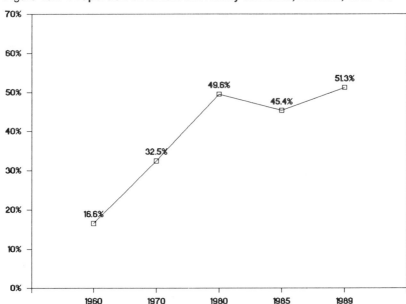

Source: Statistical Yearbook of PSR of Albania (Tirana: Komisioni i Planit te Shtetit, 1990), pp. 154–55.

an organized social and political force. There were no women's organizations before the war. The first mass women's organization was the Antifascist Women's Union of Albania, founded in 1943, during the War of National Liberation. In 1946 this organization changed its name to the Women's Union of Albania (WUA).

For forty-five years, WUA was the only women's organization in the country. Constructed on the model of the women's organization in the former USSR, the WUA was designed to serve as a transmission belt for the communist Labor Party of Albania. Under that system no mass organization could be independent. The structures of all such organizations, their range of activities, their working methods, and their leaderships were all dictated by the highest organ of the party, the Politburo.

As it was totally dependent on the party-state, the WUA could not truly represent women's interests. It was always a political instrument in the hands of the top party leadership, with almost no voice in its own policies. Of course, women were often seen on platforms at solemn meetings, serving the same function as the potted plants: decora-

Figure 15.2 **Proportion of employed women with vocational secondary education and higher education, Albania, 1965–89**

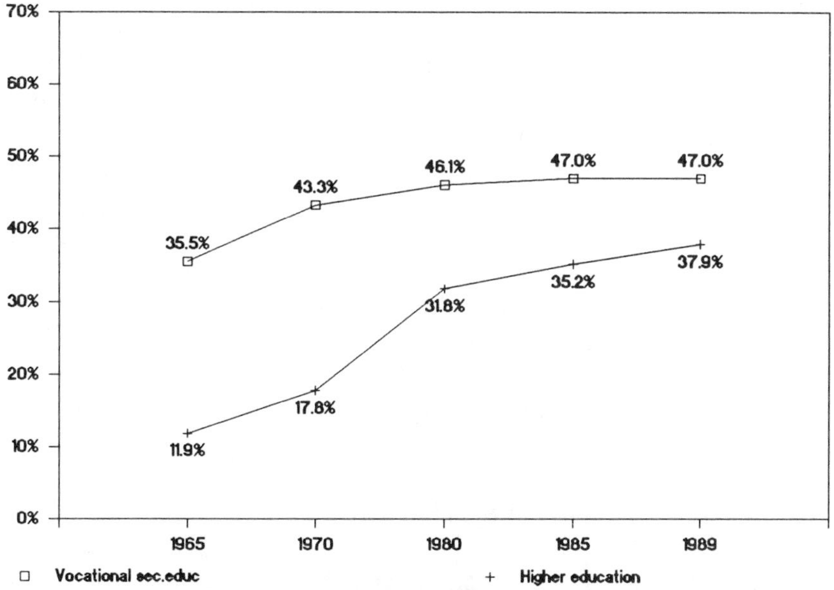

Source: Statistical Yearbook of PSR of Albania (Tirana: Komisioni i Planit te Shtetit, 1990), p. 87.

tion. Within the WUA, women could not articulate or defend their own interests. Their energies could not be organized in a real mass women's movement; their struggle for emancipation could take them no further than the Labor Party. For more than four decades Albanian women remained victims of the party's propaganda, which portrayed even the rights guaranteed to women by the constitution as gifts of the party, not legitimate rights that the party was bound to recognize.[7]

Yet, one cannot deny that the WUA played a significant role in the lives of Albanian women. Through meetings and campaigns aimed at putting women's issues on the political agenda, efforts to improve the material and cultural conditions of their lives, and various publications, the WUA did open the eyes of many women and involve them in political and social life. It did nothing to create a women's movement in Albania, however, and its activities were confined largely to urban women, a small segment of the female population.

The gap between women's legal position in the political life of the country and their actual participation in the society's political institutions was as great in Albania as in the other East European countries.

By law, they had a place at almost all levels of the national machinery; in fact, their influence in national politics was minimal.

Take the participation of women in the national and local governments. The candidates for deputies and local councilors were all chosen by the Democratic Front, another transmission belt of the Labor Party, and certain quotas were set for women, usually about a third of the total. Nevertheless, women deputies never managed properly to voice the opinions and the interests of half of the electorate in the highest legislative body, the People's Assembly, nor did they play an effective role in the local executive bodies. This situation was due largely to the criteria for their selection and the function the Assembly had to serve. Before a draft law or decree was submitted to a vote in the People's Assembly, it had to be "debated" and decided upon in the Politburo. Any draft law submitted to the deputies was expected to be approved, and it was.

Gender Differences in Political Socialization

Although Albanian society is still a typical gender-stratified society in the sense in which the term is used by J.S. Chafetz—that is, a society in which all males have greater access than females to the core values of their society[8]—we cannot deny that gender differences in political socialization have been narrowing, especially during the past two to three decades.

This statement finds considerable support in the results of a nationwide survey conducted in the fall of 1991. One thousand men and women responded to questions aimed at measuring their knowledge of political affairs, their interest in national and international news, and other indicators of political behavior.

Knowledge of political affairs was measured by the number of reasonably accurate answers to questions about several international organizations, the names of political personalities inside and outside the country, and so on. Figure 15.3, which shows the proportions of men and women respondents who had never heard of certain international organizations, and other responses to similar questions tell us that women are significantly less informed than men about politics.

When asked, "In general, what media source do you regularly use *most* often to learn about important events and problems in your country?" men named newspapers and most women mentioned television.

Figure 15.3 **Percentages of Albanian men and women who had never heard of five international organizations, 1991**

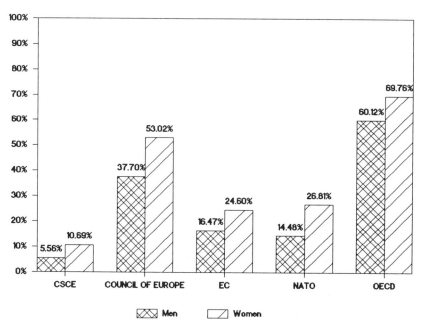

This difference, I believe, can be explained simply by the fact that men and women do not have equal roles and responsibilities in everyday life, particularly in family life, so they do not have the same access to various sources of political information. Men are usually treated as guests in their homes; they appear at mealtimes, and if they are home in the evening they often do nothing but read newspapers. Women, who bear the burden of all household tasks, have so little time for books and newspapers that often the late-evening news on television is their only source of information.

Knowing that very few women in Albania have positions of power in the machinery of government or leadership positions in political organizations, we were astonished to find that women have about the same level of interest in politics as most men. In our sample, 15.5 percent of women and 19.2 percent of men said they had a great deal of interest in politics; 37.9 percent of women and 28.8 percent of men said they had a fair amount of interest. And alas, about the same percentage of men (31.1) and women (35.0) answered they were not very much interested in political matters.

Figure 15.4 **Relative frequency with which Albanian men and women discussed political matters, 1991**

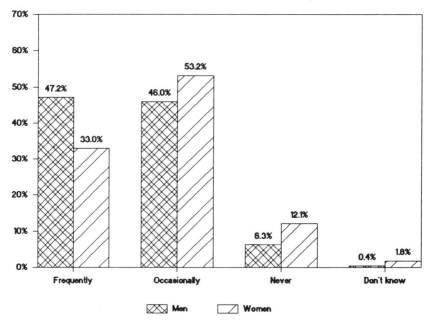

When asked, "When you get together with friends, would you say you discuss political matters frequently, occasionally, or never?" more men than women said "frequently," while more women than men answered "never." The differences in the "occasionally" responses were not significant (Figure 15.4).

The fact that women discuss political issues less frequently than men does not mean that they are less interested in politics than men. Women, having less time to read, may have less information, and their higher percentage of "don't know" answers suggests that they may also be less willing to take a stand on matters that may be controversial.[9] I do not believe, however, that women are less interested in political matters than men. Especially in times of transition, when the whole society is being swept by waves of drastic economic and political changes, gender differences in concern about political matters narrow. In view of their gender roles, women seem to be more vulnerable than men to the negative consequences of the economic and political changes the country is undergoing, so they are motivated to change traditional patterns and attitudes, even in areas traditionally regarded as men's business, such as politics. If women discuss political issues less frequently than men, we must remember that they have far fewer opportunities to do so. Doing housework, more often than not after a full day at the workplace, is not the same as strolling with friends or sitting for hours with them in a coffeehouse, as most men do.

Differences in the political socialization of men and women in Albania are more clearly seen in their everyday political behavior. The respondents in our survey were also asked whether they often, sometimes, seldom, or never performed certain activities, such as writing a letter to the editor of a newspaper or contacting a public official. As Table 15.1 indicates, far fewer women than men engage in such activities. In undeveloped rural Albania, however, we found much greater differences in political behavior between urban and rural women than between men and women in general.

Our survey was conducted in the period between the first two free elections in Albania (March 31, 1991, and March 22, 1992). In neither election did Albanians register a 99.99 percent turnout, as they did for several decades under the one-party communist regime. About 10 percent of the electorate did not vote in the March 1992 election, about the same proportion as that of our respondents—11.7 percent of men and 11.9 percent of women—who indicated that they were not likely to vote. These responses lead me to believe that women turned out to vote at about the same rate as men, as they regularly do in several Western European countries.[10] When we asked, "If there were a general election next Sunday, which party would you vote for or might you be inclined to vote for?" we noted a slightly different attitude in women than in men. Although most women expressed a preference for one of the many political parties, many said they saw little difference between them, so they would vote for candidates they could believe in, regardless of party. A similar attitude has been found elsewhere.[11]

We also found it very interesting to see how differently men and women consider their own views in political matters. When we asked our respondents, "Where would you place your political views on a ten-point scale?" we received the responses shown in Figure 15.5. Women clearly tend to place themselves near the center of the political spectrum; very few identity themselves with either the far right or the far left. Men seem to be more polarized then women, with a striking tendency toward the right. More than a third of male respon-

Table 15.1

Percentage of Albanian Men and Women Who Engaged in Certain Political Activities, 1991

	Often		Sometimes		Seldom		Never	
	Men	Women	Men	Women	Men	Women	Men	Women
Writing a letter to the editor of a newspaper or contacting a public official	2.7%	1.5%	5.7%	5.8%	25.2%	20.0%	66.5%	72.7%
Working with other people in the community to try to solve some local problem	4.3	2.3	12.8	9.9	31.5	22.3	51.4	65.5
Attending a public meeting or rally	15.2	8.3	29.3	17.0	32.3	34.4	23.2	40.2
Circulating a petition in support of a cause	10.1	5.3	12.8	10.1	23.1	20.0	54.0	64.6
Taking part in a public demonstration or march	12.4	4.6	16.8	11.2	23.2	20.7	47.6	63.5
Working in a political campaign	7.5	5.4	10.5	5.0	20.3	15.5	61.7	74.1

Figure 15.5 **Percentages of Albanian men and women who located their political views at ten points on a scale from left to right, 1991**

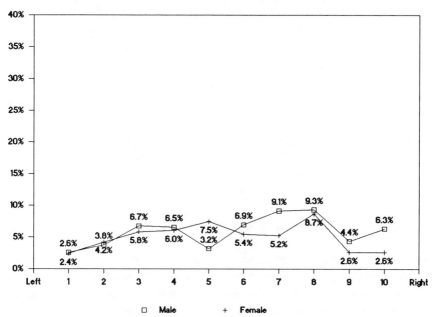

Research survey conducted fall 1991 by Fatos Tarifa.

dents placed themselves to the right of center (between 6 and 10), whereas less than a quarter of female respondents did so. The tendency is even more obvious when we refer to the extreme points (9 and 10) to the right of the scale. The right wing accounts for more than twice as many men as women in our sample, but only a small minority of both genders identified with the far left.

Finally, we found that a large number of respondents—more women than men (47.4 and 38.3 percent, respectively)—were unable to place their views on the scale. This finding came as no surprise, for two reasons. First, for many decades such terms as "left" and "right" were absent from the political vocabulary of Albanians. The totalitarian system tried hard to create an image of Albanian society as homogeneous; all Albanians were presumed to reject any ideology other than Marxism-Leninism. The 1976 constitution officially proclaimed Marxism-Leninism to be "the ruling ideology" (art. 3); soon it was to be the only ideology.[12] Second, in a time of transition from a dictatorship to a multiparty system, "left" and "right" can be confusing to many people. The opposition was characterized as a right-wing political force. Since the old communist regime was a dictatorship, however, it too could be defined as right-wing; yet its supporters were considered extreme leftists.

In interviews conducted before and after the 1992 election we found that many women adopted the political views and attitudes of their fathers or husbands. To a great degree they are still accustomed—sometimes forced—to accept the paternal guidance of the man in their lives. As one woman in Tirana put it, "A woman's duty is to share her husband's ideas and beliefs, not to argue about politics, which is not a woman's proper business." A village woman said: "That morning, on the way to the polling station, my husband kept insisting that I should vote for the Democratic Party, otherwise I'd have no place in his home."

The Arena for Women's Political Activity

It seems paradoxical that though women's education level and employment rate have risen, though the status of wives has improved considerably, and though women's interest in political issues has increased, their participation in political life has declined enormously. Women in Albania today are disappearing from politics.

The experience of the years since 1991 indicates that the transition period is a time not only of serious economic and political problems but also of disintegration of all social relations and institutions, and that women are the big losers.

In the economic sphere, the political changes brought about a complete breakdown of Albania's trade with the East European countries, which had accounted for 60 percent of its foreign trade. That situation brought Albania to the edge of catastrophe in 1991. In 1992 unemployment reached 70 percent and the inflation rate was around 300 percent. For days on end there was no electricity, no running water. During the winter of 1991–92 there was no way to heat houses and schools. Without humanitarian aid from various countries there would have been no food at all in the stores. As a result, for the first time since World War II Albania faced mass emigration. More than 700,000 people—one of every five Albanians—have left their country since 1991.

Unemployment is higher among women than among men. Many women, having no way to protect their economic and social rights, have resumed the homemaker role. The enormous increases in prices have lowered not only the standard of living but also the psychological well-being of Albanians, and especially of women. In the countryside the picture is even more discouraging. The collective farms have been disbanded. Each family has been allotted its plot of land, but no farm machinery is available. The work is backbreaking, and the farm wife finds her life sinking into the old patriarchal pattern. In these circumstances the rural birthrate has risen again and the percentage of girls in secondary schools has declined.

The political changes in Albania have disrupted everybody's life, and the transition period is far from over. It will be a long time, probably longer than elsewhere in Eastern Europe, before Albania finds its way to stability. But that is not the issue. The issue is the impact that the economic and political reforms have had on the status of women, and particularly on their participation in political life. Let us consider two facets of the problem: political organization and representation in governmental bodies.

Political Organization

The Women's Union of Albania dissolved some months after the introduction of the multiparty system. For some time there was no women's organization. A few women activists from both the old WUA and the newly formed opposition parties competed to recruit various segments of women, especially intellectual women, and to organize them into new groups oriented toward their political views and party affiliations. Three organizations emerged: the Women's Democratic League (WDL), the Women's Forum of Albania (WFA), and the Reflection Women's Club.

The WDL was organized under the auspices of the Democratic Party with the immediate aim of paralyzing the WUA and persuading women to vote for the Democratic candidates in the first elections. All women in the Democratic Party are automatically members of the Women's Democratic League. Thus the WDL is not an independent group but a party organization. One is reminded of the Labor Party's old transmission belts.

The WFA, formed a few months later, claims to be an independent organization, affiliated with no political party. The Reflections Club, formed at the beginning of 1992 as an association of some thirty or forty intellectual women in Tirana, also claimed to have no political agenda. Judging from its program, it seemed to be the first feminist organization in Albania, created to encourage a feminist movement among women students and intellectuals.

Though the situation in regard to women's political organization in Albania seems to be more colorful today, women's issues still have not been placed on the political agenda, and their political interests are not institutionalized or protected by strong organizations. The three women's organizations not only have limited memberships but are invisible in the political arena. Furthermore, they have no influence at all in rural areas, where the great majority of women live. Yet these new women's organizations have raised important issues—the reproductive rights of women, family planning, social welfare, divorce—and have urged their consideration by the general public, the various political parties, and the government.

Immediately after the establishment of the multiparty political system, the former trade union was split into two different groups, the Independent Trade Union and the Free Trade Union. Women are invisible in both.

The case of Albania shows clearly that women's participation in politics cannot be considered apart from the life of the society; it very much depends on the level of democracy the society has attained and on its economic development. In present-day Albania, both democratic and economic standards are very low.

The political and economic turbulence of the years since 1991, in particular the violent crises of 1997, have removed Albanian women even further from the world of politics than they were before. The social tensions before and after the establishment of the multiparty system, the rapidly rising crime and unemployment rates, and the deepening poverty and uncertainty have focused women's concerns on the welfare of their families. Even women who had been politically active in the past turned away from politics during or soon after the political changes, creating a vacuum in the country's political life that has not yet been filled. Though the anticommunist opposition movement in Albania created a climate favorable to the development of a new role for women in politics, few women entered the political arena and even fewer remain.

The new opposition parties that mushroomed in Albania did not find it easy to recruit women, both because of the aggressiveness of their attacks and counterattacks and because of the worsening economic situation. A large number of men who left the Labor Party joined one or another of the newly formed opposition parties, but most women simply opted out.

The figures available on women's membership in the various political parties are very unreliable. At the present time women seem to be fairly well represented in the three largest and most influential groups, the Socialist Democratic, and Social Democratic parties. In all others women are all but absent.

Moreover, there is a wide gap between women's entry into a political party and their inclusion in its leadership. No party leader in Albania is a woman, and it is difficult to find a woman in a top leadership post. As in many other countries—even in the Scandinavian countries, where the percentages of women in the parliaments are comparatively high—the same iron rule prevails: the higher the rank in the organization, the lower the proportion of women.[13]

The gap between men and women in political life has grown so wide that we could characterize present-day Albanian politics as a world in which men and women live completely separate lives.

Representation in Governmental Bodies

Gender inequality in Albanian politics seems to be most marked when we consider the representation of women in the National Assembly and in other decision-making bodies of state machinery. As in many other East European countries, the number of women elected to the parliament has declined precipitously. As Figure 15.6 makes clear, the proportion of parliamentary seats held by women after the elections of March 1991 and March 1992 was lower than at any other time in the entire period since World War II—two and a half times lower than it was in 1945, when it was all of 7.3 percent. It may well rank among the lowest in the world.

With the establishment of the multiparty system, Albanian women definitively lost their quota of one-third of the seats in the National Assembly. In the new political system, each political party makes its own decision and bears its own responsibility in regard to gender representation among its seats in the National Assembly.

The system adopted for the 1992 parliamentary elections was a mixed one: 100 deputies were to be elected by an absolute majority and the remaining 40 by proportional representation. In the 100 constituencies, only 8 of the 521 candidates nominated by the 11 competing parties and the independent candidates were women, and only 3

Figure 15.6 **Percentages of female members of Albanian parliament, 1945–92**

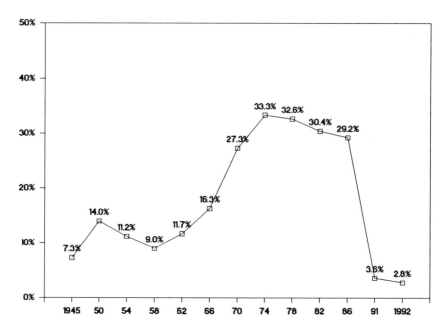

Source: Statistical Yearbook of PSR of Albania (Tirana: Komisioni i Planit te Shtetit, 1990); *Zari i Ponullit,* April, 1991; *Rilindja Demokratika,* April 1992.

women were elected as deputies. The 5 parties that won the right to go on through the proportional system included only 10 women among the 87 candidates on their lists, and of these 10 women, only one was elected. Table 15.2 shows the number of men and women candidates of each party in both the majority and the proportional representation system. The very limited number of women nominated gave them no chance to take a significant number of seats in the Albanian parliament during 1992–96. Of the 140 members of the National Assembly, only 4 were women. The picture remained virtually unchanged with the 1997 parliamentary elections. Of the 155 members of the National Assembly elected in June-July 1997, only 7 are women. In this election, the Socialist Party (SP) returned to parliament with a majority of seats and formed a coalition government with five other left-of-center parties. Because of the difficult economic situation, high crime rates, and political instability, social issues—generally including women's

Table 15.2

Number of Men and Women Candidates for Albanian National Assembly, March 1992, by Party

Party	Majority system (100 constituencies)		Proportional system (by lists)	
	Men	Women	Men	Women
Democratic Party	94	3	31	6
Socialist Party	99	1	27	2
Social-Democratic Party	97	–	2	1
Republican Party	94	–	7	1
Agrarian Party	46	–	10	–
Communist Party	28	3	–	–
Party of Unity for Human Rights	28	1	–	–
Christian-Democratic Party	11	–	–	–
Ecological Party	7	–	–	–
Party of People's League	3	–	–	–
Universal Party	1	–	–	–
Independent	5	–	–	–
	513	8 (1.53%)	77	10 (11.49%)

Source: Unpublished report of the State Commission of National Elections, April 1992.

issues—have nearly disappeared from the political agenda. Even though there are two women holding portfolios in the cabinet, the cabinet composition is expected to change shortly.

We may assume that if each party had nominated more women, the proportion of women elected would have been higher—not simply because women voters would have supported women candidates but because members or supporters of each party would have voted for the party's candidates. This is a safe assumption because the proportion of women elected in 1992 (2.86 percent) was almost identical to the proportion of women nominated (2.96 percent).

If women are to be more significantly represented in parliament, parties have to be persuaded to nominate more women as candidates. In my view, in Albania, as well as in other East European countries where women are rapidly loosing ground they have held in the past, a gender quota system should be applied to the nomination of candidates, to promote women in politics and give them access to governmental power.

Before the collapse of the communist system, at least one woman always headed a ministry and several women were deputy ministers and department heads. In the four governments since the March 1991 elections, including the current one, not one woman has held a portfolio or any other high-ranking position in a governmental body or institution. At a time when women's experience in the fields in which they have acquired expertise—education, medical care, culture, welfare—is desperately needed, they are shut out.

The stress caused by the grave economic situation and the political instability of the country have added to women's difficulty in understanding their real position in political and social life. And it has slowed their efforts to mobilize to defend their rights and advance their interests in society and in politics.

Notes

1. *The Code of Lekë Dukagjini* (New York: Gjonlekaj, 1989), pp. 38, 22, 44.

2. Fatos Tarifa, "Marriage and the Family in Albania Today." Paper presented at the international conference "The Future of the Family in Europe," Vienna, 1990.

3. D. Gaudart, "The Emergence of Women in Research and Development in the Austrian Context," in *Women in Science: Token Women or Gender Equality?* ed. V. Stolte-Heiskanen et al. (Oxford: Berg, 1991), p. 10.

4. L. Omari and S. Pollo, eds., *Historia e Shqipërise*, vol. 4 (Tirana: Akademia e Shkencave/RPSSH, 1983), pp. 84, 176.

5. *Statistical Yearbook of PSR of Albania* (Tirana: Komisioni i Planit të Shtetit, 1990), p. 82.

6. Ibid., pp. 153–55, 87.

7. Fatos Tarifa, "Albanian Women in a New Social Context." Paper presented at the regional seminar "The Impact of the Economic and Political Reform on the Status of Women in Eastern Europe and the USSR: The Role of National Machinery," Vienna, April 8–12, 1991.

8. J.S. Chafetz, *Sex and Advantage: A Comparative, Macro-structural Theory of Sex Stratification* (Totowa, NJ: Rowman & Allanheld, 1984).

9. S. Bourque and J. Grossholtz, "Politics an Unnatural Practice: Political Science Looks at Female Participation," in *Women and the Public Sphere: A Critique of Sociology and Politics,* ed. J. Siltanen and M. Stanworth (New York: St. Martin's Press, 1984), p. 119.

10. Ibid., p. 121; J. Hills, "Women and Voting in Britain," in Siltanen and Stanworth, *Women and the Public Sphere,* p. 137.

11. Bourque and Grossholtz, "Politics an Unnatural Practice," p. 121.

12. F. Tarifa and E. Cela, "Albania—Transition from 'No' to 'Yes,' " *Conscience and Liberty* 2 (1991): 17.

13. T. Skard and E. Haavio-Mannila, "Mobilization of Women at Elections," in *Unfinished Democracy: Women in Nordic Politics,* ed. Haavio-Mannila et al. (Oxford: Pergamon Press, 1985), p. 42.

16

Difficulties and Opportunities in the Transition Period

Concluding Observations

Marilyn Rueschemeyer

The transition in Eastern Europe to a postcommunist polity and economy dramatically affected the position of women. Any evaluation of the developments toward democracy and a market economy in these societies has to take their situation into account.

The improvements in some areas of the economy and for some segments of the population have been paralleled by havoc and disintegration imposed on others; large numbers of people are unemployed, and some suffer from severe poverty. Moreover, the emphasis on national, ethnic, and religious themes by politicians and the clergy have not only signaled alternative points of identification for citizens but diverted attention from severe social problems. Strife and animosity among ethnic, religious, and national groups have not only been revived; they have been created—or re-created. At the same time, these developments feed on unclear and threatening economic prospects. New economic plans underemphasize or ignore their potential effects on many segments of the population. Class and gender differences in outcome seem unavoidable. Yet the hope is that the new market economy will somehow improve the lives of all people in the long run.

Developments in the late 1990s have not fundamentally changed the situation of women in East European politics. This is true even though in a significant number of countries, the political and economic changes have been increasingly consolidated. Many of the difficulties affecting the early transition years continue, though their impact on women's political engagement varies across countries and issue areas.

The contributors to this volume do not reject the introduction of a

285

market economy into Eastern Europe, but they do expect that it will automatically work miracles. How the transition takes place, how regulations are introduced, how developments affect various social groups (economically and psychologically), and how the policies relate to deeply held values—these issues determine not only economic success but also the development of a more just social order, as well as the very identification of people with the new political system. One only has to look at the variations across market economies—the differences between Latin America and Scandinavia, for example—to see the many forms such an economy can take and the varying impacts on the citizens of a country.

We are especially concerned about the effects of the transition on the position of women in Eastern Europe. We observe that the expectations and worries of large numbers of women are considered relatively unimportant—so unimportant that they are not even addressed by most of the major political parties. We note that in the move away from authoritarian rule toward a democratic society, large numbers of women are not effectively represented. It indeed appears that women, together with the lowest socioeconomic strata, are among the losers in the recent transformations. The social and economic supports they had are gone or are threatened. Furthermore, in several of the East European countries, women represent a larger percentage of the unemployed than their male colleagues, and have a more difficult time regaining employment once they lose their jobs. The situation of mothers with young children and of older women seeking work is especially severe.

A basic problem is that all East European societies now are too poor to sustain the old supports, which, though they varied greatly in quality, included virtually free health and educational services and child care. Under the new conditions created by economic and political transformation, it is hard to imagine that the resources required for such measures will be easily available. The hope, again, is that the new political economy will eventually produce a pie large enough to enable all to live well. But the early policy directions—which are likely to be decisive for a long time to come—must be charted under conditions of painfully felt scarcity. The economic constraints of politics, then, are considerable. But there are still choices to be made, and these choices reflect not only pressures to concentrate on economic development but, to a considerable extent, existing power relations.

As we have seen, the current situation varies greatly from country to country. And no country has yet an established national agenda for future developments with respect to the role of the state in the economy, with respect to the state's responsibility for employment, child care, and social equity, with respect to the role of the church and the family.

Women, too, are debating the issues that affect them, even in countries where those issues are receiving scant attention from the political powers. Differences in perspective generally are not only rooted in cultural traditions; the different opportunities available to women, their educational level and occupational training, their financial resources, and of course the supports provided by the state—all these things affect their future possibilities and their assessments of what is of worth to them. Clearly, too, differences with respect to employment, education, and earnings affect the impact of economic restructuring on women. These differences exist among women, and similar differences exist between women and men.

In most of the countries of Eastern Europe, all adults were expected to work; both men and women were educated for jobs and had roughly the same access to occupational training. Surviving gender differences in education, skill, earnings, and position in the occupational hierarchy, however, continue to affect the attitudes of employers and employees now. Although these differences could theoretically be modified in the new regimes, in the reality of the transition, it appears that they are being accentuated.

The earliest years of transition—initiated through continued oppositional activity in Poland or through changes especially of economic policies in Hungary—and more generally the developments after the historical divide of 1989 had a great impact on what is happening now. In Poland the Catholic church gave great support to the activities of the oppositional union. Its role is extensive and largely conservative. Aside from the ongoing prestige of the church in Poland throughout the communist period, its power is potent in part because the church was an important player in the relation between party-state and Solidarity. As the chapters on Poland indicate, many women played important roles as invisible supporters, taking over a variety of practical tasks. They rarely held leadership positions, however, and none of the groups that negotiated with the government was led by a woman. Titkow writes that women provided essential liaison support with the Catholic church. At the same time, attitudes toward the role of the family and the woman's position in it were being formulated from the beginning under the influence of the church.

The former German Democratic Republic, in contrast, was a country with a Protestant past, with wide acceptance of pro-choice policies, of single motherhood, and of near-universal employment outside the home. During the early protests against the regime, women participated in marches; later they took part in the round tables where negotiation and administration took place before the elections of 1990. Furthermore, an independent women's movement that gave voice to women's unresolved concerns from a variety of perspectives was consolidated. Though women's interests were addressed then, the independent women's movement achieved only minor success in the elections, having won only limited space on the joint list of new movements. At the same time, the Federal Republic has to deal for the first time with a large population that has no affiliation with any church; and the more progressive West German women's advocates now have broader support.

The oppositional Charter 77 in Czechoslovakia was an intellectual movement that explored women's issues, among them renewed attention to the family. Wolchik notes that women, though a minority of the charter's signatories, were frequent spokespersons for the organization. They were also involved in the formation of the Civil Forum and the Public Against Violence. Moreover, women founded and led new dissident organizations in the last years of communist rule.

To a considerable extent, these early years reflected some of the most important trends in the society, including those related to the previous status and position of women. But other factors soon came into play, and these factors, too, affected future policies and the role of women in political life. Czech women became increasingly marginal in politics, though their position is still quite different from that of women in some of the other countries represented in the volume. Their marginalization had many reasons, to which we will return; but the aggressive nature of party politics, the self-perception of women in the political battles described by Regulska and Tarifa, and the reluctance in most countries to introduce quotas' for women were certainly discouraging factors.

In the former German Democratic Republic, the tensions of competitive party politics and the losses that both women and men experienced in that process were compounded by the nature of unification with West Germany. The GDR joined an ongoing institutional enterprise, a process that many East Germans now experience as an imposition of West

German institutions and power relations on Eastern Germany. This transition period presented Eastern Germany with a comparatively conservative agenda with respect to women, along with rather dramatic changes in the role of women in political life in Western Germany.

We see, on the one hand, that initiators of political and social change in a society win or retain some authority and control over institutional change, and so their positions on social issues gain in importance. On the other hand, in the fight over political influence and control, other factors and issues become important or are created in the battle.

Some of the political orientations and policies that are instituted in the process have a direct impact on women; others do not necessarily directly affect the position of women but affect their lives indirectly. The battles over abortion and policies designed to reduce or extend the time allowed away from work after childbirth reflect attitudes toward issues that are quite clearly grasped. But the implications of other policies are less clear and the ramifications may be apparent only after considerable time has passed.

The return or re-creation of national and ethnic identities may divert attention from pressing social problems and encourage traditions that have been long abandoned. With respect to women, the most salient policies—or lack thereof—are connected with the need for economic development and the introduction of market mechanisms. As a result of the early economic reforms in Hungary, for example, some workers, mostly men, took on second jobs, though some women also took advantage of available business opportunities. When men took on additional jobs, or when women worked only part-time, even the small share of household tasks and especially of child care that husbands had assumed was drastically reduced. Increasing poverty in the initial transition years in Hungary, and in many of the other countries of Eastern Europe as well, also means that more tasks are done within the household—canning, sewing, and the like. When women have the main responsibility for these tasks—as they do in most of Eastern Europe—they find it difficult to accomplish much outside the home, not to speak of establishing a career if that is their choice.

As Tarifa makes clear, the introduction of private plots and the abandonment of the cooperative farms in Albania have added to women's burdens. Since it is impossible in the present economic crisis to mechanize the work that is done on private property, the overall workload has increased, and rural women have returned to their role as homemakers in an environment that Tarifa describes as conservative and patriarchal.

In Bulgaria, Kostova suggests, economic problems are accorded priority as they come up, and that situation makes women a subject of no interest or of hidden interest, since the new economic program encourages them to be passive members of households, rather than active individuals. She observes that though the transition government has no particular policy defining the role of women, the current economic model treats the family as a unit, not as a group of individuals. With these observations, Kostova points to a major development in nearly all the countries of Eastern Europe.

It is not that all social and economic power centers directly or consciously stand in opposition to women's interests. But major organized interests in the economy and in society typically are concerned with other goals, and women's concerns seem just an irritating side issue. As the prospect of market competition and privatization looms larger, several enterprises have abolished day-care programs. Here the goal is typically to allow the corporation to survive economically, not actively to discourage women from participating in the labor force. But we know that in fact such decisions have a powerful impact on women employees, a devastating effect on single parents with children, and that these policies embody assumptions about the flexibility of women's roles that women themselves may not share. As we have seen, they are premised on a view of women as members of families and not as individuals with rights and needs of their own. Those traditions that stress women's roles outside the labor force are in line with these economic decisions, but in any case, such actions by enterprises, by the state, or by the municipality result in a view of women as less reliable workers than their male colleagues; they justify and encourage the hiring of men.

Among the most salient issues affecting the lives and future possibilities of women in East European countries are abortion, the continuity of child care and other social supports, and the integration of women into the labor force. In any one country, women are divided on these issues. But to indicate that a substantial segment of the population is against abortion does not tell us who is supporting what or what the majority of women want for themselves. In Poland the church has actively pushed for antiabortion legislation (which Wałesa signed into effect in 1993), but the reaction of so many women against these initiatives has challenged its very authority in Polish society. In 1996, a more liberalized abortion bill was signed by the president. The subsequent challenge by the Constitutional Tribunal, however, presents the new government with a problem that reflects the ongoing tensions in Polish society surrounding this issue. Other chapters on Croatia and Slovenia, for example, also suggest great tensions between the church and women. West Germany sanctioned abortion only under certain conditions, whereas East Germany allowed it. After severe and long battles, the Bundestag modified the West German regulations so that the new codes, though still not as liberal as those of Eastern Germany, make it easier for women to obtain abortions. An initially strong anti-abortion code has also been modified in Hungary, but the pressures for hardening the regulations remain strong. In Romania, the 1966 decree outlawing abortion and the sections on abortion in the criminal code were quickly revoked by the new government.

These initiatives concerning abortion were part of a constellation of activities that took a variety of forms but essentially called into question changes that were initiated during the communist period, changes that were anti-Christian and supposedly antifamily as well. As Fodor describes it, the Hungarian Christian Democrats want the state to interfere to make certain that women's role as bearers and educators of children is strengthened. These critics of equality under communism see women as having had the care of the family in addition to their work obligations, but now, with the end of the communist regime, they are able to stay at home and take up their proper role once more. Such traditional views are held by women as well as men.

Others criticize communism for not achieving real equality, for the difficulties of women's lives, the inadequate services, the poor condition of their housing; but such critics do not have a conservative agenda with respect to state responsibility for adequate health care, education, and child care, or with respect to the role of women. It seems clear that most women do not simply want to return to the family and drop out of public life. Research findings in several countries indicate that many women would like to reduce their hours at work, that they would rather be at home with their children for the first two or three years, but that only a minority want to become permanent homemakers. Even in Romania, with its former fanatical pronatal policy and its policies on women in the labor force, most women want the right to a job. They want this right because they need to earn money, and they want to have the possibility of working to escape boredom at home; for forty years, Fischer reminds us, women have been influenced by their hopes of equality and escape from the drudgery of household tasks.

Similar arguments are made about the disappearance of day-care centers. When children spent their early years in day care, according to the critics, they inevitably suffered. Indeed, many centers were overcrowded and lacked flexibility in their programs. In Western Germany, conservative ruling Christian Democrats are quite comfortable maintaining the existing inadequate nursery system because of their belief in the importance of home care for children. But citizens of Eastern Europe had a wide variety of experiences with child care and found some of the facilities quite adequate. In any case, further reductions in services make it difficult for women to search for work. The policies now being formulated have long-term effects on the lives of women.

Nearly all the contributors to this volume suggest that after the end of the communist period and the introduction of market mechanisms, poverty increased among certain groups, notably among single parents with children and older women who were not able to keep their jobs. In some countries the situation was desperate. At the time Tarifa's chapter was written, the unemployment rate in Albania was 70 percent; for days in a row there was no electricity, no running water, no food without humanitarian aid. A job for at least one member of the family, then, was of critical importance. Because of cultural traditions, because of the resources put into certain industries, and also because of discrimination against women, it was the man who usually received the work and the woman who took on responsibility for everything else that had to be done in the household. Titkow comments that the pride that most Polish women take in successfully managing daily survival, both under communism and in the postcommunist period, is related to their lack of perception of the symptoms of discrimination in social and occupational life. But whether or not women feel great gratification and satisfaction in what they have to do during the transition period, the protection of the family during this time is one of the most important reasons women give for their reluctance to become involved in political activities.

Furthermore, the authors suggest that the experience of women with the political life of Eastern Europe under communism is related to their reluctance to get involved now. First, women now have the possibility of retreating from participation in politics, and they overwhelmingly choose to do so. Second, during the communist period women saw no sense in spending their energies in the political arena because there was little space for innovation or power sharing. And third, it was the state that formulated major policies with respect to women's issues. At the same time, it was the state that gave supports to women so that they had no need to become involved in self-help or quasi-political groups even if they could have done so. Such past experiences have an impact on women's willingness to become involved in political life now. Yet we also note that in some countries women were very active during the initial transition period, hopeful that they could address issues of concern to them and gaining experience in new types of organizations.

It seems that in the early transition years, feminism tended to be equated with the imposition of communist rule on the one hand and with the fanatical man-haters of the West on the other. "Gender equality" is a term that most politicians, male and female alike, hesitated to use. Quotas for women in political representation are generally shunned because they are associated with the politics of the past. And the women who came into politics then, it is said, were only tokens, less qualified and less experienced than men. To many, then, the fact that the representation of women in politics is far lower than it was during the communist period is no cause for concern—women can now retreat, and the elected politicians do not have to work with tokens who cannot make the same contributions to political activity as their male colleagues.

We know that the delegates to East European parliaments, male and female, had limited power during the communist period. Would it have been better, then, to have no parliaments at all? Even granting the fact that there were women sitting in parliament with different backgrounds than their male colleagues, we also know that some of those women were highly educated and experienced people who could now make important contributions to their societies. Some of these women are unacceptable because of their past associations with the party; a very small number of others are slowly entering political life.

Defining the criteria of acceptability is part of the political game. The problem is that policies are being formulated that affect the lives of women, and they are being formulated by a majority of men in the context of their own political problems and aspirations. The practice of calling women feminists or communists because they press for social supports and the right to work has political implications, and the people who oppose these goals are well aware of the effects of their accusations. Ironically, throughout the years, women in Eastern Europe have been uneasy with Western feminist goals as they understood them.

In the communist societies of Eastern Europe, the official women's organizations reflected government policy, instead of representing an independent voice to express the concerns of women. Even if they took on a number of important educational activities or offered help in the residential areas, it is probably fair to say that they were not considered organizations that addressed the most important needs of women. With the end of communism, most of these organizations transformed themselves, but in general they lost membership. In the meantime, other women's organizations representing a wide variety of concerns and interests were formed—professional, cultural, entrepreneurial, charitable, and Christian groups of all sorts. Many of these groups deny that they are feminist, and as Wolchik suggests, some attempt to revive women's domestic role. Programs for feminist studies have been initiated, sometimes with the help of Western scholars who supply materials. Some feminist groups have formed. They are generally small, confined to urban areas, and well aware of their minority position. Their connection to parliamentarians varies from country to country. Especially in the early years of the transition, the few women parliamentarians tended to hesitate to represent women; they were—and still are—generally too few even to form an interparty coalition on women's issues. And even when that is not the case, as in the German parliament, party regulations generally discourage voting against one's party. Fodor also notes that strict regulations bind interparty alliances in Hungary. Poland does have a women's parliamentary group that cuts across party lines and that includes a majority of the women delegates. Though we see these women as an important potential source of support in efforts to address the issues that women consider most urgent, some women are discouraged about what can be accomplished in political parties and prefer to lobby through grassroots local organizations. These, groups, too, are still rather underdeveloped.

Though it is impossible to tackle in this conclusion all the parties and their policies—or lack thereof—on women, two groups seem to have more specific agendas than others. (That does not mean they necessarily receive the votes of the majority of women.) The Christian Democratic, church-affiliated, and nationalist parties tend to support the strengthening of the family and a return to women's traditional role. The reformed communist, socialist, and social democratic parties generally emphasize gender equality at least with respect to employment practices and social welfare policies; some of them make an effort to incorporate more women in political life, though very few parties have a quota system. The liberal parties, though their policies vary even more than those of parties to the right and to the left, tend to support the right to abortion and attempt to be cosmopolitan in their concerns and connections, but generally do not advocate interference on behalf of women in the labor market or incorporate a women's agenda in their programs. An important issue that separates liberals from reformed communists is the attitude toward the role of the state. Some parties combine perspectives that seem incompatible. In Romania, for example, the program of the National Liberal Party indicates an obligation to redress the past sacrifice of the family and at the same time assumes that both parents work inside and outside the home.

Women parliamentarians in several countries now have the same educational backgrounds and occupational experiences as their male colleagues. Although they are still a small minority, women have gained considerable experience since the early transition years. In interviews in 1992 and 1997 with women deputies in Romania, Fischer observed improvement in the professionalism of these women in the legislative environment, reflecting the increased political maturity of both the women themselves and their male colleagues. Fischer found that most of the women now see themselves as specialists on women's issues and want to address women's social and economic problems. Still, in other countries, such as Bulgaria, Kostova observes that women delegates seem to have no strategies or programs that differ from those proposed by the party they represent. In Germany, such "feminist" issues as interference in the labor market on behalf of women are fought out in a different context, as mentioned above.

Women are generally better represented in local politics than at the national level, though women's participation dropped there, too, after 1989. In Czechoslovakia before the split, for example, women represented 16 to 21 percent of the deputies in the local councils. Regulska notes that the experiences of Polish women in local and regional offices are important for future political activity. Women who do participate in local and regional politics gain experience, are in a position to create networks for future support, and potentially have an impact on policies that affect them. Interestingly, Regulska writes that at the national level Polish women have become more vocal; the abortion issue especially increased solidarity among women and generated nationwide support. That has been true in other countries as well. Women's political organizations have made important contributions in fending off antiabortion regulations and other harmful legislation affecting women's rights. Nechemias notes the legislative success of women in Russia in establishing a new family code.

The small number of women in political life is not astonishing given the conditions with which they have to deal and the attitudes of men toward their participation. Many women decided to retreat into private life. But of even greater concern are the women who initially became members of parties (as in the former German Democratic Republic) or who had been successful in elections (the women interviewed in Romania) and then chose to drop their party membership or not run again in the next election. Women in the former GDR were disappointed in the parties, even in democratic development as they saw it. In Romania, the most important reason given was the belief that they accomplished little in parliament and that it was not worthwhile sacrificing so much personally and putting that amount of effort into political work. With increased representation and political experience, however, more women believe they can contribute something important to the political development of their country. Nechemias points to the success of women in Russia in 1993, which sent twenty-three out of sixty women elected to the Duma. Despite their subsequent losses in the next election, their earlier success resulted in other political blocs seeking women candidates for their party lists.

Some general developments should be noted. First, the early and uncritical love of everything Western is slowly eroding, and people increasingly evaluate political changes by their effects on human lives. Women especially are worried about transformations that in their eyes are too radical or too rapid. Regulations and interventions associated with the old regimes can be transformed to accommodate current conditions without endangering the new forms of government or returning the old *nomenklatura* to power. Concrete measures to address the social problems that arise in the process of change are crucial for people's ability to identify with nonauthoritarian regimes.

Second, these societies need skilled citizens and in general do pay attention to individual achievements. In the process, individual rights are also increasingly recognized. That recognition gives encouragement to women who are well educated, skilled in their occupations, or productive in their professions. At present these developments coexist with both collective orientations and family-oriented policies.

There are indeed issues that are in dire need of the support and energy of women parliamentarians. The states have abolished or seriously reduced important supports, and local governments may lack the funds to provide them. Without such supports employment for women becomes illusory. Hence the political involvement of women is crucial if decision makers are to be pressured into addressing these issues and maintaining adequate supports in future years. Retreat from the political scene is dangerous, as several of the authors suggest, especially when resources are meager yet the agenda for the future is being set. These years are crucial for women because present economic and social policies will have a profound impact on women's lives now and for decades to come.

We believe that increasing the position of women in political life is necessary for a real, functioning democratic society. Furthermore, as Kostova and others suggest, the neglect of women's issues may become a blemish on the emerging democratic order. Even within the narrow limits of social policies supportive of women's interests, political action and decision making remain important, even crucial. This has been apparent in the second half of the 1990s to women engaged in political life at all levels, even with their frustrations, even if their achievements are incremental, and even if they succeed in only holding at bay restrictive policies that have such enormous impact on their lives. For politics in all its forms—choice on the basis of collective action—constitutes the main counterweight to social and economic power in society. To provide men and women with real choices with respect to these issues is to enrich the democratic basis of Eastern European countries. But that is a hard goal to achieve, as all these chapters so clearly indicate, without substantially increasing the political involvement of women.

Selected Bibliography

Adamik, Maria. "Hungary: A Loss of Rights?" *Feminist Review,* no. 39 (Autumn 1991): 166–70.

Antic, Milica G. "Democracy between Tyranny and Liberty: Women in Post-Socialist Slovenia," *Feminist Review,* no. 39 (Autumn 1991): 149–54.

Blanchard, Olivier, Rüdiger Dornbusch, Paul Krugman, Richard Layard, and Lawrence Summers, *Reform in Eastern Europe.* Cambridge, MA: MIT Press, 1991.

Buckley, Mary, ed. *Post-Soviet Women: From the Baltics to Central Asia,* New York: Cambridge University Press, 1997.

————. ed. *Perestroika and Soviet Women.* New York: Cambridge University Press, 1992.

Bystydzienski, Jill M. "Women and Socialism: A Comparative Study of Women in Poland and the USSR." *Signs* 14 (Spring 1989): 668–84.

Clements, Barbara Evans, Barbara Alpern Engel, and Christine D. Worobec. *Russia's Women: Accommodation, Resistance, Transformation.* Berkeley: University of California Press, 1991.

Dölling, Irene. "Changes in the Daily Life of Women in the Five New German States." Paper presented at a conference on women in Eastern Germany, Center for European Studies, Harvard University, 1991.

Einhorn, Barbara. "Democratization and Women's Movements in East Central Europe: Concepts of Women's Rights." Paper presented at the Research Conference on Gender and Restructuring: *Perestroika,* the Revolutions, and Women, World Institute for Development Economics Research, United Nations University, Helsinki, September 2–3, 1991.

————. "Where Have All the Women Gone? Women and the Women's Movement in Central Europe." *Feminist Review,* no. 39 (Autumn 1991): 16–36.

Ferree, Myra Marx. "Equality and Opportunity: Feminist Politics in the United States and West Germany." In *The Women's Movements of the United States and Western Europe,* ed. Mary Katzenstein and Carol McClurg Muller, pp. 172–95. Philadelphia: Temple University Press.

Fischer, Mary Ellen. "Politics, Nationalism, and Development in Romania." In *Diverse Paths to Modernity in Eastern Europe,* ed. Gerasimos Augustinos. Westport, CT: Greenwood 1991.

Funk, Nanette, and Magda Mueller, eds. *Gender Politics and Post-Communism: Reflections from Communism and the Former Soviet Union.* New York: Routledge, 1993.

Heitlinger, Alena. "Framing Feminism in Post-Communist Czech Republic," *Communist and Post-Communist Studies*, 29 (1996).

―――. *Women and State Socialism: Sex Inequality in the Soviet Union and Czechoslovakia.* Montreal: McGill–Queen's University Press, 1979.

Jancar, Barbara W. "Women in the Opposition in Poland and Czechoslovakia in the 1970s." In *Women, State and Party in Eastern Europe,* ed. Sharon L. Wolchik and Alfred G. Meyer, pp. 168–85. Durham, NC: Duke University Press, 1985.

Janowska, Zdzislawa, Jolanta Martini-Fiwek, and Zbigniew Goral. *Female Unemployment in Poland.* Economic and Social Policy Series, no. 18. Warsaw: Friedrich-Ebert Foundation, May 1992.

Kligman, Gail. "The Politics of Reproduction in Ceauşescu's Romania: A Case Study in Political Culture." *East European Politics and Society,* Fall 1992; 364–418.

―――. *The Wedding of the Dead.* Berkeley: University of California Press, 1988.

Kolinsky, Eva. "Political Participation and Parliamentary Careers: Women's Quotas in West Germany." *West European Politics* 14 (January 1991): 56–72.

―――. ed. *The Greens in West Germany.* Oxford: Berg, 1989.

―――. ed. *Women in West Germany.* Oxford: Berg, 1989.

Kostova, Dobrinka. "The Transition to Democracy in Bulgaria: Challenges and Risks for Women." In *Democratic Reform and the Position of Women in Transitional Economies,* ed. Valentine M. Moghadam. Oxford: Oxford University Press, 1993.

Lapidus, Gail W. "Gender and Restructuring: The Impact of Perestroika on Soviet Women." In *Democratic Reform and the Position of Women in Transitional Economies,* ed. Valentine M. Moghadam. Oxford: Oxford University Press, 1993.

―――. *Women in Soviet Society: Equality, Development, and Social Change.* Berkeley: University of California Press, 1978.

Lemke, Christiane. "Women and Politics in East Germany." *Socialist Review,* no. 81 (1985): 121–34.

Lovenduski, Jane, and Jill Hills, eds. *The Politics of the Second Electorate: Women and Public Participation.* London: Routledge & Kegan Paul, 1981.

Meyer, Alfred, and Sharon L. Wolchik, eds. *Women, State, and Party in Eastern Europe.* Durham, NC: Duke University Press, 1985.

Mežnarić, Silva, and Jelena Zlatkovic. "Gender and Ethnic Violence; The Case of Kosovo." *International Review of Sociology* 2 (1991): 113–21 (special issue).

Millar, James R., ed. *Politics, Work, and Daily Life in the USSR.* Cambridge: Cambridge University Press, 1987.

Moghadam, Valentine M., ed. *Democratic Reform and the Position of Women in Transitional Economies.* Oxford: Oxford University Press, 1993.

Nelson, Daniel, ed. *Communism and the Politics of Inequality.* Lexington, MA: Lexington Books, 1983.

Nickel, Hildegard. "Sex Role Socialization in Relationships as a Function of the Division of Labor: A Sociological Explanation for the Reproduction of Gender Differences." In *The Quality of Life in the German Democratic Republic: Changes and Developments in a State Socialist Society,* ed. Marilyn

Rueschemeyer and Christiane Lemke, pp. 48–58. New York: M.E. Sharpe, 1989.

Plakkova, Olga. "Women's Views on the Past and the Future of Women's Organizations." In *Contemporary Problems of Women and Family: Youth and Upbringing.* Bratislava, 1990.

Rosenberg, Dorothy. "Shock Therapy: GDR Women in Transition from a Socialist Welfare State to a Social Market Economy." *Signs* 17 (Autumn 1991): 129–51.

Rueschemeyer, Marilyn. "New Family Forms in a State Socialist Society: The German Democratic Republic." *Journal of Family Issues* 9 (September 1988): 354–71.

———. *Professional Work and Marriage: An East-West Comparison.* London: Macmillan; New York: St. Martin's Press, 1981.

Rueschemeyer, Marilyn, and Hanna Schissler. "Women in the Two Germanys." *German Studies Review,* DAAD special issue, 1990, pp. 71–85.

Rueschemeyer, Marilyn, and Szonja Szelenyi. "Socialist Transformation and Gender Inequality." In *East Germany in Comparative Perspective,* ed. David Childs, Thomas Baylis, and Marilyn Rueschemeyer, pp. 81–109. London and New York: Routledge, 1989.

Rueschemeyer, Marilyn, and Christiane Lemke, eds. *The Quality of Life in the German Democratic Republic: Changes and Developments in a State Socialist Society.* New York: M.E. Sharpe, 1989.

Rule, Wilma, and Norma C. Noonan, eds. *Russian Women in Politics and Society.* Westport, CT: Greenwood Press, 1996.

Scott, Hilda. *Does Socialism Liberate Women?* Boston: Beacon, 1974.

Shaffer, Harry. *Women in the Two Germanies: A Comparative Study of a Socialist and a Non-Socialist Society.* New York: Pergamon, 1981.

Shaul, Marnie S. "The Status of Women in Local Governments: An International Assessment." *Public Administration Review,* November/December 1982, 491–500.

Siemienska, Renata. "Women and Social Movements in Poland." *Women and Politics* 6 (Winter 1986): 5–36.

Szalai, Julia. "Some Aspects of the Changing Situation of Women in Hungary." *Signs* 17 (Autumn 1991): 152–70.

Szelenyi, Ivan, Szonja Szelenyi, Bruce Western, and Tamas Kolosi. "The Making of Political Fields in the Transition to Post-Communism: The Dynamics of Class and Culture in Hungarian Politics, 1989–1990." Manuscript.

Tarasiewicz, Malgorzata. "Women in Poland: Choices to Be Made." *Feminist Review,* no. 39 (Autumn 1991): 182–86.

Verdery, Katherine. *Transylvanian Villagers.* Berkeley: University of California Press, 1983.

Wolchik, Sharon L., *Czechoslovakia in Transition.* London: Pinter, 1992.

———. "Men and Women in Parliamentary Elites in Czechoslovakia." Manuscript.

Woodruff, D. "The 'Woman Question' and the State Question: Current Soviet Debates." Department of Political Science, University of California, Berkeley, Manuscript.

Young, Brigitte. "German Unification: The Politics of Abwicklung at Former East German Universities and Its Effect on Gender." Manuscript, 1992.

Index

Poland
  abortion in, 28–30, 56, 290–291
  concerns of women in, 45–50
  female labor force in, 20–26
  female political participation in, 28,
    290–296
    local, 35–38, 40–45
    obstacles to, 46–47, 51–56
  post-communism in, 39–40
  role of Catholic church in, 287
  women's movement in, 30–31
Polish Feminist Association, 31
Polish General Public Opinion Poll, 29
political participation, 290–293
  in Albania, 270–272, 278, 280–284
  in Bulgaria, 250–253, 255–259, 263
  in Croatia, 215–217, 219, 221
    attitudes on, 230–231
  in Czechoslovakia, 117–118, 119–122,
    130–136
    attitudes on, 128–129
  dropping out of, 296
  in East Germany, 92, 94, 99, 101–103
  in Hungary, 140–148, 155–160
  limited responsibilities through, 83–84
  local, 34–38, 39, 41, 50, 295–296
  nonpartisan vs. party, 130–132
  and party membership, 70–77
  in post-1989 Germany, 94
  in Romania, 172, 174–176, 182–187,
    190–192
  in Russia, 13, 16–21
  in Slovenia, 202–203, 211, 213
    attitudes on, 200–205
  in Yugoslavia, 240–245
  See also quota system
political representation. See political
  participation
political socialization, 270–278
population growth, 250–251; See also
  birthrate
Postal Worker's Union, 106
The Prague Mothers, 124
propaganda, 10, 127, 171
prostitution, 173–174, 188
Prunskiene, Kazimiera, 14
Public Against Violence, 130
  women's involvement in, 118, 120, 288
Public Employees and Transport Worker's
  Union, 106
Public Employees' Union, 106
Pukhova, Zoia, 14

quota system, 283
  in Bulgaria, 258
  in East Germany, 100

quota system (continued)
  opposition to, 84–85, 203, 293
  in Poland, 41
  in Romania, 175–176
  in Russia, 9
  in Slovenia, 202
  in West Germany, 78, 79, 82–83

Radičová, Iveta, 120
Rakhimova, Bikhodzhal, 13
rape, 246
Reflection Women's Club, 270–280
religion. See Catholic church, Islam
Report on the Situation of Women in
  Poland, 31
reproductive rights, 39–40, 154, 159, 280;
  See also abortion
retirement, 153
Roman, Petr, 178, 179
Romania
  economy, 200
  female political participation in, 182–187
  postcommunist, 170–179
  role of women in,
    before WWII, 168–170
    under communism, 170–172
    under postcommunism, 179–181,
      187–190
    under Ceauşescu, 170–176
Romanian Communist Party (RCP), 170,
  171, 170–175, 178
Romanian Ministry of Labor and Social
  Protection, 190
Rostock, 101
Russia, 296
  female political participation in, 13, 16–20
  postcommunist, 11–13, 15
  under Yeltsin Administration, 20–21
  women's organizations in, 14–15, 21–22
Russian Association of Crisis Centers for
  Women, 21
Russian Party of Unity and Accord, 16
Ryšlinková, Jana, 110–120

salaries. See wages
Schenk, Christina, 104
Secretariat of the Socialist Unity Party, 92
Securitate, 177
Sejm
  and abortion, 28
  women in, 27, 38–39
Semenova, Galina, 13
Serbia. See Yugoslavia
Serbian Citizen's Union (SZU), 244, 245
Serbian Socialist Party (SPS), 243, 245
sex education, 150–155